SALVATION IS FREE THE POWER IS NOT

AUTHOR, COMMUNICATOR AND FUNCTIONARY
RYAN DAVIS SHAW

ISBN 979-8-62-836814-5

ryandavisshaw.com
livetenten@gmail.com

Printed in the United States of America

Experiencing Heaven's power—here on earth

— RYAN SHAW

Contents

1 a volcano meets a tornado

IT'S 11:00 A.M., AND I need to get up. I've had only three hours of sleep, and I am so hungover. Wait a minute. I'm not hungover. I'm still drunk. I can't have that. I have back-flips to do on my wakeboard today. I better have a few shots of Jägermeister to avoid the hangover. I'll grab a forty-eight pack of "I am Canadian" for the boat on the way out to the lake. Don't forget the ice.

One night, years later, I will grab a forty pounder of whiskey, a rope, and a chair, and head down to the basement. The only decision left: climb up on the chair sober and then kick the chair out from under my feet—or drink the forty pounder of whiskey to go out in a blaze of cowardly glory—to be left hanging.

Let's call this my "last night."

This is how my life came to a terminal crossroads on my "last night." I was consumed with an unidentifiable desire to leave this misery called . . . life. The destruction to my family and friends was nuclear during this time period. I was all alone, or at least that's what felt real to me. I hurt for as long as I can remember, and I don't recall a single day of *true* freedom during this season of my life. When the pain mixed with the pride of life and a fistful of fifty-dollar bills, the recipe became terminal, and my life became dark. Very dark. The darkest years of my life started at age seventeen after I left my mom and dad's home. It lasted until my "last night" when I was age thirty-four. Scars tell a story.

I have sexually defiled my body on many occasions. I can't count the number of street/bar fights that I have been involved in. I have been through numerous relationship breakups including divorce. I have been charged with two DUIs. I have lost my driving papers seven times and have had a suspended license for a period of over five years combined. I have been through four criminal court cases, the latest ending in 2012 in Supreme Court, where I stood on the Court of Queen's Bench pleading guilty to an indictment charge with a maximum penalty of fourteen years. I've been hospitalized more times than I can count for severe bodily injury, and three times for suicide. During this seventeen-year time frame, I was diagnosed several times with bipolar disorder, ADD, and ADHD. The most recent diagnosis was multiple personality disorder. I endured countless broken relationships with women during this time period, but nothing compared to the seventeen years of relational desolation I had with Mom and Dad, and my sister and her family.

On my "last night," I had a fully advanced stage 4 terminal wounding coming to death's end. The whisper of death at the time was so peaceful. Like a drug running through my veins.

THE "LAST NIGHT"

On my "last night," I found myself all alone with a couple pieces of silverware, a coffee table, and a few chairs in a rented and empty condo—dirty too from all the traffic that had stripped the place empty. I had a bottle of whiskey and a rope from the toolbox of my work truck. I went downstairs to set up the rope in the floor joists above. The strategy was the only decision left: climb up on that chair sober and rope up or have one last liquid party to go out wasted instead. After weaving the rope through the joists, I stepped back down off the chair. I took the bottle of whiskey upstairs to ponder my last decision. Drunk or sober?

Just as I got back upstairs . . .

Ding-dong. The doorbell rang. I wasn't expecting anyone.

What? Who's here?

Larry walked right in, unannounced as he usually does. He saw me sitting on the chair. There was nothing new about the state I was in. I didn't have to explain anything about my condition. He knew my situation without any words. He had watched this misery for over ten years, and it was likely very exhausting to deal with. We sat for an hour with hardly any words. What do you say to a guy at 10:00 p.m. at night when you know he's made the decision and there are no answers at that point? I was paralyzed. Explaining my case was irrelevant. But what could he do? The cycles had been so frequent that Larry knew, if not tonight, it would be another night, and he couldn't stop it. This would only be a delay. Larry left with no plea, no advice, and no answers. Out the door he went with only a trail of love behind him. I sat dormant. It was silent again. I went back downstairs with my decision made.

"I'll go sober."

I climbed up on the chair. The air was so heavy that it felt like I could touch it. As I stood there on the chair with the rope around my neck . . . all of a sudden . . .

My head became quiet.

The noise had completely stopped for the first time in my life . . .

A jolt of power just shot through me . . .

What just happened?

For the first time in my life, it felt like a six-tonne weight of darkness had lifted off me. In that instant, it felt like an entire life's worth of depression, oppression, rejection, and addiction released right off me—just absolutely gone. The moment was so peaceful. Almost unexplainable, really. After that, I had repeating thoughts in my head saying, "It's over . . . The pain ends tonight." The voice was just repeating over and over in my head.

Then, just as fast as I felt the peace, I felt rage. I didn't know what the rage was all about, but I was angry at something. I got off the chair, and I went back upstairs and opened the patio door. I threw the bottle of whiskey, and my cell phone against a wall in the backyard, destroying both. Then I came back inside of the condo. Something crazy had just happened. I had some sort of life-altering power surge and release downstairs. But right after that moment, I also realized that something had led me to that place of devastation just moments earlier.

Shortly after this realization, I returned to the feeling of weightlessness. I felt like I had just walked through a door in the wall, passing from the side of death to the side of life. It reminded me of the movie *The Truman Show*. He eventually walks through a secret door in the wall to discover his entire life inside the walls was a setup. Everything I had known to be true was false, and the whole project had been exposed. The arrangement of my life had been fabricated by design—a total lie. In that moment, I didn't know what or who had controlled my life up to that point on the chair. I did, however, know that something had been deceiving me through the life lenses of the worldly glasses I had been looking through.

Suddenly, different words started repeating in my head again. "Die to yourself tonight, and the misery will stop for good." It was the whisper of truth this time. It wasn't telling me to kill myself. This voice was telling me to die to myself figuratively. "Die to this life, die to this world. It's done, and the misery ends tonight."

In the twinkling of an eye, and for no apparent reason that I could think of, my thoughts were different, and I had a different power in me. I had an empowering new energy source giving me such clear thoughts about what I had to do next. I had to die to my past entirely, without a remnant or a trace of the old life, people, or habits that were keeping me in this prison.

I wasn't sure what it all meant that night. All I knew was, in that moment, I had an encounter that gave me a new life. I left it all behind that night. I died to my pride, my reputation, my circumstances; and anything from the old life was left behind. I knew that something had taken over for me. I realized that it was a total surrender to a power source I was *not* yet familiar with. At 10:45 p.m., I went to bed, never the same.

The next day, I woke up, and my whole world as I knew it was completely different. The weightlessness was still as present as the night before. The pain wasn't going to make my decisions for me anymore. I felt free from the spirit of death. I knew that the old order of life had died the night before. At that point, I wasn't sure what the new order was, because I was all alone. It's not like an instruction book showed up at the front door from FedEx that morning. All I knew was that I had been empowered to completely die to the old order.

Three days later, I ran into a good friend whom I hadn't seen in many years. After the usual small talk, we started talking about some of the more intimate details of our lives. I explained this newfound freedom to him. He looked so amazed and told me that he had spent years "praying for me." I didn't really know how that related to my newfound freedom, but it didn't really matter to me at that moment. He had explained how happy he was that I had come out of the darkness I was living in. He reached into his truck and handed me a book to read. I'm sure you know what I was thinking right about then (eyes roll inside my head) Okay . . . thanks. I wasn't much of a reader. At first sight, the book didn't interest me whatsoever, but I took it out of respect, and we parted ways after some closing chitchat.

Days later, I got curious and then decided to open the book to read "a few pages." Well, I couldn't put the book down. I read the entire book in two days, which was a world record for me. From that day on, one miracle after another started manifesting almost every day. Eventually, the source of what was responsible for this all-powerful encounter that night revealed Himself to me as God my Father, the Creator of the heavens and the earth and all that is in it. It's been six years since what I call my "last night." I was broken, financially drained, suicidal, and totally alone in every facet of life. I wanted to leave this misery called life in the worst way.

Today, by God's mighty grace, I live free of the pain and oppression that owned my life. God has completely set me free from the grip of death that was strangling me. I live a victorious life for Christ now. By harnessing the all-powerful encounter that night and embracing God's love through relationship with Him since, I have found the freedom. I have also discovered power alongside this freedom. My life has never been the same.

On the other hand, and on the same journey, He's shown me that multitudes of others on this planet are being strangled by the same pain and strongholds each and every day, living in the wrong order—broken order, which ultimately leads to *out of order*. Evidently, this may even include individuals who have had the same encounter as I have had and believe. What? Yes, that's right. Those who still experience maximum amounts of continuous pain and bondage may still include those who believe in God, as well as those who haven't encountered or accepted Him. In either case, whether you have received Him or not, you may be saying,

> *Then where is all this power and freedom in God? If sometimes it works and sometimes it doesn't, then what's the point? This sounds like hogwash to me.*

I would totally understand if you were thinking this right now, and I don't blame you. I had those thoughts once myself. Whether you believe or not, I really recommend you keep reading on, and let me further explain in the chapters to follow. We were built for so much more. Our Father loves us. <u>This has very little to do with how He feels for us</u>. There is a big difference. I'm going to assume that we all realize how much our Abba Father cares for us, because that would be an entire book alone to describe. Our Father delights in us; that's an absolute fact. But it doesn't end there. This book is about coming into agreement with God. It's about entering into Jesus's name. It's about running to God, and not running away from God. A lot of Western culture pastors and leaders want to leave it at that. "Rest in the love of the Father. That's all you need to do." That statement is not untrue. It's huge. But leaving it at that is "isolation" and only one point in the entire Bible.

We need to talk about what's next, after we realize how much God delights in us, because it doesn't end there. Love requires a response. It's absolutely impossible to have a relationship with our Father if we leave it at that. If we don't have a relationship, then very little will transpire in our lives after our salvation moment. As believers, we are responsible to respond to the revelation He gives us, whether it be through conscience, whether it be through His instruction, or whether it be through His creation. Let's respond—-in love. Nothing to come from these words will be worth the paper it's written on if every single point and principle is not centered in a heart of love. In fact, the rest of this entire book will be pressing into the very meaning of the word *love*. *Love* is an action—not an emotion. We only have to read one chapter in the Bible to see that—1 Corinthians 13. "One-way" love FROM our Father is not the answer. Nor is it the entire story. It's time to tap into the power of the Holy Ghost to bring the body of Christ alive like never before—through a response of *love*.

2 the conspiracy

SALVATION IS FREE, BUT the power is not. What does that even mean? It means salvation is free, but tapping into His power that brings the victorious life is not. "This sounds 'religious.' Doesn't the power automatically come with belief?" Let's keep reading. We may be saying, "What's the difference, and why does this even matter?" Oh, it definitely matters, and we will discuss why.

If we are uncertain of what that first sentence even means or why it matters at all, that is okay. We may be a group of believers that have a few subconscious and slightly hypocritical thoughts bouncing around our heads about salvation, healing, power, and His glory. Sometimes, we may not even realize that we have the hypocritical thoughts either or what they are—hence the subconscious part. Hypocritical thoughts don't come into our heads because we have our "minds made up." They come in because we don't have "made-up minds." These thoughts will feel hypocritical until we actually understand the difference between salvation, the power that should come with salvation, and the conspiracies within.

When we don't have a made-up mind, we can struggle with the scriptures, and we will wrestle with these thoughts. We can also battle with tiny seeds of uncertainty about the victorious life and how to find it or if it's even for me. Perhaps we think it's for someone else that is "lucky enough" to be selected on a rare occasion. If we are unable to find the answers, we give up and end up terminating these thoughts altogether. Then we make the final decision in our minds: God is God, and He alone decides who gets the victory and when. If it's my time, then I guess it will be my time, because God is God.

I realize that we will never be certain about all of the details in the scriptures.

> *Now what I am commanding you today is not too difficult for you or beyond your reach. It is not up in heaven, so that you have to ask, "Who will ascend into heaven to get it and proclaim it to us so we may obey it?" Nor is it beyond the sea, so that you have to ask, "Who will cross the sea to get it and proclaim it to us so we may obey it?" No, the Word is very near you; it is in your mouth and in your heart so you may obey it. (Deuteronomy 30:11–14)*

And again,

> *The secret things belong to the Lord our God, but the things revealed belong to us and to our children forever, that we may follow all the words of this law. (Deuteronomy 29:29)*

That being said, I'm confident that we can have made-up minds about these two topics. I would agree with a portion of the last few sentences, in relation to God's timing and placing of His power. But is that the entire story? Absolutely not. Do we play a big part, to some extent, to how this could play out? Of course. God has a huge purpose for each and every one of us. The "extent" to how this could play out will change our lives entirely, here on earth, and that's the entire point. When we can't seem to find the answers we are looking for in terms of victory, we tend to shuffle these thoughts off to the side. We forget about them. We give up and get distracted with other things in our lives that we feel are more attainable. Then we continue to live our days in that belief, with very little change in our lives. Eventually, we are left with this question: Where is the victorious life we hear about when we go to church, listen to a podcast, or read a book?

This question may be one of many little hypocritical thoughts bouncing around in our heads. How do we put discernment to these thoughts? Does God just roll the dice every day to see what numbers come up and then select the person to give the victory to based on the numbers that faced up on the dice? Or does God pull down a heavenly lever on a special slot machine all day? If L-I-S-A comes up on the screen after that pull, then she wins the favor of the minute? Or maybe . . . it's the mood He's in that day.

SETTING THE STAGE
Salvation and Power

This will be our starting point. We are going to work through two topics in a general fashion for now and then more specifically in the chapters to follow. Salvation and Power.

SALVATION (QUICK LOOK) "A"

We will all receive bits and pieces of discernment every other day about God and the Bible. This will form our wisdom base during our journey from points A through Z. We will use points A to Z as a "figurative" scale to measure time. This scale will represent the time line of our physical lives *here on earth*, from our <u>salvation moment</u> to our physical death, to make this point easy. As believers, do we really understand faith in the middle or the journey from B down to Z per say? Do we really know what the letters A or Z actually represent spiritually or how to connect the dots of all those letters in the middle to see an outcome?

A is the start. Our salvation moment. Not the start of our lives but our moment of salvation. A is also the eternal life we receive the minute we truly choose Jesus Christ as our Lord and Savior. Eternal life isn't Z in the time line, because eternal life is established right at the start in the belief at A. Z is when Jesus returns or when we go to be with Him. We must realize that salvation and eternal life go hand in hand, in the same moment. Then we need to realize that there is something left after A. This is B through Z! If we didn't have something after A, then there would be no purpose, and it would be a dead journey from that point on. That is not God's intention for our lives. If salvation and eternal life happen in the same moment, then what happens from B to Z (the rest of our physical lives here on earth after our salvation moment)?

THE POWER (QUICK LOOK) "B TO Z"

A common question is, "Don't we have automatic 'access' to God's power and favor after we actually have our salvation moment? Isn't that the whole point?" Yes, it's the whole point, and no, we don't have automatic access to <u>all</u> of the special places available in the salvation decision alone. This is where the conspiracy can happen. Salvation is free—but the Power is not. B down to Z is our journey after salvation. It's the pursuit to discover and embrace the ultimate amount of intimate relationship with our Father and His Son and the Holy Spirit—all as one. It's the area where we really live out our purposes as God's children. This is where we pursue His power. If there is no pursuit, then there will be no results.

The pursuit is what brings us access to His power at various levels as we journey. The pursuit is what unleashes the radical power of the Holy Spirit in and through us. The more intensely we pursue Him, the more we will access the highest form of His supernatural manifestation, presence, and power here on earth before His final return. These types of experiences don't generally happen that often without the pursuit. This is a journey that usually starts at B, then C, and then D, and so on—getting more intense if we decide to keep pursuing. Being dedicated enough to pursue an intimacy even close to the letter Z would give us mind-blowing access to His supernatural realm, here on earth.

Letters from B down will be "kingdom-life moments." They, too, will be awesome . . . but Z . . . or getting even close to Z . . . that will blow our hair straight back if we have hair. Z is where "few" will ever enter the Bible says. Z is tapping right into the kingdom of God itself here on earth. Z will be a secret spot—touching the spiritual veil, if you will, or passing through it for a moment. This would be like accessing the Holy of Holies in the Old Testament. This type of access is not free. Not even close. It comes at a cost. Access to this power is not luck. It's not for preselected "chosen" people, as we will see. It's not for young people only. It is available for anyone dedicated enough to pursue God and the power He has waiting for us. God intended us to live with His radical power in these journeys, no matter what stage of life we are at. Radical power will mean set-apart favor. The two will go hand in hand.

QUICK RECAP—IDENTIFYING THE POSSIBLE CONSPIRACIES

Let's recap. We took a quick look at salvation and power. Let's look at some of the possible conspiracies or inaccuracies that may exist in these two topics:

Salvation—We may think that belief alone isn't the only "requirement" for salvation, that there is more required according to the "tough" parameters mentioned in some of the scriptures.

Salvation—We may think that belief alone gives us access to His power.

Power—We may think that His power is too rare or too random for me to experience.

Power—The various ideologies to "access" or receive His power here on earth, *if* it even exists at all.

These are a few of the conspiracies that may be bouncing around our heads giving us these hypocritical thoughts we talked about earlier. We will take a closer look at these topics in the chapters to come. Unfortunately, many believers see our walk here on earth as "A" being salvation and "Z" being the end, or eternal life—thus failing to understand what the "B–Z" actually is. "B–Z" is the journey after our salvation moment. It's "purpose." It is the whole reason that God built us in His image.

Mark Twain said it like this:

The two most important days in your life are the day you are born and the day you know why.

Until we realize that this power is about God's purposes, we will struggle with our own purpose. We truly will. We will also find it difficult to access His power until we get our eyes off ourselves. We will live lost lives as we try to pursue the ever-dying things of the world. We will plant and plant and plant, but the proper harvest will never show up. The power available will be a partnership together with God to fulfill our purposes in the kingdom Gospel plan. We will get to enjoy being the vehicle to carry around and steward God's power for Him. With this power will come favor and the victorious life as well. This is meant to glorify Him. Also, tapping into His power makes our ministry to the lost very simple to describe. In one line in fact,

I appreciate all of the theoretical reasons you want to tell me why God doesn't exist, but I have seen way too much of His irrefutable love and power in my life to ever deny Him or His existence.

Perhaps we are saying, "What's with this power I hear about? Stuff like physical healings, spiritual healings, overcoming pain and addiction, victory in our family circumstances, promotion, financial breakthroughs, love, prophetic gifts, set-apart wisdom, restoration in marriages, anointed abilities, and the manifestation presence of God here on earth—experiences like seeing angels or hearing God's voice or having dreams and visions from the Holy Spirit. And seeing Jesus? Are you kidding me? This stuff never happens to me or anyone around me."

Power always comes with a cost, either spiritually or worldly. The reality is no matter where we are in life, we can, and we will access His mind-blowing power. We need to believe it's there first, and then we need to go after it, to access it. If accessing more of His manifestation power and Glory here on earth doesn't really interest us, then fair enough. We may not be interested in reading on. On the other hand, if living out more of our actual purpose does interest us and we haven't been experiencing His power, let's continue on and look at salvation and His power in more depth. Let's be a generation that rises up to glorify our King with His power. It's accessible for all of us if we are willing to pursue it. We will need His power to be a set-apart people in the body of Christ.

> For I am not ashamed of the Gospel, because <u>it is the power of God</u> that brings salvation to everyone who believes: first the Jew, then to the Gentile. (Romans 1:16, KJV)

The only two things that will matter in our walks is His love and His power. Every other detail will be a religious waste of focus. Let's empty out the religion to make space for His power. It's time to sell out for Jesus. When we sell out for Jesus, we will live radical power-filled lives that will blow our minds for His glory.

3 digging into salvation

THIS NEXT PARAGRAPH WILL be *very important* to harness, and it may even be offensive for some to hear. We will look ahead to the scriptures as we dig in. I want to be very clear in this next part because I don't want there to be any confusion or sounds of hypocrisy as we continue on—especially the part about salvation and the absolute importance of obedience.

The point at the end of chapter 1 is this: It's possible to have an encounter with God and actually believe in Him *but not be operat-*

ing in His order. Yes, that's right. There is a large population of people living like this in the believing community. It happens every day—thus forfeiting access to the supernatural power that we can have here on earth. This gives the church limited power in the big picture, especially Western culture. The power lies entirely within the <u>order of operation</u> that we actually choose to live by—God's order or the world's order. We need to get this sorted out in our lives. That being said, we <u>can</u> believe without operating in His order—that's a fact. We can be operating in the ways of the world as believers.

Think of it like this:

Let's use an example such as the ideals of the Civil War. Perhaps we believe, without a doubt, for one of the two different sides that battled. Say, years later after the war, a riot breaks out between the two groups. If we choose not to go out to the front lines and riot, or we choose not to get involved on the streets at the protest, does that mean we do not believe in the side we support? Absolutely not. It just means we are not participating in the action or "the order" of the group we believe in. There could be many different reasons we don't participate in the action. The action will bring a result, one way or another, if we participate in the riot or the protest.

Well, it's the same with believing in God. We *can* believe in Jesus and be living without His power in our lives. It's unfortunate if we believe and do not actually participate in His order. There won't be much of a "result" to harness in terms of His power here on earth. His power is where we find the new-level breakthrough and the victorious lives we are looking for. We discover God's purposes for our lives in this realm as well. We are not talking about "superficial" lives that look victorious in the "world's" eyes. We are talking about victorious kingdom lives for God's purposes. There is a huge difference. One will have significance, and the other one won't.

Belief only promises salvation. That's why we can still see a believer not living the victorious life here on earth, as mentioned at the end of chapter 1. We need to understand that "belief" and accessing His "power" are two different topics entirely. Belief *should* cause change or, in other words, cause us to follow a different order. But again, it doesn't always, or sometimes, it's very little at first. This could be another hypocritical thought that we wrestle with sometimes.

This point does not make His power more important of a topic than salvation by *any* means. In the past, I used to think that salvation was far more important of a topic than operating in His power. Then God revealed something to me on this matter. He reminded me that it's His very power working in us, and through us, that actually brings salvation to His children as a part of His sovereign kingdom plan through discipleship. So in retrospect, one is as significant as the other. The two are equals in terms of importance and should be working together—and that's why we should be pursuing it. In any case, without God's incredible love and mercy to start with, we wouldn't be talking about either one of these two points. But because we can, the point still remains.

It's like this:

Belief *without* His order can still = salvation.
Belief *with* His order can = salvation + access to His power and Glory, which will give us the victorious purpose-filled lives.

Salvation is free; the power is not. We can't assume that just because salvation is free that the power is as well. Salvation has one purpose, and kingdom power here on earth is for another purpose. The bull's-eye on the target is to bring them together for the "whole purpose." This is a results-orientated pursuit as we will see. We must not get salvation and power interlocked or confused as being the same thing automatically.

SALVATION (THE IN-DEPTH LOOK)

Let's take a deeper look into the salvation process again on its own so that we can be firm in our foundations. Let's be properly equipped to understand how to merge His power into our "saved" lives. For salvation, which is eternal life, *there is only one single requirement: to truly believe in the Son of God as our Lord and Savior.*

This is an absolutely free gift from God. We don't work for or earn a "free" gift. The word *gift* doesn't make it free. Not all gifts come for free. The word *free* makes it free. Belief in Jesus is the one and only single requirement for salvation and eternal life A (heaven). When we truly believe, it doesn't necessarily mean we are working in God's order. Again, it just means we believe. If we are a little bit cranked up about the theology here, then let's look at Luke 23 in the Bible. This was Jesus on the Cross in His very last moments between two very bad criminals. One criminal was to the left, and one was to the right of Jesus. The one criminal was mocking Jesus still, but the other criminal had something very different to say to Jesus in his very last moments before he died. As recorded in the Bible,

> But the other criminal rebuked him. "Don't you fear God," he said, "since you are under the same sentence? We are punished justly, for we are getting what our deeds deserve. But this man has done nothing wrong." Then he said, "Jesus remember me when You come into Your kingdom." Jesus answered him, "Truly I tell you, today you will be with Me in paradise." (Luke 23:40–43)

This criminal was not baptized, he did not pray, and he did not honor God in any part of his life. He never went to a church or sang praises to God before he was nailed to the cross beside Jesus. And yet we see by belief alone this man would go to paradise with Jesus that day. We can appreciate the reality of the free gift God has given to us through the belief in His Son, Jesus, for the salvation part. Nothing else can give us this gift. Not works, not good behavior, not deeds— *nothing but belief.* If we feel any differently than above, then we strip the power of the *Cross* and the blood that was shed for us through grace and become no better than the Pharisees that Jesus Himself rebuked.

On a sidenote, I never debate anyone's salvation position. This is for God alone to decide. In other words, whether this person or that has salvation, or if they *truly* believe or not. Debating "salvation" positions will only cause confusion and get us all twisted up in God's Word. It will cause us to get critical about others as well. As far as I'm concerned, we have taken our eyes off the prize when we start debating belief or not. It is not our job to get critical about whether we believe or not.

Our job is to spread the good news in love with the evidence of His power to back it up. God will do the rest.

I will, however, follow up with more scripture to support salvation and how it is different than power as we look to the text ahead. We will also look at more text to confirm the one and only way to receive salvation. As we continue on the topic of salvation, we may be questioning the significance of the following types of verses all throughout the Bible:

> *Or do you not know that the unrighteous will not inherit the Kingdom of God? Do not be deceived; neither fornicators, nor idolaters, nor adulterers, nor effeminate, nor homosexuals, nor thieves, nor the covetous, nor drunkards, nor revilers, nor swindlers, will inherit the Kingdom of God. (1 Corinthians 6:9–10)*

> *I know your deeds, that you are neither cold nor hot. I wish you were one or the other! So, because you are lukewarm—neither hot nor cold—I am about to spit you out of My mouth. (Revelation 3:15–16)*

> *Truly I say to you, whoever does not receive the Kingdom of God like a child will not enter it at all. (Luke 18:17)*

If we find *any* scriptures in the Bible that we think disqualify us from eternal life in heaven (other than scriptures that talk about "not believing" in Jesus as our Lord and Savior), then we need to have a closer look to get a better understanding of the scriptures and what they truly mean. The criminal on the Cross beside Jesus was likely many of those things mentioned in 1 Corinthians 6:9. By knowing the scriptures with more clarity, we will unlock the knowledge to truly find the answers we are looking for, whether we like them or not. We need to come to one *major* understanding of the scriptures in terms of salvation. That one particular piece of information is this:

> Any one scripture that has anything to do with pursuit, works, deeds, striving for, pressing in, trials, tribulation, achievements, service, dedication, commitment, obedience, failing in obedience, love, no love, personality traits, lifestyle, personality flaws, behavior, failing in sin, victories, or targets to shoot for . . . will have nothing to do with receiving salvation.

By capturing the last paragraph, I can be relieved of the grueling task of yanking out every single disqualifying verse in the Bible that we may want to challenge this point with. This also brings a new level of peace and clarity in the scriptures when we finally understand this point. Belief alone will be the one and only qualifier for the magnificent gift that God has given to us through His Son, Jesus Christ, on the Cross.

> But for that very reason I was shown mercy so that in me, the worst of sinners, Christ Jesus might display His immense patience as an example for those *who would believe in Him and receive eternal life*. (1 Timothy 1:16)

On the contrary, this doesn't mean that the disqualifying or obedience verses get forgotten or shuffled aside by any means. It just means they don't qualify or disqualify us for the eternal gift of salvation. Look at Peter, for example. He denied Christ three times, and yet Jesus would start the Church age through him shortly after his denial.

"Order" is action in obedience. If obedience had anything to do with our salvation, then none of us would receive the eternal gift. If we only knew how much different obedience looks in God's eyes as compared to our eyes. The standard is way different. "This week, I am obedient enough. Last week, I wasn't." "If I did more right than wrong for the last five years of my life, then hopefully I receive the approval at the end." Where do we draw this ridiculous line if our salvation had anything to do with our obedience? This sounds ludicrous, doesn't it? This is where the confusion and hypocritical thoughts come in—big-time. With confusion comes uncertainty when we read verses such as

> Not everyone who says to me, "Lord, Lord" will enter the kingdom of heaven, but only the one who does the will of the Father who is in heaven. *(Matthew 7:21)*

Doing the will of our Father won't give us access to eternal life. I know—this is completely backward to what we think we know. Also, I'm not nearly suggesting that we don't do the will of our Father. The will of our Father is the whole point. Just not for salvation. We read that belief alone is the only qualification. Anyone who thinks that they are obedient enough to receive the free gift of salvation better go through a spiritual overhaul. What does the Bible say about *belief alone?*

> He has saved us and called us to a holy life—<u>not because of anything we have done</u> but because of His own purpose and grace. This grace was given us in Christ Jesus before the beginning of time. *(2 Timothy 1:9)*

> For it is by grace that you have been saved, through faith—and this is not from yourselves, it is the gift of God—not by works, so that no one can boast. *(Ephesians 2:8–9)*

> For it is with your heart that you <u>believe</u> and are justified, and it is with your mouth that you profess your faith and are saved. *(Romans 10:10)*

> For God so loved the world that He gave His one and only Son, that whoever <u>believes</u> in Him shall not perish but have eternal life. *(John 3:16)*

> They replied, "<u>Believe in the Lord Jesus</u>, and you will be saved—you and your household." *(Acts 16:31)*

I write these things to you who believe in the name of the Son of God so that you may know that you have eternal life. (1 John 5:13–14)

Whoever <u>believes in the Son has eternal life</u>, but whoever rejects the Son will not see life, for God's wrath remains on them. (John 3:36)

We could go on and on with verses about "salvation" or "qualifying" or "disqualifying," which again would be a grueling typing expedition for a guy like me. The good news is that we don't need to. It's not that I'm too lazy and that I don't want to find them to make the point; it's just that it's not necessary. The beauty about understanding this <u>principle</u> is that we can consciously apply it to any one of the hundreds of "qualifying" or "disqualifying" verses. This discernment will also allow us to break through the divisive ideologies of the different church denominations and stances. It won't matter what every other church says about this or that, or if it's different.

Salvation is salvation, and power is power. We can stand firm in our understandings, regardless of the different "opinions" that may be based on one-sided scriptures or denominational tradition. Again, only when we understand both topics and then learn how to merge the two together *can* we be at peace and break through the religious hypocrisies that exist. Salvation only comes by truly believing in Jesus Christ as our Lord and Savior. Nothing else.

For we are God's handiwork, created
in Christ Jesus to do good works, which
God prepared in advance for us to do.

—Ephesians 2:10

4 digging into the power

**THE POWER
CONSPIRACY**

IT'S UNFORTUNATE, REALLY, WHEN belief exists with little to no order. This isn't God's intention for our lives. This posture doesn't generally birth any better victory in this life than before we actually believed. To an even bigger point, it gives God no glory when we live powerless, unvictorious lives, contrary to what anyone says. Perhaps we live so narcissistically; we could care less if we glorify our Father or not. In this posture, we won't even give thought to His power in our day-to-day lives. The sole purpose of our existence is to bring glory to God. This comes from the evidence of His love that comes through His power.

> *I raised you up for this very purpose, that I might display My power in you and that My name might be proclaimed in all the earth. (Romans 9:17)*

Thinking that we should be kicked to the curb or suffering 24/7 for the rest of our lives is a religious "false humility." There is no Biblical evidence of anyone staying stuck for the entire journey before they started seeing God's power show up and show out. Even with the famous story of Job in the Bible, most scholars believe his journey of hardship only lasted nine months. Generally, when we are not willing to stay committed to His order or we give up, we walk around with this self-loathing "false humility." This happens because we didn't have the faith to receive His favor, or we didn't want to pay the price or wait on God. And now because we walk around defeated, we would rather walk around with this false humility than admit that we gave up or wouldn't pay the cost. We do this as a defense mechanism to protect us from the underlying disappointment. Seeing God's power show up and show out, of course, describes the believers that were willing to press in with Him during the trials and tribulations of life. This describes the believers who would not give up. This describes the believers who are not ashamed of the Gospel. This describes the believers who would wait on God and not jump back into the ways of the world to get the instant gratification of the flesh. This describes the believers that actually knew God's promises in His Word and would eagerly wait for these promises to come to fruition in their lives through faith. This describes the believers who stayed committed to building God's house instead of focusing on their own homes only. This does not describe the ones who gave up, resisted His order, or thought their ways were better than God's ways. I can't speak for those people. Those who trusted in Him and operated in His order always found powerful moments of victory one way or another, even to death, which is a victory when in Christ. That being said, not everyone who has died in the name of Christ has experienced kingdom power during their lives on earth. Hard to hear but true. We will discover why.

I knew the defeated life all too well before my "last night." I also know that this is hard for anyone to hear, including me, but the power and favor aren't free; they come with a cost. Sometimes, the first cost is humbling ourselves to hear the truth. Humbling ourselves or being humbled hardly ever feels good. We need to put ourselves aside for a moment to see that having the evidence of God's power in our lives is more about Him than it is about us. If we are consumed with self, we won't care about God's calling on our lives. Nor will we care about His power. If we are believers living in a selfish posture, we will be critical about the ones seeking His power. Then we will make ignorant claims that our walks should be about "relationship" with Him only, instead of His power.

We make these claims because we have given up on His power. Also, this stance comes from a lack of understanding of the scriptures and selfishness. This is because we don't realize that nothing comes to us, including relationship with our heavenly Father, without His power. The only way we will know our Creator is through the *power* of the Holy Spirit! Fruits of the Spirit start with power! Wisdom and understanding of the scriptures come from His power. It all has to do with His power at different levels. The very creation that we live in came from His power. None of us are self-made people, whether we know it or not, and we don't even have the basics without God's power. We won't even be able to get out of bed in the morning without God's power. As we rely on His power for deeper relationship, we look to show evidence of His power to others as a part of the kingdom Gospel plan. This only happens when we take our eyes off ourselves.

THY KINGDOM COME

"Thy kingdom come, thy will be done, on earth as it is in heaven."

You know what I hear in that verse? I hear God saying, "Okay, but *you* first." Why? This is because our Father is more than clear in His Word. His kingdom will come into us if His will is actually done. But not until. "Thy will be done" requires submission to see His power and glory show out in our lives.

> Now listen, you who say, "Today or tomorrow we will go to this or that city, spend a year there, carry on business and make money." Why, you do not even know what will happen tomorrow. What is your life? You are a mist that appears for a little while and then vanishes. Instead, you ought to say, "If it is the Lord's will, we will live and do this or that." *(James 4:13–15)*

It doesn't mean we have everything figured out in our lives according to our earthly calculations. Really, it means we have nothing figured out.

> My message and my preaching were not with wise and persuasive words, but with a demonstration of the Spirit's power, so that your faith might not rest on human wisdom, but on God's power. *(1 Corinthians 2:4–5)*

When we have everything figured out, we are prideful people. Why would we get preferential treatment living disobedient, worldly, and pride-filled lives that are not submitted to Him?

The Bible says,

> Submit yourselves, then, to God. Resist the devil, and he will flee from you. Come near to God and _He will come near to you_. *(James 4:7–8)*

> If we died with Him, we will also live with Him; if we endure, we will also reign with Him, _if we disown Him, He will disown us_. *(2 Timothy 2:11–12)*

> If you seek Him, He will be found by you, _but if you forsake Him, He will forsake you._ *(2 Chronicles 15:2)*

When God comes near to us, this is His kingdom power and favor. This is the "kingdom of God" as written in the scriptures. The kingdom of God has already come to the earth for us. When the scriptures allude to "coming into the kingdom" or "thy kingdom come," they are not just referring to us coming into the "family of believers" or coming into our "glorified eternal living places" *only*. These scriptures are intended to point out God's power coming into us through the Holy Ghost, as we will see in the text.

Let's be clear about verses that say, "God is near us, or with us," or "When we draw near to Him, He draws near to us." When God comes near to us, this is His presence; but this is also His manifested power and His favor, and a new level of living. These verses don't mean that God will be around us in some sort of mysterious way that we don't understand (it will certainly feel like that, if we don't lean into Him in a radical way). This is real life presence, power, and action happening in our lives when our Father comes near to us. He will make it more than obvious that it is Him. It seems clear from those last verses and many others that we would actually have to do something, though.

Perhaps put in the effort to draw near to Him? Perhaps do *His* will? Perhaps develop the deposits He has put in us. Perhaps leave our old lives behind. Perhaps live a life of excellence. Perhaps take our hands off the control of our lives and let Him take over. Perhaps take Him seriously for the first time in our lives? Perhaps this is where all the qualifying and disqualifying verses start to make sense for the first time. This sounds like action to me.

> *No, the Word is very near you; it is in your mouth and in your heart so you may obey it. See, I set before you today life and prosperity, death and destruction. For I command you today to love the Lord your God, to walk in obedience to Him, and to keep His commands, decrees and laws; then you will live and increase, and the Lord your God will bless you in the land you are entering to possess. But if your heart turns away and you are not obedient, and if you are drawn away to*

*bow down to other gods and worship them, I declare
to you this day that you will certainly be destroyed.
You will not live long in the land you are crossing
the Jordan to enter and possess. This day I call the
heavens and the earth as witnesses against you that
I have set before you life and death, blessings and
curses. Now choose life, so that you and your children
may live and that you may love the Lord your God,
listen to His voice, and hold fast to Him. For the Lord is
your life, and He will give you many years in the land
He swore to give to your fathers, Abraham, Isaac and
Jacob. (Deuteronomy 30:14–20)*

God coming close to us isn't automatic just because we believe
in Him. Let's not be deceived. Also, being a "good" person <u>only</u> won't
bring on this type of power and favor either. Our earthly standard of
"good" is so much different than God's. This doesn't mean we don't
be good people <u>by any means</u>. Being good to others is a *huge* calling
on our lives. It just means that it's not the only qualification that will
bring us set-apart and powerful lives, especially when it's done apart
from God and His order. It becomes a prideful pursuit at this point.
The devil has the unbelieving community tricked with this theology.
That's why many people don't surrender their lives to Christ. This
theology is "universalism" with no allegiance to anything, including
Jesus Christ.

*And whatever you do, whether in word or deed, do it
all in the <u>name of the Lord Jesus</u>, giving thanks to God
the Father through Him. (Colossians 3:17)*

If I've heard it once, I've heard it a hundred times. The most
popular claim coming out of an unbeliever's mouth is that "I'm a
good person, and I'm good to others." This is their justification to
live apart from God or their need for a Savior. Often enough, we
can hear the same claim from a believer's mouth. At this point, we
become our own gods, <u>if that is our only standard</u>. Let's not let that
be our only standard when it comes to our pursuits with Christ. We

will trick ourselves out of all other forms of worship that bring His power and victory into our lives. The scripture says,

> Love the Lord your God with all your heart and with all your soul and with all your strength and with all your mind; and, "Love your neighbor as yourself."
> (Luke 10:27)

Let's not forget to do the first part of that verse, because the last part becomes insignificant without God in the center of our lives. There will be no power in the last part if the foundations aren't set in the first part. This is because the power is from the Holy Spirit. If there is no allegiance to Jesus, then we will not access His power. At least not kingdom power, anyway.

> The Lord your God will circumcise your hearts and the hearts of your descendants, so that you may love Him with all your heart and with all your soul, and live. The Lord your God will put all these curses on your enemies who hate and persecute you. You will again obey the Lord and follow all His commands I am giving you today. Then the Lord your God will make you most prosperous in all the work of your hands and in the fruit of your womb, the young of your livestock and the crops of your land. The Lord will again delight in you and make you prosperous, just as He delighted in your ancestors, if you obey the Lord your God and keep His commands and decrees that are written in this Book of the Law and turn to the Lord your God with all your heart and with all your soul.
> (Deuteronomy 30:6–10)

Access to His power and favor is going to require work and deeds in action. The devil doesn't want us to talk about deeds. He's blinded the Church with deeds. He's caused us to think it's religious to talk about deeds and set-apart living. That's because we are confused with the scriptures. We don't *truly* know what the dos and don'ts verses give us—or don't give us. This is a major issue in the Western church. A large portion of believers have salvation and power mixed up or blended together at some sort of level whether we know it or not. Take a verse like this:

> *For of this you can be sure: No immoral, impure or greedy person—such a person is an idolater—has any inheritance in the kingdom of Christ and of God. Let no one deceive you with empty words, for because of such things God's wrath comes on those who are disobedient. (Ephesians 5:5–6)*

What do we do with a verse like this? I will *never* downplay, depreciate, or minimize the importance of obedience. That is not what this is about. This entire study is a closer look at love. Love is obedience. That being said, which one of us thinks that we can actually qualify for salvation by *not* doing the things mentioned in the last verse? We can't qualify ourselves in—and we can't qualify ourselves out of salvation—outside of *belief* alone! We need to see that these types of verses—texts that have qualifiers and disqualifiers attached to them in kingdom of God, heaven, or kingdom of Christ verses—are not giving us the yes or no approval into heaven or eternal life after Jesus returns for us. They give us the yes or no for power—kingdom power. Also, disobedience will bring discipline—whether we want to hear it or not. That's what the last line of that verse means. Again . . . which one of us thinks that we can be obedient enough to inherit salvation? Obedience doesn't qualify us for eternal life. We would strip the power right out of His blood, on the Cross, if we think there is something we could do or not do, outside of belief, to qualify for eternal life with Him.

Last night, I was rehearsing in the media department of our church, for the upcoming service, with the worship team. In between sets, I got speaking to one of the members about power. He actually brought it up in a roundabout way. Long story short, he said, "But what about the person that gets randomly 'slayed in the Spirit'? God will decide these moments, not us."

You see, that statement is only half true. That's the entire point of this study. First, God is the Commander in Chief of the universe.

He alone will decide the five *W*s in terms of releasing His power. The Bible says that the Holy Spirit will distribute this power as He sees fit. But that's only half of the story. We do play a part. If someone <u>truly</u> gets slayed in the Spirit, as it's called, it's not "random" or a lucky moment. This is because there have been many steps of surrender in that person's life leading up to that exact moment. This person has emptied themselves to God. They are in the most extreme posture of surrender and submission to our Father. That's the first step of action or obedience.

Also, I've noticed that these moments usually come on us when we are in some worship night or a powerful fellowship gathering. There are likely many more people who have taken those same steps leading up to that worship night. They have attracted the Spirit's power into the room. These are two more steps of obedience—worship and fellowship together. God says, "Where two or three gather in my name, I will be with you." I doubt this person would have been slayed in the Spirit had they chosen to go to an R-rated movie that night instead of a worship gathering. Just saying. That is why it's not "random." This is the omnipresent power of God being manifested to kingdom-of-God power. This comes by being plugged in and taking several steps of obedience in His order. This is action and deeds in submission. This is a set-apart life. This is obedience in love.

From day to day, we seem to hear a lot about the salvation message, which is absolutely fundamental, because salvation is the very first step. Every now and then, we will also hear the David and Goliath type of stories. Do we ever have time to bring all the letters together from A to Z? Do we learn and understand how to merge salvation and power *together* in the same message, and actually put it to work? Do we even care? We need to understand that salvation and power are two entirely different topics altogether. Perhaps we think one is automatically the other. If we don't have answers to these questions, we can be left frustrated in our walks.

Perhaps faith in the middle or the process in the B–Z part of our journey gets neglected in the discussions today. Why is this? This is because the process to discover and actually have access to what's available in B to Z is <u>work</u>. B to Z, or the "faith in the middle," gets neglected for the most part because B to Z is <u>work and a *new order* to live by</u>—but it's not easy. Change can be painful. As a society, work is not what people want to hear. This is the part that doesn't get talked about very often. This is because we want everything quick and for the least amount of work or for free. Also, *a new order* seems to be offensive to most. A new order isn't all that popular to talk about, because we don't want to change our cushy, addicted, or comfortable living patterns most of the time. "Don't judge me." Then when we can't overcome our struggles, we get cranky and complain about them. We start to blame God and wonder where He is and why we aren't getting any good breaks. Then we give up on God and His promises. There is a problem with neglecting to talk about the "*process*" in obtaining what's available in the B–Z journey. That problem is we will miss the calling God has put on our lives if we don't. We will miss the "purpose" we are so desperately searching for deep within. We will miss the power and favor God wants to release into our lives. So . . . in this book, I say . . . let's talk about it. Knowledge is power.

> For the earth will be filled with the <u>knowledge</u> of the glory of the Lord. *(Habakkuk 2:14)*

THE POWER—B TO Z (THE IN-DEPTH LOOK)

> To this end I strenuously contend with all the energy Christ so powerfully works in me.
> —*Colossians 1:29*

To properly discuss and bring discernment to power, and the *process* that takes place to tap into His power, we must know what His power even is. Let's review power in more depth. Day to day, we will all live out an assortment of different experiences within them. Each day, we have natural experiences, or we will have days mixed with natural and supernatural experiences. Both the believer and the unbeliever can live natural lives only. We have already talked about this. Just because we believe in Jesus Christ doesn't mean we will have supernatural experiences in our days. We will only tap into the power of God here on earth when we start operating in obedience with excellence. The manifestation power is the "super" part. God's "super" mixed with our "natural" give us the "supernatural" experiences. This is the spiritual realm of His presence that exists all around us through the Holy Spirit.

Jesus said that we would do better things than Him after His death and resurrection. Hard to believe, but the scriptures don't lie. What was to come after His death and resurrection? The Holy Spirit, of course, fifty days after Jesus's resurrection. This was called Pentecost. Is the Holy Spirit better than Jesus then? Of course not. Jesus was simply saying that instead of having "spot" power, depending on where He was at, this power would be accessible to everyone and everywhere when the Spirit arrived. This experience would be access to His kingdom power.

The Bible says,

> *What I'm about to tell you is true. Anyone who has faith in Me will do what I have been doing. In fact, he will do even greater things. That is because I am going to the Father. (John 14:12)*

What? Jesus promised that we would do greater things than Himself. Jesus turned water into wine, healed the lame and the blind, walked on water, had special wisdom, healed a paralyzed man, calmed a storm, and taught with great authority. The list is endless, really. It's almost unfathomable to think that we would have "access" to this type of power. How in the world could we do greater things than these? Jesus explained the answer in the last verse, and He also says,

> *But now I am going to Him who sent Me. None of you asks Me, "Where I am going?" Rather, you are filled with grief because I have said these things. But very truly I tell you, it is for your good that I am going away. Unless I go away, the Advocate (the Holy Spirit)*

will not come to you; But if I go, I will send Him to you.
(John 16:5–7)

All that belongs to the Father is Mine. That is why I
said the Spirit will receive from Me what He will make
known to you. (John 16:15)

The Holy Spirit (power) was sent to the earth for us, to be all around us with the intentions of entering us, as the scriptures just confirmed. The Holy Spirit would be our Advocate and our Helper. The Holy Spirit would be our power source. The Holy Spirit would be available to everyone, everywhere, in every moment of every day. The Spirit would be a deposit in us the minute we decided to trust Jesus Christ as our Lord and Savior. I believe that one of the most misinterpreted parts of the Bible, in terms of the sending of the Holy Spirit, is that once the Spirit enters us, we have kingdom power automatically working in us. That's in part why we are left with all of these hypocritical thoughts or uncertainties as we mentioned earlier when it comes to salvation, the power, and His manifestation glory. The fact is, we have to develop this deposit through submission and obedience to God in His order to see this deposit come alive in our lives as power.

Students in law enforcement will be given a firearm after they graduate the academy and become a police officer. They will have power on their hip, but many will work an entire career without having to use it on duty. What if a SEAL is carrying a grenade that he never throws? In either case, both will have power on them, but there will be no execution of this power if action is not taken. Just because the power is available doesn't mean we are using it. Just because there is favor available doesn't mean we will receive it. Just the same, we can have the Spirit in us, but we may not ever execute to see its power released.

What if we don't rely on our Advocate for help? What if we don't take our hands off the steering wheel of our lives long enough to let the Helper actually help us? What if we don't execute in any way to see this power and favor come alive in our lives? What if we don't develop the deposit of His Spirit in us? We can't assume that just because we believe and have been given access to the Holy Spirit, we have His kingdom power working in us. I believe once the Spirit enters us, God has sealed us with salvation and deposited His Spirit in us. Once we are sealed with salvation, we must go after His kingdom power after that. Kingdom power isn't automatic. The Spirit can be in us, but we can quench His power through disobedience and distraction. Or we can resist Him altogether. We know this from the scriptures. This, in turn, becomes a powerless walk.

> Do not grieve the Holy Spirit of God, by whom you were sealed for the day of redemption. *(Ephesians 4:30)*
>
> Do not quench the Spirit. *(1 Thessalonians 5:19)*
>
> "You men who are stiff-necked and uncircumcised in the heart and ears are always resisting the Holy Spirit; you are doing just as your fathers did." *(Acts 7:51)*

When we quench the Spirit, we quench His power working through us. When we pull away or resist Him, we pull away or resist His power. Plain and simple. So just because it's accessible doesn't mean it is automatically working in us. We have a big part to play. We will all experience different levels of His power, <u>according to how we live our lives</u>. The kingdom power of God, here on earth, comes with a cost. It will not be the most popular way to live. This is what the qualifying and disqualifying verses were intended for—especially the "kingdom of God" verses. We must realize that kingdom verses mean power and *not eternal life*. Every single kingdom of God verse mentions qualifiers or disqualifiers, or something to come. We know that this cannot mean eternal life or heaven in these particular references. The Bible talks about the one and only qualifier for salvation. We discussed the *only* one qualifier for eternal life in the last chapter. If kingdom of God verses had anything to do with eternal life or our eternity in heaven, then the scriptures would totally contradict themselves. The scriptures never contradict themselves. The scriptures will look contradictory sometimes until we actually understand them. For instance, let's review two verses to appreciate how they may look contradictory:

> He has saved us and called us to a holy life—<u>not because of anything we have done</u> but because of His own purpose and grace. This grace was given us in Christ Jesus before the beginning of time. *(2 Timothy 1:9)*

> Or do you not know that the unrighteous will not inherit the Kingdom of God? Do not be deceived; neither fornicators, nor idolaters, nor adulterers, nor effeminate, nor homosexuals, nor thieves, nor the covetous, nor drunkards, nor revilers, nor swindlers, will inherit the Kingdom of God. *(1 Corinthians 6:9–10)*

The first verse talks about salvation, and the second verse talks about His power. At first glance, they both might appear to be talking about salvation and heaven. These two verses may look contradictory to some if we don't understand the difference between salvation and power verses. Kingdom verses always talk about works or no works, sin or no sin, or something to come. This cannot be talking about salvation because of the "Timothy" verse that says, "He saved us . . . not because of anything we have done." This shows us that we can't *do* or *not do* something for salvation outside of belief alone. This is a *huge* flaw in the understanding of the scriptures. We must have a *made-up mind* about the conspiracy within kingdom verses or, again, qualifying or disqualifying verses and how they relate to salvation and power.

POWER

What does the kingdom of God mean then? Kingdom of God is His spiritual <u>power</u> available for us to "access" here on earth.

> For the kingdom of God is not a matter of talk but of power. *(1 Corinthians 4:20)*

These verses suggest that by some sort of "works" or acts of obedience away from sin, we might have access or inherit the kingdom of God. Salvation is free; the power is not. The power comes with a cost. We will need to plug in to access it. Here's a simple illustration:

Let's say you head down to the mall to buy a new cell phone. If it's a new iPhone, you will receive the nice white box wrapped in plastic. You unwrap the package to reveal your new phone. Wow! Awesome! You power on your new phone and go through all of the orientation steps to set it up. After you get through the "setup" portion, you will discover that your brand-new phone has very little battery power in it. This phone will have to be plugged in very soon, or it will lose all of its power and be dead. If the phone goes dead, does that mean that you didn't go through the orientation and start-up process with your new phone? No. Does it mean that the battery is gone or that it doesn't have one? Of course not. It just means it has to be plugged in to be filled back up with power. See where we are going with this? Faith without deeds (plugging in) is dead or is a powerless walk. That does not mean we are not saved still. I think we may be surprised who we see in heaven when that time comes. I also think that we will be surprised to see the different levels of responsibility and reward in heaven and in our glorified lives, according to how we lived our lives here on earth.

I believe that when we accept the Living Word of God and the works of Jesus on the Cross, we get sealed with salvation and are given the Holy Spirit as a deposit. The Spirit is the new battery we are given inside of us. Then we go through orientation and setup, which is a few steps in the start-up of our new journey. Maybe we get a Bible, or perhaps maybe we get baptized, or maybe we join a church. As life continues on from day to day, we discover that the batteries that we were given (the Holy Spirit in us) start to get lower and lower. Why is this? And what is draining our batteries? Life, sin, trials, and tribulations drain the batteries in us or the Spirits power in us. In order to get our batteries charged back up, we must "take action" and "plug in." This doesn't automatically happen if we don't take action. If we refuse to plug in to some sort of action (God's order), we will get weaker and weaker, and eventually, our "power" will run out.

We will live natural lives with no evidence of God's power in them. Does that mean the Spirit is gone or that we are not still sealed? No. It means that we need to take action with God to access His power to fill back up. What's the power source? Plugging into His order in obedience. This "activates" the Holy Spirit's power within us. This starts to develop what was deposited in us. The more we plug in, the more power we will have. The plugging in is work, action, and relationship, and so on. This is where the "qualifying" or "disqualifying" verses take meaning in our lives. This is where we discover kingdom-of-God power. It is the omnipresent Spirit of God that was sent to the earth to be in us and to be all around us—hence the omnipresence. There will be a cost to plug in and receive this omnipresent power in a <u>manifested</u> form. Salvation is free; the power is not.

OMNIPRESENT TO MANIFESTED

> "Am I only a God nearby," declares the Lord, "and not a God far away? Who can hide in secret places so that I cannot see them?" declares the Lord. "Do I not fill the heavens and the Earth?" declares the Lord.
> —Jeremiah 23:23–24

Picture yourself entering a huge building. We come into the building sealed and with the Spirit deposited in us. Perhaps our batteries are low, or in other words, the power is almost gone. The building has power all through the walls, floors, and ceiling. There is power (kingdom power—the Holy Spirit) all around us (omnipresent). It's "near" and "very close." It's everywhere like the scripture mentions above.

But because there is drywall and other coverings on the walls, floors, and ceiling, we have no way to touch it or access it. It's everywhere, no doubt, and all around us. But there is only one way to access it. Accessing this power is plugging into it. Plugging into this power outlet is the work, effort, or the cost we will pay to access the power. Power isn't free.

Picture the drywall or whatever other coverings shielding the power, as sin, life, distractions, noise, trials, and tribulations—a veil of some sort that puts distance between us and the power. Plugging into this power is operating in the order of Christ. This moves His power from an omnipresent form to a manifested form. This is kingdom-of-God power. When we are tapped into His power, it's now in us. When the power is in us, it can now flow through us. If then you touch someone else while still plugged into this power, this power will flow through you and into the other person. This is kingdom life. To get the kingdom life, we will need to be plugged into His kingdom way of living, which is His order. Remember, kingdom life on earth is different than salvation. These are two different topics. Salvation is salvation through belief, and kingdom life is tapping into His power through His order.

DEEDS

Wait a minute, though. Didn't James have something to say about this when he talked about deeds in his writings? What's with these deed messages? Such a conspiracy again. Dos, Don'ts. Do this, and don't do that. I can't make up my mind. We can now.

The Bible says,

> In the same way, faith by itself, if it is not accompanied by action, is dead. But someone will say, "You have faith; I have deeds." Show me your faith without deeds, and I will show you my faith by my deeds. (James 2:17–19)

James is not debating salvation in his writings. We need to get this sorted out in our minds. We can discern all the deeds and works verses very easily now that we realize that the deeds weren't for salvation purposes. We can finally put these annoying hypocritical thoughts in our heads to bed. Deeds verses actually tell us that there is still something worth fighting for after "A" salvation. Deeds are for the B to Z journey (purpose) parts of our lives. Deeds determine our destiny. Deeds and works are the keys we use to unlock the doors to give us access to the kingdom power. Deeds will change our life here on earth and will also affect our eternal positions.

The Bible says,

> You foolish person, do you want evidence that faith without deeds is useless? Was not our father Abraham considered righteous for what he did when he offered his son Isaac on the altar? You see that <u>his faith and his actions were working together</u> and his <u>faith was made complete by what he did</u>. And the scripture was fulfilled and says, "Abraham believed in God, and it was credited to him as righteousness," and he was called God's friend. You see that a person is considered righteous <u>by what they do and not by faith alone</u>. *(James 2:20–24)*

Perhaps there is no better verse in the Bible to give us an illustration of how we are to pull the two messages together to see power and favor, salvation and deeds. God didn't mean that Abraham would lose or forfeit salvation without deeds. Salvation comes by belief alone. Abraham already believed. That wasn't the point. The point is that Abraham merged his belief together with his deeds into one of the most obedient acts of worship ever recorded in the Bible. It means when we merge our belief (faith) together with our deeds (God's righteous order), we would come alive in our journeys and be living a purpose and power-filled life. This means things will happen a lot differently in our lives when we operate in God's order, rather than not. After all, of anyone to ever walk the earth, Abraham gets the honor of being known and considered as the Father of our faith. His obedience and willingness to operate in deeds and in God's order would set him apart for eternity. Again, this has nothing to do with his salvation. Eternal life can't be earned or bought through deeds. The victorious life has everything to do with our level of dedication, commitment, and desires in our journeys (B to Z) with Him. If God is just an accessory for our lives every now and then, we will not see His power, favor, and breakthrough. It's just not happening. God needs to be the necessity in our lives each and every day. He needs to be at the very center of our cores.

THE ELITE

In the US military, one of the deadliest human weapons to ever exist will be in the United States Naval Special Warfare Development Group (NSWDG), commonly known as SEAL Team Six. This soldier will be the elite of the elite. This soldier will have fully advanced abilities in the SE-sea, A-air, and L-land (SEAL). The work, commitment, discipline, and mind-set to *ever* achieve such a skillset would level most men or women in the orientation stages of training. The cost on a man's life to ever earn a place within a SEAL Team Six position would be incomprehensible for most human beings. That's why they are so decorated in their fields. That's also why 99.9 percent of us will never meet or know a SEAL Team Six member. They are rare. Besides, their identities are kept exclusive to the general public for safety reasons. Well, it's the same thing with tapping into God's supernatural kingdom experiences. There will be a cost on a man's life to have access to this type of power and favor. Much like a SEAL, the level of commitment, or the cost we are willing to pay, will determine how far down the supernatural scale of B to Z we will travel. The further down the scale, the more we will experience.

Faith if not accompanied with deeds would be dead, so say the scriptures. This means we will struggle to find the victorious lives, and our walk would be powerless. We must plug into God's order, *instead* of the world's order to access His power, so that we can live victorious kingdom lives like Abraham did. Maybe the proper way to put it would be like this: We need to unplug from the world to plug into God. The two different sockets that we plug into will become very significant for the rest of our lives. Not every plug-in will give us power.

WHITEWASHED

When we merge our belief (salvation) with our deeds (God's order), we start to see supernatural works and God's power show up in our lives. This is a guarantee. God considers this to be a righteous way of living.

"And it was credited to him as righteousness," as said in James 2:23.

When talking about the "righteousness" that gets credited to us through obedient living in God's order, we must take a few things into account. This is so that we don't miss the mark in the purpose of this pursuit. The intention here is to be <u>living righteous lives . . . not living to look righteous.</u> There will be no kingdom power access with deeds performed in selfish and "religious" postures. The intent in living righteous lives is to glorify God when we access His power. It's for His purposes and not for our own selfish need for recognition. It would be a shame to put in all the effort, if only to miss the mark entirely after all that work, because we wanted the glory.

Unfortunately, this happens all the time in the believer's community. Taking a self-righteous posture when performing deeds will be a direct roadblock on our journeys. It will suck the power right out of our walks. We are now talking about "selfless" obedience versus "selfish" religion. Obedience versus religion. God wants our deeds to be done with our hearts in the right position, not for religious reasons. Jesus came for relation and not religion. There is no power in religion. If we find that our walks focus largely in part on our denominational church beliefs, traditions, or opinions, then we better "examine ourselves" in a big way as the Bible says,

> *Examine yourselves to see whether you are in the faith; test yourselves. (2 Corinthians 13:5)*

Our journeys are not supposed to be a clinic of "religious" displays filled with self-righteous, man-made, denominational rules and opinions that hold higher levels of superiority or authority than other believers in the body. Jesus mentions a people called the Pharisees that lived like this in His time. The Pharisees earned numerous rebukes from Jesus. As we study, we clearly learn not to be like them. We are not to allow our relationship with God to be reduced to a legalistic display of self-righteous behaviour or deeds done from denominational traditions. As written,

> *"How is it you don't understand that I was not talking to you about bread? But be on your guard against the yeast of the Pharisees and Sadducees." Then they understood that He was not telling them to guard against the yeast used in the bread, but against the teaching of the Pharisees and Sadducees. (Matthew 16:11–12)*

> *Woe to you, teachers of the law and Pharisees, you hypocrites! You are like whitewashed tombs, which look beautiful on the outside but on the inside are full of the bones of the dead and everything unclean. In the same way, on the outside you appear to people as righteous, but on the inside you are full of hypocrisy and wickedness. (Matthew 23:27–28)*

> *And when you pray, do not be like the hypocrites, for they love to pray standing in the synagogues and on the street corners to be seen by others. Truly I tell you, they have received their reward in full. But when you pray, go into your room, close the door and pray to your Father who is unseen. Then your Father, who sees what is done in secret, will reward you. (Matthew 6:5–6)*

Who were the Pharisees? The Pharisees were a political party, a social movement, and a group of wealthy businessmen who held high positions in the Sanhedrin. The Sanhedrin was a religious organization or an assembly of twenty-three to seventy men appointed in every city in Israel. These men were elders, and they were to be recognized as leaders in their communities. Pharisees wanted to be on the "religious" podium and on display for everyone to see. In the New Testament, the Sanhedrin led by the Pharisees were best known for their part in the series of trials that resulted in the crucifixion of Jesus. Go figure.

The Sanhedrin began with an informal examination of Jesus before Annas, the former high priest, followed by a formal session in front of the entire Sanhedrin, before Caiaphas. It was this group, the Messiah's very own people, that would hand Him over to the Romans to be crucified on the cross. Let's not be like the religious Pharisees.

OBEDIENCE/GREASY-GRACE "PENDULUM"

OBEDIENCE

As we spend our lives in the B to Z, we need God's balance in our lives. We need His balance to make sure that we stay in His "sweet spot." When it comes to deeds and obedience, we often find extremes in the believing community, to one side or the other, on the obedience versus grace pendulum. Sometimes it's hard to stay in the sweet spot or balanced on the pendulum in my opinion. Why is this? I truly believe that this spread on the pendulum comes from what we talked about earlier—uncertainty in the scriptures. We need to know our Bibles to be effective witnesses. If we don't understand the scriptures that involve "qualifications" or "disqualifiers," we try to achieve our way to salvation, which is impossible. Furthermore, we don't know what to trust in God's order. A misunderstanding now turns into a trust issue. When we can't get settled, then we stay committed to whatever side we believe in because we don't know the difference. I *think* we believe that our salvation is an absolutely free gift through the cross most of the time. But sooner or later, works and deeds start creeping into our conversations in terms of salvation. Critical and judgmental spirits, too—especially the ones that really have a heart to please God. This is obedience turned religious. When we really have a passion to follow God and His order and we don't fully understand the works and deeds scriptures, we default back to works for salvation whether we know it or not. And passionately too. This is because we don't quite understand what the deeds or qualifying verses were intended for. The problem is twofold here:

First, the works won't actually benefit us for the reason we think, without even knowing it. (Religious works won't give us salvation *or* power.)

Second, we start becoming religiously critical about the ones <u>not</u> doing the works, and we wonder if they are doing "their part" or not. What a waste! Criticism will suck God's power right out of us as well.

Obedient believers are willing to pay the price to some extent to access the kingdom of God (power) here on earth but get blocked by the religious spirit. That's like spending six months studying and preparing for one exam and then not showing up for the test. Much like the Pharisees, we won't have much access to kingdom power with critical and judgmental spirits. We don't have to read very far into the Gospels to see this. That is the religious spirit.

GREASY GRACE

On the complete opposite side of the pendulum, we find "greasy grace." In this posture, there is belief, but there is absolutely no desire to pursue the kingdom power of God through His order. Or there may be no knowledge that it exists at all. We need to remind ourselves that salvation exists in this posture, too, if we <u>truly</u> believe in Jesus as our Savior. Belief should cause change, but it doesn't always—or sometimes not at first. Sanctification doesn't happen automatically just because we received salvation. Remember the thief on the cross in Luke 23 or the ideals we talked about in the Civil War. We can believe and not operate in God's order.

Greasy grace means this: "There isn't a deed in the world that matters, because it was all done on the cross, and covered by the blood." In other words, "Let's live any way we want to, because we are believers under grace. Sin it up. This is my style of religion!" This position (done on the cross and covered by the blood) is only true for the purposes of salvation. Again, I truly believe this stance starts from the lack of understanding in the scriptures. The misunderstanding turns into a trust issue again. If we are unsettled in the verses, then we remain stuck in this posture, because we don't know the difference.

If we can't be settled in the understanding of what the deeds are for, then we scrap them. After we scrap them, we are left on the extreme side of grace only. In some cases, we just might not be willing to pay the price for the power, so we resort to "grace" only, as it relates to salvation, mercy, and the forgiveness of sins. We don't know what to trust again, because of the uncertainty. Perhaps we don't realize that His mercy should be working simultaneously with our obedience done in faith, to start experiencing more measure of God's power and favor, to see verses like Jeremiah 29:11 come to fruition in our lives. We will talk more about grace in chapter 7.

In either case, this type of posture is evident. In this position, we find that our lives remain the same as they did before we had our salvation moment. If we only knew the victory we were forfeiting in this posture. We usually stay stuck in our storms for the rest of our lives. We are unable to see victory and kingdom power, because we are not operating in His order to access His power. Without deeds brought together with the belief, like in Abraham's case, there won't be many results for the most part. When we remain like this, we continue to operate and gauge everything in the ways of the world. We don't know any differently, because we have never seen His power at work in us.

The Bible says,

> *They are from the world and therefore speak from the viewpoint of the world, and the world listens to them.*
> *(1 John 4:5)*

The government will decide. The doctor will decide. The economy will decide. My history will decide. I have this, so I will always have that. I was raised like this, so I will end up like that. My bank account says this, so my future will be that. There will be very little "super" in these "natural" lives. And perhaps that's okay for some, I suppose. Maybe we have grown weary of the work that it takes. Maybe we don't even care if we glorify God or not. Maybe our lives are so comfortable for the time being that we don't need God. Maybe we have given up on trying to experience the supernatural kingdom experiences after trying for a time. Growing weary is very common, and the Bible gave us some more advice on this:

> *Therefore, since we are surrounded by such a great cloud of witnesses, let us throw off everything that hinders and the sin that so easily entangles. And let us run with <u>perseverance</u> the race marked out for us, fixing our eyes on Jesus, the pioneer and Perfecter of faith. For the joy set before Him he <u>endured</u> the cross, scorning its shame, and sat down at the right hand of the throne of God. Consider Him who <u>endured</u> such opposition from sinners, so that you will <u>not grow weary and lose heart</u>. (Hebrews 12:1–3)*

Two problems exist with being so far on the grace pendulum as well:

The first one we just mentioned: we won't experience the supernatural kingdom life that we could be living—glorifying God to others in mission, thus living out our purpose for Him.

Second, this type of faith can get critical as well. We start getting critical about the other believers who are chasing after obedience as they pay the price to pursue the kingdom life. We start accusing acts of obedience by the other believers as being "religious" deeds. This is because of our lack of desire or understanding to press in as we stay positioned on the extreme-grace side of the pendulum.

If we don't fully understand the deeds scriptures, we can find ourselves out of balance in our spiritual journeys (B to Z). If we are off balance, we will be forfeiting kingdom power and favor, whether we realize it or not. We can find ourselves on one of the two extremes. We can end up being a critical greasy grace believer or a critical obedient believer. Let's do our best to understand the scriptures that apply to salvation and the kingdom of God. This will keep us better balanced and effective believers. This will give us the most potential to tap into the kingdom of God here on earth for the supernatural and victorious lives. This will give us true purpose in Him. Salvation is free; the power is not.

5 the kingdom conspiracy

SEEK FIRST THE KINGDOM. Accepting and receiving salvation happen in a single moment. We don't seek for our salvation. The Holy Spirit will seek us out and give us many moments to say yes to Jesus. When we truly say yes, that moment is done—for our salvation part (so long as we always remain in belief). When Jesus said the words "Seek first the kingdom," He was talking to believers! Jesus was a Jewish man talking to Jewish believers. He was talking to His very own disciples who already left everything to follow Him.

In the scriptures, we see reference to the kingdom of heaven and the kingdom of God. Most believers today see no difference in the two terminologies, at least for the most part. Maybe we haven't cared enough to dig into the kingdoms to see if there is a difference. How do we discern the two kingdoms—and does it really even matter? It only matters if we care about the Word of God in terms of our mission and living out the victorious life here on earth. Discerning these two kingdoms won't mean much to us if we aren't interested in the mission or His purposes for our lives.

Jesus, His disciples, and the apostles preached two kingdoms, and sometimes simultaneously. If we don't look close enough, they can appear to look the same, or maybe we don't understand what either one of them means. As we read the Word of God, we see that kingdom-of-God verses is mentioned roughly seventy times in the Bible, and the kingdom-of-heaven verses are mentioned about thirty-three times.

Today, most believers use the word *kingdom* in a very general and broad term. Most believers describe the kingdom as this faraway supernatural realm called heaven. The "sweet by and by" so to speak. A reference to the kingdom, in most cases, seems to allude to some sort of heavenly realm, or the heavenly host, or the final spot in which we will reunite with Jesus in our glorified lives. In this realm, we have God, His Son, the Holy Spirit, the angels, and the saints. All of our efforts here on earth would make deposits into the "kingdom" for His bigger purpose and the calling on our lives in some sort of way. This part is very true. One day, we will reside in this supernatural realm of glorified living after the return of Christ or if we die as believers before He returns. But what about our time here on earth?

The entire picture of God's kingdom will look different to those of us who are alive as compared to those who are with Him now. We can clearly see that kingdom messages in the Bible weren't specifically meant to refer to salvation in heaven or that moment when we will finally meet up with Jesus. Different messages were preached for that realm. Salvation messages. Salvation messages are different than kingdom messages. It's not to say that salvation and heaven aren't a piece of the whole Kingdom Gospel Plan. They absolutely are. It just means that we need to see that kingdom messages were meant for something else *after* the first part of the kingdom plan had taken place—the salvation. It's crucial to have this matter dealt with before we move on to discern the two kingdoms: the "kingdom of heaven" and the "kingdom of God."

Let's seek the two kingdoms and take a closer look to see what we find. As we dig deeper into the Word of God and start searching the evidence, we can see that kingdom verses are actions, qualifiers, disqualifiers, or something to come. We will see that the two kingdoms are for the same purpose but for different reasons. We see that the two kingdoms were designed for one common purpose. That purpose was for "power" here on earth. By seeking God, we will be seeking His power, one way or another, every single time. Relationship with God is power through the Holy Spirit. Joy is power through the Holy Spirit. His presence is power through the Holy Spirit. Healing hands, gifts, breakthrough, favor—it's all power in God's kingdom. Kingdom means His power, favor, an edge, an advantage, in all forms of His purpose, including a relationship with Him.

THE KINGDOM OF HEAVEN

We must realize that all scripture was God inspired. Some scriptures would be "to" us, and some scriptures would be "for" us. We need to understand this because many generations would come and go as the scriptures became available. That's why there is a difference in the terminology between the two kingdoms.

All scripture is useful for us one way or another. Let's start with the kingdom of heaven. When reading about the kingdom of heaven, we can make two distinctions very early on. First, the kingdom of heaven message was for the Jews only. Second, Jesus was power. Jesus was the kingdom of heaven in physical form.

FOR THE JEWS

> *These twelve Jesus sent out with the following instructions: "<u>Do not go among the Gentiles or enter any town of the Samaritans.</u> Go rather to the lost sheep of Israel. As you go, proclaim this message: 'The kingdom of heaven has come near.'"*
> —Matthew 10:5–7

The kingdom of "heaven" and the law in the Old Testament had to do with the <u>nation of Israel and its people</u>. As seen in the scripture above, this message was for the *Jews* only. According to the prophecies, there was going to be a time in the future when a King would come to permanently reign. If you were under that law, you were reading the promises associated with that particular law. The disciples and the Jews believed that Jesus was going to come and wipe out Pilate and Herod, and smash the Roman power. They believed He was actually there to come and sit as the King of Israel. You could see the evidence of this mind-set in the scriptures. We see that the Jews went ahead of Jesus in Jerusalem to lay down palm leaves in anticipation of His triumphal grand entry. They thought He was coming to reign, not to be crucified.

> *The next day the great crowd that had come for the festival heard that Jesus was on His way to Jerusalem. They took palm branches and went out to meet Him, shouting, "Hosanna!"*
> *"Blessed is He who comes in the name of the Lord!"*
> *"Blessed is the King of Israel!" (John 12:12–13)*

They are saying, "Finally! Here is our King! We are tired of Rome ruling over us!" The only problem was this: the general population of Jews missed some of the Old Testament scriptures, psalms, and prophecies about the fact that the King would have to "suffer" first before this future kingdom would be established. The prophets knew it, but the general population of Jews didn't. It was a very confusing time. We can see this confusion all throughout the Gospels as they questioned Jesus on such matters. Most of the Jews thought that

Jesus was just a man coming to be their King to destroy the oppression they had been living under for so long. Little did they know that the "kingdom of heaven" was at hand or near. The kingdom of heaven was the Messiah in the flesh and blood, accompanied by all His power and glory.

The scriptures say that there would be two times that Jesus would come to earth:

First, as a Lamb to die for everyone's sin.

Second, as a Lion to set up His physical kingdom forever.

Jesus came as the lamb, as we all know by reading the scriptures today. Most of the Jews didn't know this in their time. They thought He was there for the latter—to set up His kingdom. That being said, they didn't really even understand what the latter part meant either. Consequently, because of scriptures fulfilled, the physical kingdom of heaven will be established after the battle of Armageddon in the Valley of Jezreel. I have physically stood and looked over that valley in Israel. It's magnificent. After this battle takes place, Jesus will set up His millennial kingdom here on earth, in Israel for the Jews. This kingdom will be in Jerusalem. Gentiles will have access to this kingdom as well.

> On His robe and on His thigh, He has this name written: King of Kings and Lord of Lords. (Revelation 19:16)

> The second death has no power over them, but they will be priests of God and of Christ and will reign with Him for a thousand years. (Revelation 20:6)

> He will be great and will be called the Son of the Most High. The Lord God will give Him the throne of His Father David, and He will reign over Jacob's descendants forever; His kingdom will never end. (Luke 1:32–33)

When Jesus came the first time, He *could have* set up His kingdom when He was with the Jews, but He didn't. He didn't because He was under submission to our Father. He allowed the Jewish religious leaders to decide whether they would accept Him or not, in that moment, to fulfill the scriptures. According to the scriptures, the high-ranked Jewish religious leaders rejected Jesus as the promised King of Israel, their Messiah. It started with an informal hearing before Annas, the former high priest. This examination was unproductive. Annas sent Jesus over to the acting high priest, Caiaphas, who then conducted a more formal next phase examination in relation to Jesus's trial. After these examinations, Jesus was handed over to the Romans to be crucified as the Old Testament prophets had prophesied. Again, the problem is the general population of people in the time of Jesus were not complete in the teachings, or they wouldn't accept them. If they would have been complete in the scriptures, they would have known that this Man had not come to set up His kingdom yet, because He had not yet "suffered."

The Bible says,

> "So! You who are going to destroy the temple and build it in three days, come down from the cross and save Yourself!" In the same way the Chief Priests and teachers of the law mocked Him among themselves. "He saved others," they said, "but He can't save Himself! Let this Messiah, this King of Israel, come down now from the cross, that we may see and believe." (Mark 15:29–32)

We can see the general population of people, the teachers of the law, and the Jewish leaders were very incomplete in the teachings. They didn't realize that Jesus had to suffer, and that's why they were making such mockeries at Him. Also, the kingdom-of-heaven message was for the Jewish people only. This is a good indication that there are two different kingdom messages being preached. Jesus said go to the Jews only, not the Gentiles, and tell them that the kingdom of "heaven" is at hand or has come near. Or in other words, Jesus was there with some and on His way to others. Jesus was the kingdom of heaven, right in front of their eyes.

POWER

Jesus went throughout Galilee, teaching in the syna-
gogues, proclaiming the good news of the kingdom,
and healing every disease and sickness among the
people.
—Matthew 4:23

Jesus was the power source right in front of them. He was preaching, teaching, and displaying kingdom of heaven power in front of their very eyes. All power came through Him. Jesus is the kingdom of heaven. He gave them specific instructions <u>not</u> to preach this to the Gentiles, because a different message was going to be preached through Paul and the other apostles in the Church age.

In the meantime, Jesus was preaching the kingdom of heaven and saying, "Here I am." John the Baptist was also preaching that Jesus was on His way. Jesus says,

> *Repent, for the kingdom of heaven has come near.*
> *(Matthew 4:17)*

Then John the Baptist says,

> *"Repent, for the kingdom of heaven has come near."*
> *This is He who was spoken of through the prophet*
> *Isaiah: "A voice of one calling in the wilderness,*
> *'Prepare the way for the Lord, make straight paths*
> *for Him.'" (John 3:2–3)*

John the Baptist was preparing the way for Jesus as he was preaching the kingdom of heaven. "He's on His way. He's almost here."

Jesus also preached the kingdom of heaven is at hand. Or in other words, "Here I am." This message was for the Jews in Israel. We can't dismiss that the Gentile nations existed all around them, yet the kingdom-of-heaven message was for the Jews only. The kingdom-of-"God" message to come was for the Jews and the Gentiles. This is how we can know that they are different kingdoms. One kingdom is Jesus in physical form, and one kingdom is not. Also, we can see that the kingdom of heaven meant power for the Jews, and not our eternal resting place in heaven, from this one scripture alone:

> And I tell you that you are Peter, and on this rock I will build My church, and the gates of Hades will not overcome it. I will give you the keys of the kingdom of heaven; whatever you bind on Earth will be bound in heaven, and whatever you loose on Earth will be loosed in heaven. (Matthew 16:18–19)

Jesus told Peter that He was giving him the keys to the kingdom of heaven. What were these keys? Power and authority. This did not come without a cost. Although Peter had several hiccups during his journey, he did pay the price to have the privilege of being given access to the kingdom power of heaven. Peter was not given the keys to heaven itself or authority over the supernatural realm of our glorious lives in heaven with God. So this does not actually mean heaven. He was given access to the power that would come for the people who would live in the Church age. Peter would lead this new age. Here is another scripture that will clearly show us that the kingdom-of-heaven message is not a reference to eternal life, heaven, or salvation. I don't think the verses get any clearer than this one.

The Bible says,

> Jesus replied, "Not everyone can accept this word, but only those to whom it has been given. For there are eunuchs who were born that way, and there are eunuchs who have been made eunuchs by others— and there are those who chose to live like eunuchs for the sake of the kingdom of heaven." (Matthew 19:12)

Nobody on earth will ever convince me that we need to be castrated or live like we are castrated for salvation, heaven, or eternal life. This would be ludicrous. Besides, we can't do anything but believe to have the free gift of salvation as we have already discussed. What could this verse possibly mean then? It means these men would eliminate any chance for sexual sin to contaminate their lives or distract them from getting this type of power and relationship with God. That verse says, "Not everyone can accept this word." No kidding. As a man . . . not even comprehendible in the flesh. To think of a man's level of commitment in such a case. This would be one of many steps for these men, to pursue the "super" power and relationship in their "natural" lives. This would be "supernatural kingdom life"—kingdom-of-heaven power.

> The kingdom of heaven is like treasure hidden in a field. When a man found it, he hid it again, and then in his joy went and sold all he had and bought that field. (Matthew 13:44)

> Again, the kingdom of heaven is like a merchant looking for fine pearls. When he found one of greater value, he went away and sold everything he had and bought it. (Matthew 13:45–46)

Jesus is saying that His realm of power and glory is like a treasure to seek, to find, and to go after. We don't seek, buy, or sell, or look for salvation and eternity. It can't be earned, traded for, bought or sold, or searched out. Kingdom-of-heaven verses also do a lot of referencing to the least or greatest in the kingdom. This simply refers to, more or less, access to His power and favor in His glorious realm. This will be determined by how intense we seek Him out in obedience, in relation to how He has actually called us to live in His purposes.

We now see, according to the scriptures, that Jesus will set up His kingdom, the kingdom of heaven, when He returns to Jerusalem. He will set up His kingdom as the Lion of Judah, after the Battle of Armageddon, to put *all* of His enemies under His/our feet. The kingdom of heaven message was for the Jews, in their time, with Jesus. Jesus was the kingdom of heaven. He was the power. He had the power and the glory right there in the flesh. He performed miracles, with His power, that could not be counted. His teachings were always accompanied with signs of power. Some would access His power by actually following Him and walking with Him in belief and obedience. Those who were sold out in their walks while He was there would experience the power in the kingdom of heaven. Look at Peter, for example. Peter would walk on water with Jesus. This was kingdom-of-heaven power. The disciples would heal and cast out demons while dedicating their lives to walk with Jesus. When Jesus left, He left us with another way to access His power: the kingdom of God.

THE KINGDOM OF GOD

It is easier for a camel to go through the eye of a needle than for someone who is rich to enter the kingdom of God.
—Mark 10:25

Rich people will go to heaven *all day long*. This scripture has nothing to do with heaven. Giving away all our money or living without it will not give us access to heaven or eternal life. Money is a distraction to most. This verse does not suggest that we shouldn't earn our keep or have an abundance. Money can be the root of all evil, as we have heard many times. It can be a major source of idolatry and has the tendency to move us away from God. And often enough, we feel self-sufficient when we have lots of money in our back pockets. It will be much harder to experience power in the kingdom of God with the temptation of money, *if* we don't have extremely sound foundations. This verse is designed to protect us, not prohibit us. Let's move on.

Through many tribulations we must enter the kingdom of God. (Acts 14:22)

I thought all we have to do was believe in Jesus Christ as our Lord and Savior for eternal life? Oh, wait a minute. This is not a salvation verse. We need to understand that these types of verses were being preached to believers already. They have already received salvation. They have already pressed in with Jesus. We can't do anything but believe in Jesus for salvation. The thief on the cross didn't go through any trials and tribulations with God. At least, not spiritual trials and tribulations, anyway—because he didn't walk with God. The kingdom of God is going to be a special realm of living—a place of power and favor for those who are dedicated enough to press in hard enough to find it. A treasure, so to speak.

"Seek first His kingdom" in Matthew 6:33 means that we may as well go after His power first through His order after our salvation so that we can actually do His purposes in love. How are we supposed to fulfill our missions if we don't have His power? Without His power, we will not glorify Him, and we will miss the "purpose" as His disciples. We can tell people about Jesus all day long with our words, but it is His *power* behind our words that will move peoples' hearts, when it's done in love. What is love? Read 1 Corinthians 13:4. Love is action, not an emotion. Action will require power to execute. Why do we think that Jesus told His disciples to "go back and make reports about My power" in Luke 7:22? Too many believers are all talk with no power behind their words. People's hearts won't be moved like this. Most often, we want to throw out the religious "dialogue" card when it comes to our faith. "God this, God that, believe this, believe that." Our words are not going to change anything if we can't back them up.

> Because our Gospel came to you not simply with words but also with power, with the Holy Spirit and deep conviction. (1 Thessalonians 1: 5)

Jesus knew this. Words without power is religion. Religion is dead and won't move a thing. Action will require His power behind it, whether we realize it or not.

> What Jesus did here in Cana of Galilee was the first of the signs through which He revealed His glory; and His disciples believed in Him. (John 2:11)

That verse says it all. Let's read it again. God's power through His Spirit will rock the nations when accompanied with the dialogue. This is what will attract the lost to salvation because of the evidence. It's no different for us. We need to be partnered with the Holy Spirit to be effective disciples. Maybe we think we know what a disciple is. Maybe we don't really care if we disciple people. Maybe we think we are doing just fine, day to day as it sits. We are not talking about comfortable worldly lives here. We are talking about intense, power-filled, purpose-driven lives. A "proper" disciple will need His kingdom power to fulfill missions every day. In fact, we will need His power to even be deployed. If we aren't concerned with His purpose as a priority in our lives, then, of course, none of this will make sense or even matter. We will not need His power for natural worldly lives. The world will help us achieve that.

In the scriptures, we see that Jesus was "spot" power while He walked with His people during His ministry. Then after Jesus died and was resurrected, we see a new message appear. What was this new message? It was the kingdom of "God." The kingdom of God was the power-filled "spiritual" kingdom to come. This kingdom was to come so that we could access His power after He left to be with the Father. This message was preached to the rest of world and to the Gentiles nations from that day on into the Church age. That is precisely why Jesus was telling His disciples that He must go, because something else must come after Him.

The Bible says,

> Very truly I tell you, whoever believes in Me will do the works I have been doing, and they will do even _greater things_ than these, because I am going to the Father. (John 14:12)

The promise of something to come was the Holy Spirt to be given to us at Pentecost. Pentecost signals the beginning of what we know as the Church age. At Pentecost, the disciples witness the conception of the church.

(Refer to end of book for "conception" sidenote.)

POWER AT PENTECOST

At Pentecost, the disciples witness the coming of the Holy Spirit. As I mentioned earlier, some scripture was written <u>to us</u>, and some scripture was written <u>for us</u>. I think that the kingdom of heaven is <u>to us</u>, and I think the kingdom of God is <u>for us</u>. It's also very important to note that everything we are discussing in this book will be before the Second Coming of Christ—our physical lives, here on earth. After He returns, it will be a mind-blowing realm of everything that we can't put into proportion in our natural thinking. All kingdoms will come together at that point.

When Jesus started His ministry, it was with the early apostles. Those early apostles went out preaching in their earthly ministries. They preached the kingdom of heaven. According to the scriptures, God changed from the early apostles to the apostle Paul. When this shift happened, another message started being preached to the gentile nations now as well. We see this new kingdom, the kingdom of God, being preached as a spiritual kingdom.

The Bible says,

> For the kingdom of God is not a matter of eating and drinking, but of righteousness, peace and joy <u>in the Holy Spirit</u>. (Romans 14:17)

So what does this mean? It means that righteousness, joy, and peace are fruits of the Holy Spirit. Once again, from His power.

> You became imitators of us and of the Lord, for you welcomed the message in the midst of severe suffering with the joy given by the holy spirit. (1 Thessalonians 1:6)

This means that the kingdom of God is a spiritual kingdom, whereas the kingdom of heaven will be a physical kingdom here on earth. Both kingdoms will have His power in them. Same purpose, different reasons. The different reasons are the different ages. The kingdom of heaven, or the physical kingdom with Jesus in it, wasn't for all people at all times. Are we walking with Jesus today in physical form? No, of course not. We will when He returns. Jesus was only on the earth for thirty-three years. He is not actually with us in physical form until He returns again. The kingdom of God is for the Church age after Jesus left.

Before Jesus was to leave (be crucified and go to be with the Father), it seems that some of the early Jewish people had heard some sort of rumor of another kingdom to come in the future (kingdom of God). This message wasn't in full bloom yet. This message came to full bloom with Paul later on, but they did ask Jesus about it.

The Bible says,

> *Once, on being asked by the Pharisees when the kingdom of God would come, Jesus replied, "The coming of the Kingdom of God is not something that can be observed, nor will people say 'Here it is' or 'There it is,' because the kingdom of God is in your midst." (Luke 17:20–21)*

Here, we see Jesus talking to the Pharisees about some sort of rumor of a different kingdom to come. This was the kingdom of God. Jesus said it's not something that can be seen or observed, unlike the physical kingdom of heaven to be established in the future with Him in it. This would be a spiritual kingdom to be all around us and in our midst. The omnipresent power surrounding us—the Holy Spirit. The Jews were still waiting for the Messiah, and a new physical kingdom in Jerusalem, so they were confused about these kingdoms, and that's why they were asking so many questions about the kingdom of heaven and the kingdom of God. There is more scripture that show us that the two kingdoms are different and that the kingdom of God is the spiritual kingdom of power—through the Holy Spirit here on earth.

The Bible says,

> *Jesus replied, "Very truly I tell you, no one can see the kingdom of God unless they are born again." (John 3:3)*

This verse is not referring to a qualification to enter heaven, even though it looks like it. Another way this verse could be written could be like this:

> Jesus replied, "Very truly I tell you, no one can see My power, through the Holy Spirit, unless they surrender their old lives, and let Me sanctify them."

Born again is sanctification, not salvation. This is a spiritual transformation from living in the flesh to living in the Spirit. We won't see the power of the Holy Spirit in the kingdom of God unless we go through the spiritual transformation of leaving our old lives behind, through surrender. This is being born again. This is a process. It doesn't happen all at once. Surrender is not a one-time deal. This is why we see different levels of power and presence in various believers' lives. This is a habitual and continuous posture.

Born again is sanctification that comes through a choice of surrender after the Holy Spirit has made His deposit in us. This is a partnership with the Holy Spirit. It's not forced sanctification or obedience. We can avoid sanctification if we don't stay in surrendered postures of submission. We can resist the Holy Spirit, the scriptures say. If we resist the Holy Spirit, we can stop the sanctification process that allows us to be born again into a new life. This will stop the power in our lives that is available in the kingdom of God. The more we surrender, the more we will be sanctified. The more we allow ourselves to be sanctified, or born again, the more power we will experience.

The thief on the cross didn't have time in his favor to experience the sanctification process here on earth. He experienced salvation. Kingdom-of-God verses refer to His power here on earth through the Holy Spirit. Scriptures directly related to salvation, through belief only, look much different. This verse tells us that we need to move from living in the flesh to living in the Spirit, after the Spirit has put His deposit in us. Only then will we experience the power in the kingdom of God.

Again in verse 6,

Jesus answered, "Very truly I tell you, no one can enter the kingdom of God unless they are born of water and the Spirit. Flesh gives birth to flesh, but the Spirit gives birth to Spirit." (John 3:6)

In this verse, many believers think that the kingdom of God is heaven and that we must be baptized to enter heaven because of the "born of water" part of this text. Neither are the case. The kingdom of God isn't heaven in this reference, and we don't have to be baptized to go there. The thief on the cross was never baptized. He just believed in the very last seconds of his life. So these verses must refer to something else. They do. They are a reference to accessing His power—a special place, set-apart privilege, and a new realm of living. We know that they refer to His power by the evidence of what is in all of the other kingdom-of-God verses. If we isolate this verse on its own, it can look like a salvation moment only. We will look at more kingdom verses coming up.

Some people say "born of water" in that verse is baptism, and that's how the Spirit comes into us. That's not the case either. Our confession of faith in Jesus Christ, confirmed by His word, is what seals us and gives us the <u>deposit of His Spirit</u>. Then we are given the chance to develop this deposit by partnering with the Holy Spirit afterward through repentance and obedience. Baptism is a public confession of our faith after the fact. I have seen the evidence of the Holy Spirit in people before they ever had the chance to be water baptized in public. Also, I've seen the Holy Spirit come over some with the laying on of hands before they made the choice to be baptized.

"While Peter was still speaking these words, the Holy Spirit came on all who heard the message. The circumcised believers who had come with Peter were astonished that the gift of the Holy Spirit had been poured out even on Gentiles. For they heard them speaking in tongues and praising God. Then Peter said, "Surely no one can stand in the way of their being baptized

with water. They have received the Holy Spirit just as we have." So he ordered that they be baptized in the name of Jesus Christ. Then they asked Peter to stay with them for a few days." (Acts 10:44–48)

We see the Holy Spirit fell on the Gentiles, even without the laying on of hands and even before baptism. "While Peter was still speaking these words, the Holy Spirit came on all who heard the message." Even John the Baptist tells us this in all four Gospel accounts:

I baptize you with water _for repentance_. But _after me_ comes one who is more powerful than I, whose sandals I am not worthy to carry. He will baptize you with the Holy Spirit and fire. (Matthew 3:11)

And so John the Baptist appeared in the wilderness, preaching a _baptism of repentance_ for the forgiveness of sins. The whole Judean country-side and all the people of Jerusalem went out to him. Confessing their sins, they were baptized by him in the Jordan River. I baptize you with water, but He will baptize you with the Holy Spirit. (Mark 1:4–5, 8)

He will baptize you with the Holy Spirit and fire. (Luke 3:16)

The man on whom you see the Spirit come down and remain is the one who will baptize with the Holy Spirit. (John 1:33)

The deposit of the Holy Spirit is made when we confess Jesus as our Lord and Savior. The presence, the power, and the development of the Spirit's power will come through repentance, surrender, and submission afterward.

Jesus wasn't water baptized by John the Baptist so that the Holy Spirit could come into Him, even though it may look like that. Jesus had the Holy Spirit in Him, because Jesus is God and the Spirit, in the flesh, all in one! Jesus was baptized as an act of humility. Jesus was living by example—as He always did. Jesus being baptized was symbolism for us. It was to show us how we are to leave the old life behind, to develop the deposit, or to draw the power of the Holy Spirit closer to us by submission. The Spirit descending on Jesus like a dove wasn't Jesus being filled with the Spirit.

The scriptures say, in all four Gospel accounts, that the Spirit "descended" on Him like a light and like a dove. It never specifically says that it entered Him—or filled Him for the first time. The Spirit descending "onto" Jesus was the evidence to show us how the Spirit's power would come to us if we died to our old lives. In other words, the deposit would develop to power when we left our old lives behind, which is repentance. Repentance will attract the Holy Spirit. The Holy Spirit will bring power. Omnipresent power to manifested power.

Let's not get the two confused. Baptism will not deposit the Holy Spirit in us. Baptism is a confession of faith amongst fellow believers to show others that we have chosen to leave our old lives behind. Again, Jesus being baptized was symbolism to us only—of how we should live. The reason it is symbolism, or living "by example" for us, is Jesus didn't have an old and sinful life to leave behind! A public confession will help us to keep accountable within the body of Christ through others knowing that we have made this choice to leave our old lives behind to follow Jesus. Baptism will give us strength within the body of Christ through accountability and confession amongst our brothers and sisters. This will start the process to activate more and more of His power and victory through the repentance and sanctification process.

So in John 3:6, flesh to flesh and born of water sounds like we are coming out of the placenta in the flesh, when the water breaks in our mother's womb in her flesh. And why wouldn't it be? It's flesh to flesh. Born of water is when the water breaks, not a baptism, because it's still flesh to flesh. Then our spirit gets born again into His Spirit upon our confession of faith. When our Spirit gives birth to His Spirit, this is when we have the Holy Spirit deposited into us.

Guard the good deposit that was entrusted to you—
guard it with the help of the Holy Spirit who lives in
us. (2 Timothy 1:14)

We will need to guard this deposit to develop this deposit. We do this by partnering with the Holy Spirit after our spirit is born again. We will need to protect this position. This is work, pursuit, and diligence to get this power working in us. This is the spiritual kingdom of God. The amount that we are willing to pursue to partner with the Holy Spirit will determine our levels of access to His power in the kingdom of God.

By thorough examination of the scriptures, we can determine that the kingdom of heaven is a physical kingdom to come when Jesus returns for the final battle, to put His enemies under His feet as the scriptures say. This scripture is "to us." Jesus will actually be in this kingdom. We also see that the kingdom of God is the spiritual kingdom here on earth "for us"—the power. The power in the kingdom of God becomes accessible by partnering with our Advocate, the Holy Spirit, in <u>obedience</u> to His order, after we confess Jesus as our Lord and Savior.

We are witnesses of these things, and so is the Holy
Spirit, whom God has given to those who <u>obey</u> Him.
(Acts 5:32)

Obedience is the key here. No obedience, no power. No obedience, no access. The Holy Spirit won't distribute His power if we aren't letting our deeds be brought together with our belief. The belief isn't enough. We must be born again and leave our old lives behind in a posture of submission. If we have disobedience in our lives still, it doesn't mean we aren't saved or the Holy Spirit isn't with us. It just means the power won't be there. Belief doesn't give us the power automatically. And obedience can't earn us a place in heaven.

THE LEAST OF THESE

Let's look at another significant scripture that shows us that the kingdom of God is power, here on earth, in spiritual form. It shows us two distinct things that we have discussed in terms of the kingdom of God.

First, the kingdom of God is a spiritual kingdom for us to access His power here on earth.

Second, not all believers would access this kingdom.

The Bible says,

> At that very time Jesus cured many who had diseases, sicknesses and evil spirits, and gave sight to many who were blind. So he replied to the messengers, "Go back and report to John what you have seen and heard: The blind receive sight, the lame walk, those who have leprosy are cleansed, the deaf hear, the dead are raised, and the good news is proclaimed to the poor. Blessed is anyone who does not stumble on account of Me." (Luke 7:21–23)

That verse shows us power. Jesus was telling His people to go back and make reports about the power. These reports were about the kingdom of heaven and the kingdom of God. Jesus was the good news of salvation. His power would be the evidence of this good news, and that's why He was telling them to report about it.

And second, not everyone would have access or enter this realm of power. Even some believers.

The Bible says,

> This is the one about whom it is written: "I will send My messenger ahead of you, who will prepare your way before you. I tell you, _among those born of women there is no one greater than John; yet the one who is least in the kingdom of God is greater than he_." (Luke 7:27–28)

Say what? What does that even mean? It means that among any man born of woman, John would be the greatest prophet among all of man. And yet the one who is *least* in the "kingdom of God" would be greater than John. That means that John the Baptist would not have access to kingdom power because "less than the least" is *not in*. The last, minus one = not in the kingdom of God. Well, we all know that John would go to heaven because he was the greatest of all men. Jesus said so. Also, we obviously know that John the Baptist was a believer. The scriptures also say that John the Baptist would have the Holy Spirit in him before he was even born (see Luke 1:15).

As we see, we can have the Holy Spirit in us but not be operating in the kingdom power as we have mentioned on several occasions already. John the Baptist was the last of the Old Testament prophets still left. John the Baptist was beheaded before the Church age came to be. In fact, John was beheaded before Jesus was even crucified. Although a man of God, John would not experience this type of manifested power. We see that the kingdom of God is not heaven or salvation as we pull all the texts together.

(John the Baptist was *not* one of the twelve disciples of Jesus. Nor did he write any of the books of John or Revelation in the Bible. John the Baptist had his own ministry out in the wilderness preparing the way for Jesus. The writer of these books was the disciple John, one of the twelve disciples. They were two different guys. The disciple John would have mind-blowing kingdom power access.)

So we see in the last scripture,

- That few would have access to the kingdom of God.
- The kingdom of God messages was not relating to heaven, eternal life, or the physical kingdom of heaven to come in the future (on this side of His Second Coming).

Jesus was curing diseases, sicknesses, and casting out demons right before their eyes. He was putting power on display for everyone to see while simultaneously preaching and teaching kingdom messages. The kingdom of heaven was the power in Him. The kingdom of God was the message of power coming through the Holy Spirit.

THE TRANSFIGURATION

Another story to show evidence that the kingdom of God is power, and His manifestation presence for us here on earth, is the famous Transfiguration moment on Mount Hermon located near Caesarea Philippi. Three of Jesus's disciples would experience this in the very flesh, here on earth. The <u>disciple</u> John would be a part of this (this was not John the Baptist). This experience was associated with the very message that Jesus was preaching in that exact moment—the kingdom of God. Jesus said to His disciples,

> Truly I tell you, some who are standing here <u>will not taste death</u> before they see the kingdom of God. (Luke 9:27)

That verse says that a few of the boys would experience the kingdom of God power before they died. So again, we know that the kingdom-of-God verses, in these "particular" references, aren't referring to heaven or our glorified lives after the return of Jesus, because they were going to be alive for this experience with Jesus! We see that the disciples were about to get a sneak peek of the supernatural manifestation power in the living flesh called the kingdom of God.

What's the very next verse? The Transfiguration moment! Jesus gave them an early glimpse of what was to come for all humanity—the power and intense supernatural manifestations to come through the Holy Spirit after Jesus ascended to the Father. Power wasn't going to be restricted to Jesus and the prophets from this point on.

The Bible says,

> About eight days after Jesus said this, He took Peter, John and James with Him and went up onto a mountain to pray. As He was praying, the appearance of His face changed, and His clothes became as bright as a flash of lightning. Two men, Moses and Elijah, appeared <u>in glorious splendor, talking with Jesus</u>. They spoke about His departure, which He was about to bring to fulfillment at Jerusalem. Peter and his companions were very sleepy, but when they became

fully awake, they saw His glory and the two men standing with Him. As the men were leaving Jesus, Peter said to Him, "Master, it is good for us to be here. Let us put up three shelters—one for you, one for Moses and one for Elijah." (He did not know what he was saying.) While they were speaking, a cloud appeared and covered them, and they were afraid as they entered the cloud. A voice came from the cloud, saying, "This is my Son, whom I have chosen; listen to Him." When the voice had spoken, they found that Jesus was alone. The disciples kept this to themselves and <u>did not tell anyone</u> at that time what they had seen. (Luke 9:28–36)

Talk about Peter having his head in the sand for a moment. Do you blame him? When he woke up, he didn't really know what he was seeing, because he hadn't seen anything like this before or hadn't had access to this type of power, favor, or manifestation presence before. In either case, the boys were still alive—in the flesh—to have this kingdom-of-God experience, so we know these kingdom verses are not a reference to our glorified lives after His Second Coming. The boys were willing to pay the price to be privileged enough to have access to this power. They left everything to follow Jesus. The level of dedication and commitment was everything here. Eventually, ten of the twelve disciples would give their lives for the Gospel. The other two? It was believed that John may have died of natural causes on the island of Patmos after writing the book of Revelation, or somewhere else shortly after. The other was Judas. We all know how that ended. Believer gone rogue.

We must discern the "qualify" or "disqualifying" verses again—because they are not intended for salvation. We need to see what we gain in the "qualifying" verses or what we forfeit in the "disqualifying" verses. There are gold nuggets to discover in both of these types of verses, and each one of these scripture verses is designed to show us one of three things:

First, the disqualifying verses are intended to remind us that habitual disobedience *could* tear our lives to pieces. What if the disobedience got so bad that we stopped believing entirely? I have seen this happen with my own eyes. Believer gone rogue and dying as a worshipper of Satan. That's one point in these scriptures. Some may say that's impossible because of this reference in John:

> *I give them eternal life, and they shall never perish;*
> *no one will snatch them out of my hand. (John 10:29)*

Okay, that's all fine and dandy, but we need to read from chapter 1. Jesus is referring to His sheep! Those who actually believe in Him and listen to His voice. We are protected when we follow Him. He isn't talking about people who don't believe anymore or quit following Him or quit listening to His voice.

Second, if we don't do this, we won't get that. We don't get the privilege to access His power, through His presence, to live the victorious lives. This is a special realm of "set-apart" living. The power is not free.

Third, if we do this, we will get that. The power, presence, victorious lives, and new level of relationship with Him. When we pay the price to serve and honor God, as we pursue intense relation with Him, we start finding ourselves tapping into powerful lives that we didn't have before this pursuit.

In previous illustrations, we used the cell phone (plugging in) or the large building (His power in our midst or all around us) as two examples. This was to help us understand His power available and how to access it at higher levels within us. Here is another example.

Picture a regular cup. Then, picture this cup as being our physical bodies. Then picture the cup being half full of water. The water inside the cup will be the Holy Spirit within us. I'm sure we can all picture times when our cup feels full or the other times when our cup feels almost empty. To be honest, it seems that most believers in the Western culture today look worn out, stressed out and struggle to make it through a day. Not everyone but most. Or in other words, our cups are almost empty.

Why is this? This is because our cups have tiny little holes in the bottoms of them. These tiny little holes are sin, life, noise, distraction, trials, and tribulations (storms we face). These holes drain the water from our cups or lessen the power in our lives as a comparison. These empty cups won't magically fill themselves back up. What must we do? We must drill into God and His order to start supernaturally filling these cups up by drawing near to Him in a way we never have before. Not religiously but with a heart of obedience and reverence to Him and His order. The water in the cup is His power that fills up the Spirit within us. The water is the <u>power, mixed with the relationship we have with Him, all working together for the victorious life He wants us to live</u>. But again, the water (power) is not free, and it comes with a cost. In most cases, the cost won't carry a "popular" posture in our society today. Let's seek the power in the kingdom of God so that we can be effective disciples, and multiply the Gospel message in victory. His power should be the proof to back up our words, in His purpose.

6 chance to advance

FROM VICTIMS TO VICTORS

AS BELIEVERS, WE NEED to realize that the victorious life *never* comes without storms, trials, and tribulations. Thinking like this is way off. In fact, we will only see the victorious life start to birth when we come through these storms with God, in obedience. It's an illogical way to think and hardly what we want to hear. This doesn't make it untrue, and this doesn't mean we go looking for the storms either. A mature believer will see that these storms are a setup to advance us. This is when we start seeing supernatural favor and shifts in our lives.

After Job had prayed for his friends, the Lord restored his fortunes and gave him twice as much as he had before. The Lord blessed the latter part of Job's life more than the former part. (Job 42:10, 12)

I will never speak a message that will include us living high on the mountaintops every minute of every day of our lives. That's not happening. We need to be down in the valleys, or in the storms, to actually be in places where we can let our faith take serious root in Him. The Bible says,

Therefore, since we have been justified through faith, we have peace with God through our Lord Jesus Christ, through whom we have gained access by faith into this grace in which we now stand. And we boast in the hope of the glory of God. Not only so, but we also glory in our sufferings, because we know that suffering produces perseverance; perseverance, character; and character, hope. (Romans 5:1–4)

This is the only way we can actually see God's power show up, and show out, in our lives. In our walks, it's absolutely pertinent that we understand the storm process. If we don't understand the reason we face storms or what they are intended for, we will be left living like victims instead of victors. Why me? This always happens to me. I never get a good break. I was destined for this. Then we begin to expect this in our lives all the time. At this point, we become <u>bitter</u> instead of <u>better</u>. This will actually draw more storms our way until we get out of these mind-sets.

If we are taking victim postures, there will be no kingdom power in our lives. This is because God doesn't want us to be focusing on our "problems." He wants us to be focusing on His "promises." There is no obedience when we are focused on the problems *only*. We need to bring our faith together with our obedience and press into God's order to come out of these storms better than we went in. We *must* pass these tests as hard as they will be.

As you know, we count as blessed those who have persevered. You have heard of Job's perseverance and have seen what the Lord finally brought about. The Lord is full of compassion and mercy. (James 5:11)

When we position ourselves as victims, our language now changes. Problems, struggles, and defeat are all that come out of our mouths. This is how we can gauge our own positions in Christ. The fruit of our thoughts will come out in the form of words. We are actually prophesying our futures. The Bible says our tongues and words matter:

The tongue has the <u>power</u> of life and death, and those who love it will eat its fruit. (Proverbs 18:21)

"What goes into someone's mouth does not defile them, but what comes out of their mouth, that is what defiles them." (Matthew 15:11)

The lips of fools bring them strife, and their mouths invite a beating. The mouths of fools are their undoing, and their lips are a snare to their very lives. (Proverbs 18:6–7)

God wants us to be mature believers that realize that these storms must come to advance us to the next level. These storms are by design. Mature believers will know the Word of God and realize that this is a part of God's sovereign plan. Let's not blame every single thing on the devil either. At this point, all we do is look for the devil around every corner and under every bush. We blame him for everything happening in our lives. That's what the enemy wants. The devil wants us to have our eyes fixed on him, instead of having them fixed on Jesus and His promises. The distraction will keep us from accessing kingdom power.

Every victorious Bible story started with someone passing through a storm of sorts—a trial or problems that they faced. These were tests. If we pass the test with God, we will move on to bigger and better positions. God will take what is designed to hurt us to promote us. That, of course, is for the believers that won't grow weary and will stand on His promises in faith. Those believers will hold on to God's promises for all they are worth until God delivers them as He promises *all* through His Word. During these trials and tribulations, we must take our eyes off the "reason" and put them on the "revelation." God is trying to show us something every single time. He's stretching us. He's preparing us for next level living. If we take a victim position, we will not see this new level, and we will forfeit the chance to advance in His power and purpose.

> *Consider it pure joy, my brothers and sisters, whenever you face trials of many kinds, because you know that the testing of your faith produces perseverance. Let perseverance finish its work so that you may be mature and complete, not lacking anything. (James 1:2–4)*

SHAKE IT OFF

During the hard times, we need to shake off the "reasons" and focus on the "revelations." In other words, we should be trying to figure out what God is trying to do with us in these storms. If we don't, we will stay pressed down, and we will be stuck as victims instead of victors. We will stay offended and bitter, and we won't grow into the people that God purposed us to be. There are jewels to be found in these journeys.

Take the apostle Paul, for example. Paul was on a ship on the way to Rome to stand trial for preaching the Word of God. We all know what happened on this terrible Mediterranean cruise. It was a miserable time for Paul. He was in chains on a ship going to face execution. The weather was hectic as Hurricane Northeaster was approaching. When the storm hit, the ship grounded out on a sandbar, and the stern was busted to pieces. The entire fleet of 276 men were stranded on a remote and unfamiliar island. It was rainy and cold, and they were put out in every way imaginable. Could a guy's day get any worse? He was already a prisoner in chains on a ship going to Rome to stand on trial to face his fate.

God always has a sovereign plan no matter what the circumstances look like. Most people know the rest of the story. The local islanders would come out to welcome these shipwrecked sailors and prisoners. A snake would bite Paul on the hand. Paul "shakes off" the snake and doesn't die and doesn't even swell up. The people are absolutely amazed. Now they see that there is something set apart about Paul. Eventually, the locals tell the chief official on the island about this remarkable person who just shook off a deadly snake after being bitten. Paul attends the supper they host for him, and he ends up healing a member of the chief's family. The whole island of Malta comes to Paul to be healed, and a whole island revival happens. What do we see here? We see that the same hand that had been bitten turned out to be the same hand that would heal. This, amongst a major storm or setback.

Could it be that we need to "shake off" the problems to see God's promises take root in our lives? Paul wasn't going to take a victim stance. He was going to find God's purpose in the storm and press on. We need to know that everything is by design and for a purpose in our lives. *Nothing* can get to us from the devil's hands without first passing through God's hands. I once heard it like this: "The devil may bring the fire, but God controls the thermostat."

God will not allow us to face more than we can handle at one time. This is always a questionable statement to us. This becomes a trust issue. Do we actually believe God will not give us more than we can handle? It will *always* feel like it is more than we can handle if we don't rely on God's power during these trials. That's because it actually is more than we can handle without God. This creates *fear*. Also, pride factors in during these storms. If we don't trust God, then we fear. When we fear the results of the storm because we don't trust God, we try and use our own methods to come out of these storms.

At this point, it will actually be more than we can handle. The pride leads to extreme pressure. Pressure will destroy us if we don't hand it over to God. That's why we see believers living pressed down and defeated lives. We just won't give that area of our life over, no matter what, and it leads to defeat. God will always provide the victorious way out. We need to go from pressure to power. His power is made greatest in our weaknesses. When we realize this, we can take a better posture during these storms. Let's not expect to stay in these storms. That was not the design for them. When we hit a storm, it usually feels harder at first to choose God's ways instead of defaulting back to the ways of the world for temporary relief. The worlds ways feel so good in the moment, but this will be a temporary fix and lead us to an even bigger storm than what we started with.

> But as for you, be strong and do not give up, for your work will be rewarded. (2 Chronicles 15:7)

The promise of the victorious life in the scriptures is this: It tells us that if we press into God's order in a way that we have never before, we will come out of the storm better off. It will be His power that brings us through these storms better off. These results don't come automatically. It comes with a cost. I can say this with absolute conviction because I have experienced this power so many times that it's undeniable. The shifts and new level of victories *never* happened outside of the faith for me—not victories with significance in them, anyway. And to an even bigger point, these large-scale victories don't happen now unless I'm pressed into God's order merged together with my belief (faith). The belief that Christ is our Savior for eternal life isn't enough to get us through these storms better off than when we went into them. Belief gives us salvation.

We need to remember that faith has two parts. One part is for our salvation, and the other part is for His promises. The Bible says,

> Without weakening in his faith, he faced the fact that his body was as good as dead—since he was about a hundred years old—and that Sarah's womb was also dead. Yet he did not waver through unbelief regarding the promise of God, but was strengthened in his faith and gave glory to God, being fully persuaded that God had power to do what he had promised. (Romans 4:19–21)

If we don't know or *believe His promises*, we will not see them come to pass.

> For no matter how many promises God has made, they are "Yes" in Christ. And so through him the "Amen" is spoken by us to the glory of God. *(2 Corinthians 1:20)*

We also need to realize that His promises aren't automatic. Promises always come with a principle attached to them. Principles are actions that need to be executed in God's order. We need to be active in His principles to see these promises come to life. We always see the shift happen after we take steps of obedience. Only when we make God's order a <u>necessity</u> in our lives, instead of an <u>accessory</u> to our lives, will we see His power and favor shift us into these new realms of living. Like Abraham, he believed and *then* executed his deeds in faith to see through to victory. As a body of Christ, let's make a commitment to make God the center of <u>every single</u> thing in our lives. Let's be consumed in Christ. This is when we really see our lives take a radical shift. This is when our purpose will become powerful. Salvation is free; the power is not.

> I pray that out of His glorious riches He may strengthen you with power through His Spirit in your inner being, so that Christ may dwell in your hearts through faith. And I pray that you, being rooted and established in love, may have power, together with all the Lord's holy people, to grasp how wide and long and high and deep is the love of Christ, and to know this love that surpasses knowledge—that you may be filled to the measure of all the fullness of God. *(Ephesians 3:16–19)*

7 thy kingdom come

I WAS ONCE ASKED what my biggest fear was.

I asked, "Naturally or spiritually?"

She said, "Both."

I said, "Naturally, it would be turbulence on an airplane."

"And spiritually?" she said.

I answered, "Unfulfilled potential."

Later on when I was alone, I reflected on this question for different purposes. When I thought about this discussion, I realized that the answer to one of my questions was within her question. Fear. The answer was in one of my favorite scriptures. It's best written in the KJV version:

> *For God hath not given us the spirit of fear; but of power, and of love, and of a sound mind.*
> *(2 Timothy 1:7, KJV)*

With fear, we have unfulfilled potential. With a sound mind, we have faith and His power. A sound mind is also described as self-discipline in the other translations. Self-discipline would be faith at work in His order. His order would mean power. Power would mean kingdom life and fulfilled potential. Look at the twelve spies in the Bible, for example. The Israelites left Mount Sinai and journeyed through the desert to a place called Kadesh. God told Moses to send twelve men, one from every tribe to the land of Canaan, to spy it out. This was the promised land for God's people. Twelve spies, including Joshua and Caleb, left for the promised land to see if it was an abundant land. They saw that it was. After forty days, the spies returned home after scoping out the land.

The spies reported, "It is a good land, but the people are strong, and the cities have high walls." Ten of the twelve spies were scared and said, "The people there are huge, like giants! We seem like grasshoppers to them."

Caleb said, "Let's go right away. We can conquer them." Joshua and Caleb overcame their fear because they knew they had God's power behind them. They trusted God's power. The Israelites would not listen to them.

Joshua and Caleb said, "Do not disobey God, and do not be afraid."

What did God do? He said to Moses, "After everything I have done for the Israelites, they still do not obey me. So they will stay in the wilderness for another forty years, and here they will die. Only their children, and Joshua and Caleb, will live in the land that I promised to give them."

Talk about unfulfilled potential for a couple million Israelites that would never reach the promised land where God actually wanted them to go. Or in other words, a new realm of living, power, and favor. Fear cancelled out the abundance God wanted to give them. Joshua and Caleb would overcome their fears and trust in God's promises and hold on no matter what. With fear, we will have limited power. With sound minds and discipline, we will see fulfilled potential, blessing, and power.

Think of the limitless potential in God's order through the power of the Holy Spirit. This is "thy kingdom come." What type of supernatural kingdom life experiences can we expect to start seeing once we start aligning our deeds with our belief? Anything, really, when it's aligned with God's promises. Think back to chapter 2. Let me save you the inconvenience of going back. I'll utilize the copy and paste function.

"What's with all this power I hear about? Stuff like physical healings, spiritual healings, overcoming pain and addiction, victory in our family circumstances, promotion, financial breakthroughs, love, prophetic gifts, set-apart wisdom, restoration in marriages, anointed abilities, and the manifestation presence of God here on earth—experiences like seeing angels or hearing Gods voice or having dreams and visions from the Holy Spirit. And seeing Jesus? What? This stuff never happens to me or anyone around me."

The good news is that it can—and *it will*. Few will pay the price to intentionally dig in and carry their crosses. Again, I think a big reason for this is the lack of understanding in the scriptures. That doesn't mean we can't start. What are we willing to let go? What are we willing to believe? And what are we willing to go after?

> *Lord, who may dwell in Your sacred tent? Who may live on Your holy mountain? The one whose walk is blameless, who does what is righteous, who speaks the truth from their heart; whose tongue utters no slander, who does no wrong to a neighbor, and casts no slur on others; who despises a vile person but honors those who fear the Lord; who keeps an oath even when it hurts, and does not change their mind; who lends money to the poor without interest; who does*

not accept a bribe against the innocent. Whoever
does these things will never be shaken. (Psalm 15:1–5)

When we actually do carry our crosses, this is the type of set-apart power and favor we can expect to see. If we won't actually carry our crosses, then we will see very few results. I know this is hard for all of us to hear, but the scriptures don't lie, and this is the reality. What do we think the scripture means when it tells us we must carry our crosses? Does that mean that we won't see salvation if we don't carry our crosses the right way? Here we go again. Back to deeds for heaven. Carrying our cross is the willingness to seek Him more intensely as we journey from B to Z. It would be the willingness to pay the price to experience kingdom lives—or in other words, be disciples. Are we willing to be rejected? Are we willing to let go of being popular in the eyes of man? This doesn't mean we fit God into our lives when it suits us or when we have a little bit of time left over in our days. This means that God is in the very center of everything we do, every single day. God becomes our everything. God isn't an accessory in our lives; He is the necessity in our lives. Until we really get this, we will not see this type of kingdom power and favor. We likely won't even see lower levels of victorious living and breakthrough happening in our lives.

The Bible says,

If anyone comes to Me and does not hate father and
mother, wife and children, brothers and sisters—yes,
even their own life—such a person cannot be My dis-
ciple. And whoever does not carry their cross and fol-
low Me cannot be My disciple. (Luke 14:26–27)

Until we really understand the difference between salvation and His power, in terms of the qualifying verses, we will be stuck in the understanding of these types of scriptures. That verse doesn't tell us to hate our family. We must use our discernment to sort through verses like this so that we don't become all religious with our deeds and the purposes for them. Salvation is different than being a disciple. That's the whole point of this entire study. Being a disciple is work, deeds, seeking Him, believing in Him, following Him, telling others about Him, listening for His voice, and seeking a deeper relationship with Him. We do this in His order. Or in other words, action, and deeds in worship.

The way we choose to live our lives will absolutely determine the level of preferential treatment we see. Also, we absolutely have to believe that each and every one of us qualifies for the good things in His promises as we pursue obedience. If we do not believe in these promises, through faith, working in His principles in obedience becomes purposeless in terms of getting to the promised land or seeing victory in our lives. We must have faith, at least as small as a mustard seed, to advance.

Again, faith is a two-part process. Faith for salvation, and faith for His promises. Obedience, with faith, is everything in terms of the results we will see from God in the area of power and favor. "Faith and obedience, faith and obedience, faith and obedience." I don't think we could say it enough times. So in the aforementioned verse, sometimes we may have to let go of people for certain moments in our lives to pursue His purposes and to fulfill our missions. If we won't choose God first, we won't see this type of power and favor in our lives.

This is how that same verse is written in Matthew:

> Anyone who loves their father or mother more than Me is not worthy of Me; anyone who loves their son or daughter more than Me is not worthy of Me. Whoever does not take up their cross and follow Me is not worthy of Me. (Matthew 10:37–38)

Believing in Christ as our Lord and Savior does not automatically make us disciples. It makes us believers. The two are very different, and contrary to popular belief, one isn't automatically the other, as we have talked about earlier.

Again, taking action and being disciples are the target we should be shooting for if we want to live a victorious power-filled life. That's what brings the purpose into our lives as well. This is where we truly feel the "belong" part. We will talk about action in section 2 and 3 coming up. Section 1 is to get our minds made up about this subconscious conspiracy in terms of salvation and His power. When Jesus said, "Follow Me," to these men, they left everything. They left families, homes and children, and jobs for seasons of their lives to "carry their crosses." That's what that verse above means. They let nothing get in the way. These men believed in God's promises and sold out for Jesus in obedience to pursue them. These men wouldn't blend in with the world and live loose lives anymore either.

This is high-level stuff. This is SEAL Team Six dedication. Most believers in Western culture won't come even close to this type of submission and dedication. Our lives are much too comfortable in a sense. On the other hand, that's why these men were given preferential treatment and favor. This was a learned walk of obedience with Jesus, to have these kingdom experiences. These experiences didn't happen automatically for the boys. They had to pass some mega tests, and battle through some major storms in faith, before seeing the kingdom power reward.

We must realize that kingdom life wasn't just "available" during the time of Jesus or only if we actually walked with Jesus in physical form. Jesus told us something better was coming so that we could continue to live this type of kingdom life for the rest of our days here on earth. That is, if we were willing to carry our crosses and pay the price for this type of access to the kingdom power. The disciples did mind blowing miracles and had awesome kingdom power access after Jesus departed to be with the Father. Few would be willing to pay the price to have this type of kingdom power access.

The Bible says,

> Enter through the narrow gate. For wide is the gate and broad is the road that leads to destruction, and many enter through it. But small is the gate and narrow is the road that leads to life, and only a few find it. (Matthew 7:13–14)

Few will find it. Do not confuse this verse with salvation. Few would pay the price to carry their cross. Remember, the thief <u>hung</u> on the cross for his punishment. He never actually <u>carried</u> his cross. He never had any type of relationship with Jesus, and yet he would go to be with Jesus in paradise that day. Also, even though we believe, if we don't put our faith to work, our paths could still lead to destruction. This means we could still live lives that would show no evident signs of victory and overcoming here on earth. That's destruction to me. We can also see in Matthew's writing that "few entering through the narrow gate" is not a salvation scripture by looking at different scriptures in the Bible. Matthew says that few will enter. This can't mean heaven. The reason for this is what John writes:

> *After this I looked, and there before me was a great <u>multitude that no one could count,</u> from every nation, tribe, people and language, standing before the Lamb. They were wearing white robes and were holding palm branches in their hands. And they cried out in a loud voice: "Salvation belongs to our God, who sits on the throne, and to the Lamb." (Revelation 7:9–10)*

Multitudes that no one could count from every tribe, nation, and language are in heaven in John's vision. That sounds a lot different than "few will enter." Let's get the qualifying verses straightened out so we can understand the scriptures that talk about deeds, qualifiers, and costs. The scriptures don't contradict themselves.

"MY GRACE IS SUFFICIENT"

"My grace is sufficient for you." What does this mean? And what is grace exactly? Grace is another topic that I feel is not fully understood scripturally. I feel like most believers understand two-thirds of what grace really is. By only understanding two-thirds of grace, we again forfeit kingdom life power here on earth. Grace is His undeserved love, mercy, forgiveness of sins, eternal life—and His power. Yes, power. Kingdom power.

With great <u>power</u> the apostles continued to testify to the resurrection of the Lord Jesus. And God's grace was so powerfully at work in them all that there were no needy persons among them. (Acts 4:33–34)

And that by His power He may bring fruition your every desire for goodness and your every deed prompted by faith. We pray this so the name of our Lord Jesus may be glorified in you, and you in Him, according to the grace of our God and the Lord Jesus Christ. (2 Thessalonians 1:11–12)

This is an amazing piece of text that brings faith together with deeds through grace that brings power so that we can glorify God. I mean, that verse alone puts the entire kingdom Gospel mission into one text. That verse alone explains everything from chapter 2 until right now. The apostle Paul was big on the grace message. This was because Paul preached the kingdom of God. Paul experienced all sorts of kingdom power after his belief moment. He found the most grace in his weakest moments. In other words, in Paul's greatest time of need, he saw God's power show up and show out the most so that he could complete his missions. In fact, Paul's very experience of coming to belief was in a kingdom power moment on the path to Damascus before he became a believer. This was a dramatic reversal from enemy to advocate. This was a complete conversion in a kingdom power moment.

As the Bible says,

Meanwhile, Saul was still breathing out murderous threats against the Lord's disciples. He went to the high priest and asked him for letters to the synagogues in Damascus, so that if he found any there who belonged to the Way, whether men or women, he might take them as prisoners to Jerusalem.

As he neared Damascus on his journey, suddenly a light from heaven flashed around him. He fell to the ground and heard a voice say to him "Saul, Saul, why do you persecute Me?"

"Who are you, Lord?" Saul asked.

"I am Jesus, whom you are persecuting," He replied. "Now get up and go into the city, and you will be told what you must do." (Acts 9:1–5)

Most know the rest of the story. Saul was a Christian killer who would be transformed into Paul, to become one of the greatest apostles to ever walk the earth. In fact, Paul went on to write almost half of the New Testament. This got me to some <u>serious</u> thinking. Two things, in fact.

One, there is mercy for anyone of us.

Two, I said, "Father, this sounds like the experience You gave me. Although I wasn't killing Your people, You gave me this type of experience as well, in a single moment of Your glory. What gives? How did we access Your power if we weren't even believers or following Your order? Is the message that You gave me to write in this book a misinterpretation or meant for something else?" As quickly as I asked the question, I felt the answer from Him.

"Ryan, that's what the two-thirds part of My grace is. It's My love, and My mercy irrespective of how you are living your life in that moment as an <u>unbeliever</u>. Sometimes, it's one mind-blowing, powerful experience, and other times it's a series of many small nudges. Sometimes, it's a combination of both. My grace was not cheap. I gave My Son. It cost Us everything. We paid the whole cost so that you guys could experience it for free. Salvation wasn't free for everyone. Ryan, the power (grace) I gave you on your "last night" was a "freebie" because of My unconditional love and mercy. Those moments to My people is the "free" gift. Salvation and My mercy is free, Ryan. That's the two-thirds part. You can receive it if you say yes and believe. Most often, I use My power to open up an opportunity for people to say yes to Me. But after you say yes to receive the free gift of salvation, the power will cost after that, if you want it. The last third of My grace is the power and favor that you can seek *for a set-apart life,* for the remainder of your physical journey with Me here on earth. But it costs."

At that point, tears came to my eyes. What a merciful Father.

I know that the above conversation sounds "petty" and "elementary," but that's how He said it to me. I suppose He had to say it like that because I'm petty and elementary. That's the only way He could get me to understand. Our Father is real, not some unrelatable Lord that we can't talk to or understand.

As we continue on, we must have our minds made up. "Grace" in the scriptures also means His power.

The Bible says,

> But He said to me, "My grace is sufficient for you, for My <u>power</u> is made perfect in weakness."
> (2 Corinthians 12:9)

God brings completion to the first half of that sentence in the second half of it. He says My grace is also My power. The one-third grace isn't a power that we will <u>aspire</u> to have. It will be a power that we must be <u>determined</u> to have. Paul was determined to find and rely on God's power. Thy kingdom come will require set-apart lives in obedience with our loving Father. We will see this power and favor when we are submitted to Him in all forms of worship.

We need to understand the two-thirds and one-third ratio. Please appreciate that this is a figurative and simple scale just to help us relate. The two-thirds grace is the undeserved salvation, mercy, and forgiveness of sins through the works of Jesus on the Cross. We would receive this in a freewill decision to say yes to Him. The one-third grace is the power and favor (goodness) to seek after our salvation moment in A. We will need to be determined to access this power and set-apart favor, through obedience, in the B to Z portion of our journey to receive it like the disciples did. We will need to consciously say,

> Not by my might, or my power, but by Your Spirit Lord.

This is a part of the letting go process.

As written,

> So He said to me, "This is the word of the Lord to Zerubbabel: 'Not by might nor by power, but by My Spirit,' says the Lord Almighty. What are you, mighty mountain? Before Zerubbabel you will become level ground. Then He will bring out the capstones to shouts of 'God bless it! God bless it!'" (Zechariah 4:6–7)

God was saying, in effect, "Not by your power, or by your might, but *by My power*. Empty yourselves unto Me, and I will bring My power and favor your way." Relying on His power is submission, especially when we think we have the means to fix our own problems. God will always bring us through better if we will take our hands off the steering wheel. We will need to let God drive our vehicles. When we see His power, our lives will drastically change—shifts, new directions, breakthrough, victories. This is a new realm of living. This new realm of living is absolutely possible for anyone dedicated enough to pursue it. This is not some sort of fiction story.

SUBMISSION

> During the days of Jesus' life on earth, He offered up prayers and petitions with fervent cries and tears to the one who could save Him from death, and He was heard because of His reverent submission.
> —Hebrews 5:7

My will be done, or Thy will be done? Submission. The first submission with God is belief. We have been through belief on several accounts already. Is submission in our belief moment a one-time event? Certainly not. When we submit our lives over to God <u>and His order</u>, we need to continue in our submissive postures.

The amount of submission we apply to His order will determine the five *W*s when it comes to seeing these powers come alive in our day-to-day lives: who, what, when, where, and why. And sometimes how. The Holy Spirit alone will determine all these variables in the distribution process as He sees fit. The Holy Spirit will distribute this power through His "gifts." Also worth noting is the word *gift* doesn't mean free. The word *gift* means . . . gift. Power comes with a cost. "Gifts" are just the "method" He uses to distribute them, the spiritual pipeline He uses to transport His power in and through us.

God works in such a unique way. Literally, as I sat in the coffee shop writing this book, a guy came in who works with a buddy of mine. When he saw me sitting over in the corner, he got his drink and came over to my spot. After some introductory pleasantries, he asked me what I was doing. I told him I was writing a book, which always poses the next question:

"Oh, really? What are you writing about?"

I told him, "It's a faith-based book. Salvation is free. The power is not."

Of course, one thing led to the next, and we were right into "spiritualism" (as he called it).

This guy is in sales. I notice a common theme with sales guys, especially more mature sales guys. They always agree with you. This is because there may be a time in the future where we may need what they sell. So agreeing—even though they don't actually agree—is their way to network for their future. I'm fine with that because I'm not trying to get anyone to agree with me (as I said earlier, "I have seen way too much of His irrefutable power in my life to ever debate our Father's goodness or to try and convince people about God. I will, however, tell them about His power and His goodness—and then let God take over, from there).

At first, he said, "I believed once, and for many years." As I watched his face as he told me that, it actually looked very sincere. He continued (in his words, not mine), "But then me and the old lady started having troubles and ended up getting a divorce."

He continued on. "When we started having troubles, we obviously quit going to church together. It was a nasty process. The divorce didn't go well, and it was a miserable time. I never ended going back to church after that. The new girl I'm shacked up with doesn't go to church, so I've never really been back. But you don't need to be in church to believe in a 'higher power,' anyway."

I totally agreed with him on those two points. That doesn't make it beneficial just because I believed what he said. The fact is, he's right. We don't need to go to a church to believe in a "higher power." I asked him what that "higher power" was.

He said, "Oh, I'm spiritual. It's all the same. It's all the same god. Each culture has their own name for the same god or higher power."

He quickly jumped off the subject to tell me more about his life.

"Besides, I'm so busy now. She has kids and I have three. With my new job and all the kids' events, I don't have time for any of that stuff. Two kids have dance. The one boy has hockey, karate, and guitar. We are just run off our feet seven days a week. And with this new job, I'm barely staying above water. But, hey, what doesn't kill you makes you stronger, right?"

I said with a smile on my face, "I don't quite see it that way, but we don't have to see it the same." I encouraged him to start seeking God again, and we parted ways with a side-five, man hug, chest bump. Ha.

Isn't that the case in society today? Noise, distraction, stress, stress, stress. Noise, distraction, stress, stress, stress. My work, my money, my new girl, my kids, my social media a million times a day, my, my, my . . . *my*! We live in an age of never enough. *My* will be done, or *thy* will be done, was happening in real-life stereo in the exact moment that I was writing about submission. A real-life confirmation. Also, I've actually seen this guy three times in the last twenty-four hours, so God must be telling me to put him on my prayer list. I don't even know this man. Two things that instantly come to mind about society after this encounter, just minutes ago:

First, how noise pollution and "busyness" can keep us so far away from God, especially when we hit a storm. We actually use this noise to distract us or use these distractions for temporary relief during the storm. Perhaps this distraction can pollute us so bad, over time, that we actually stop believing one day. That being said, even if we still believe, we certainly won't see kingdom power living like this. Living like this is out of order. This is not God's order under submission. Not even close. "Higher power" is a classic bailout for "My power because I am my own god now" or "I give up and don't want to talk about it." My heart truly hurt for this man.

Second, the distortion in the understanding of the saying "What doesn't kill us only makes us stronger." The devil has convinced society that just because we are not dead, we are stronger afterward. It's denial. The key questions here are, have we actually survived the storm? And has the storm actually passed? We are right where Satan wants us. In the eye of the storm, where it is the most unapparent. Also, are we actually stronger? That's the distortion. Stronger is not what I saw in this case.

This circumstance is like a degenerative muscle disease. The destruction comes slowly, and that is why it is so effective. If it doesn't happen all at once, it's hard to see that the destruction is happening at all. This guy is about to have a "volcano meets a tornado" season of life. I'm all too familiar with the season. It lasted over seventeen years. The evidence of this guy's season was so apparent with all that just came out of his mouth. He was so beat down and full of defeat it was oozing out of his pores. He was tapped out financially, stressed out of his brains, and hurting in every way imaginable. It was written all over his face. This is an extreme case of someone's life that is completely out of order or not under submission to God's order. It's not something to be critical about. It's something to pray about. Perhaps he doesn't believe anymore. I have compassion for him because I was there for so long.

Often enough, we see these patterns in believers too. This is because there is no "Fear of the Lord" which brings submission in lifestyle to God's authority. We believe, sure, but we say, "Don't talk to me about my lifestyle." Or we say, "Don't you dare talk to me about the way I live." There is absolutely no fear of the Lord in these postures, and that's why we live defeated spiritual lives. God doesn't stop loving us or give up on us when we live in these postures. He just leaves us alone until we decide to let Him take over. We need to see that love and favor are two separate things in the eyes of God.

> He will be the sure foundation for your times, a rich store of salvation and wisdom and knowledge; _the fear of the Lord is the key to this treasure_. (Isaiah 33:6)

Our Father will love us *no matter* what. That is never a question. That doesn't mean we will see preferential treatment if we are living disobedient lives, consumed in the world, making all of the decisions by ourselves without God. Why would God reward disobedience? Do we reward our own children when they are disobedient? Of course not. That doesn't mean we quit loving them either. Fear of the Lord doesn't mean we are scared of God. It means we position God in the highest spot of honor, reverence, and priority in our hearts every single day.

> Therefore, since we have these promises, dear friends, let us purify ourselves from everything that contaminates body and spirit, perfecting holiness out of reverence for God. (2 Corinthians 7:1)

Fear of the Lord will bring us under submission, in His order. When we are in His order, we will see His power. There are no two ways about it. This will be "thy kingdom come" if we do the "thy will be done" part. As believers, we need to take proactive steps to supress the noise that comes from the enemy through the world. We need to put our spiritual earmuffs on.

NOISE SUPPRESSION

Noise suppression and submission isn't only for the guy who just came into the coffee shop, or for the "family" struggling in such extreme circumstances across the street. This is for every single one of us, including me. This is daily maintenance. Habitual reflection in, and on, God's Word and His order. We are all equally accountable.

None of us, including me, are experts at this. That's why this is a journey. That being said, it's the truth. We won't experience kingdom power living *sloppy, distracted, noisy,* and *sin-filled, wordly* lifestyles. We must supress this noise. We must learn God's Word and actually apply it.

The Bible says,

> *They are not just idle words for you—they are your life. (Deuteronomy 32:47)*

> *Do not merely listen to the word, and so deceive your-selves. Do what it says. Anyone who listens to the word but does not do what it says is like someone who looks at his face in a mirror and, after looking at himself, goes away and immediately forgets what he looks like. But whoever looks intently into the perfect law that gives freedom, and continues in it—not for-getting what they have heard, but doing it—they will be blessed in what they do. (James 1:22–25)*

Perhaps we should discuss the word *journey* a little deeper as well. It's bizarre how many believers will try and discredit God's power and favor amongst each other. We will set up arguments of why we are disqualified for the very thing we want and need. "Oh, just because you saw power and favor doesn't mean that everyone will. We are all on a different journey."

Again, only half of that statement is correct. Let's not be con-fused. God is the same God for each and every one of us. He doesn't change or show favoritism, the scriptures say. His promises are for everyone. Let's take salvation for example. The promise of salvation will be the same for every human that will ever live. *Believe.* The jour-ney to get there will be significantly different for us all. It's the same promise, though. Let's not try and trick ourselves out of the power and favor that is available to everyone with a silly "journey" stance.

We will all take different journeys to get to the same end results. The key here is we need to actually be journeying instead of using the different "journey" stance as an excuse of why we don't have God's power in our lives. Usually, the people that want to discredit God's power and favor are the ones that are living defeated lives in the false humility that we talked about earlier. Trying to discredit God's favor for our lives is like saying the air we breathe isn't for everyone. It's like saying that we will all be on different journeys, so not all of us will be privileged enough to have air. God made the air for each and every one of us. He also made His promises for each and every one of us. We try and discredit His goodness, because deep down, we know we aren't willing to live the type of lives that will access His power and favor. We would rather use the "journey" stance as an excuse, instead of admitting we have grown weary or won't dedicate ourselves enough. At least for the time being.

I don't think that most of us believers purposely choose disobedience. I don't think we are bad people; I think that we are distracted people. The distraction comes from all the noise in the world around us. This noise is deadly because it's barely obvious. When it's barely obvious, it becomes very destructive. Experiencing power or being selected to be a vehicle of the Holy Spirit's most powerful gifts is going to be rare. It will be a very privileged place. In fact, seeing any of His power, even at lower levels, won't be all that common either. We need to find a dedicated and balanced "all-in" heart position in God's order to access the power needed to be effective in these gifts. The Bible is actually very specific about these gifts and seeking them.

Remember the verse in Matthew 6:33? "Seek first the kingdom." Another way to put it would be to seek first My Order, which accesses My power through My gifts. It's telling us to be eager about it, because God wants us to multiply with His power through these gifts. We cannot multiply without this power in any way. We can do worldly things, sure. The devil will help us out with that. But if God isn't the center of every single success, it will be an absolutely purposeless pursuit with no significance. It will end up in disappointment every single time. Let's be eager to seek Him and the gifts for His glory so we can stay on track on our missions.

THE GIFTS

The Bible says,

> Now you are the body of Christ, each one of you is a part of it. And God has placed in the church first apostles, second prophets, third teachers, then miracles, then gifts of healing, of helping, of guidance, and of different kinds of tongues. Are all apostles? Are all teachers? Do all work miracles? Do all have gifts of healing? Do all speak in tongues? Do all interpret? <u>Now eagerly desire the greater gifts.</u> (1 Corinthians 12:26)
>
> Follow the way of love and <u>eagerly desire</u> the gifts of the Spirit, especially prophecy. (1 Corinthians 14:1)

God is showing us to seek, and to be eager for, His spiritual gifts that release His power. These gifts are designed to multiply disciples. We may ask, "If God wants multiplication, then why doesn't He just automatically power us up in His gifts and let us go?" This would be tyranny. Forced obedience. We would be like a bunch of robots. God designed us in His image. God is not a robot, so He wouldn't create us like one. God gives us free will to choose. If we didn't have a choice, then we would have no purpose in the pursuit, and our walks would be meaningless. There would be no execution of love like this. It's all about glorifying God in mission with these gifts in love.

Fortunately, these gifts will benefit our lives as well. We will be seeing new-level victories and advancement in our lives. We will see growth, freedom, and joy like never before. This is God's desire for us. All of these breakthroughs will be laid out as seed for other people to see. This is what draws people in to multiply in love. As these supernatural works take place in our lives, we will be dropping seeds of God's glory into the unbelieving community. They will want what we have if it's done right and in love. We will also be edifying the believing community not currently experiencing this power. We will want to show proof of hope in a hopeless world.

The Bible says,

> There are different kinds of gifts, but the same Spirit
> distributes them. There are different kinds of service,
> but the same Lord. There are different kinds of work-
> ing, but in all of them and in everyone it is the same
> God at work. Now to each one the manifestation of
> the Spirit is given for the common good. To one there
> is given through the Spirit a message of wisdom, to
> another the message of knowledge by means of the
> same Spirit, to another faith by the same Spirit, to
> another gifts of healing by that one Spirit, to another
> miraculous powers, to another prophecy, to another
> distinguishing between Spirits, to another speaking
> in different kinds of tongues, and to still another the
> interpretation of tongues. All of these are the work of
> the one and the same Spirit, and He distributes them to
> each one, just as He determines. (1 Corinthians 12:4–11)

The Bible is telling us that there will be a time and a place when the Holy Spirit releases His power to us through these spiritual gifts. There will be different levels, different times, and different responsibilities within these gifts as we operate in them according to His will. This is the "different journeys" part. Different journeys that boast the same results of power, favor, and victory. This is the supernatural and set-apart life we should expect to live when our deeds start aligning with our beliefs (merging the two together).

> For we are God's handiwork, created in Christ Jesus to
> do good works, which God prepared in advance for us
> to do. (Ephesians 2:10)

Again, this message *may not* be for everyone. Maybe we have grown tired or weary. Maybe we don't know that this power exists. Maybe we are comfortable enough with our lives for now, because we are set up pretty good and comfortable in a worldly sense. Maybe we just aren't interested enough to put the work into these deeds to start seeing the victorious life take root in our journey.

Again, there is a cost with deeds. Deeds are worship done in obedience and most often involve some level of hurt at first. Correction hurts, getting sober can hurt, putting down the food can hurt, apologizing can hurt, helping someone can hurt, and forgiveness can hurt. The pursuit for power will be results oriented. The pursuit will not look "popular" in the world's eyes. Operating in His gifts will be a privilege. Sometimes, we are so desperate for a breakthrough and so unwilling to do anything for it. The more we press in, the more we will see. That is a fact. We need to put our spiritual earmuffs on to block out the noise of the world designed by Satan to get us off balance and one-sided. In other words, consumed with the ways of the world and all it has to offer only. We need to unplug from the world and plug into God in a serious way.

This may sound religious to the majority, and that's fine. That's because we don't understand deeds and power. We won't accept that we need to be set apart, a cut above so to speak, to see preferential treatment. We won't accept that uncommon obedience produces uncommon power, reward, and destinies for us. In that case, we claim this is "religious." Generally, the people who claim this is religious are living with defeated mentalities. Was Abraham religious when he climbed the mountain with his son, with a knife in his back pocket? Talk about committed. I can't even imagine. Apart from Jesus and the Cross, this was "Thy will be done" at its climax. Set-apart victory doesn't come in a life full of mediocrity and compromise. God is looking for disciples that will stand up to live a set-apart life *in excellence.*

> *For the eyes of the Lord range throughout the Earth to strengthen those whose hearts are <u>fully committed</u> to Him. (2 Chronicles 16:9)*

> *Therefore, "Come out from them and be separate, says the Lord. Touch no unclean thing, and I will receive you." (2 Corinthians 6:17)*

I know this from my very own walk and watching others when the breakthroughs happen. They all say the same types of things after the breakthrough. I was fasting. I was in a heavy season of reading and prayer. I was serving. I was worshipping. I was at a men's retreat. It's consistent too. The reports always come with the works that people elected to pursue. Pursuits that they weren't doing before they got the breakthrough that they needed.

> *You, God, are my God, earnestly I seek You; I thirst for You, my whole being longs for You, in a dry and parched land where there is no water. (Psalm 63:1)*

If we draw near to Him, He promises to draw near in return. And not just in "presence only." Visible, powerful, and blatantly obvious so that we know without a doubt that it is <u>His hand at work</u>.

> *He did this so that all the peoples of the Earth might know that the hand of the Lord is powerful and so that you might always fear the Lord your God. (Joshua 4:24)*

Once we experience God's power, we will not want to miss out on it after that. Obedience becomes very attractive at this point. Being a committed believer isn't "tricky." It's hard. God doesn't make the pursuit impossible to figure out. He makes it hard to execute, though. We will need His power to execute. Once we have this power, we will have His anointing. Once we have His anointing, the hard work will become easier and easier. Salvation is free; the power is not. God wants His best for all of us. Let's be a generation of believers that is willing to do the "Thy will be done" part so that we can tap into His kingdom that has already come.

SECTION 2

8 out of order

WHAT DOES "ORDER" MEAN? There is right order of operation, and there is wrong order of operation. One order of operation works well, and the other doesn't. Not following correct order leads to broken order. If the broken order is not rectified, the consequence can become *"out of order."* This is a volcano-meets-a-tornado season of life. Believers can experience this season. We can also stay permanently stuck in this season, as well.

Everyone understands order to some degree. When we get wounded or hit a storm, and we all will at some point, it's the order of operation that follows and then the degree in which we understand this order that will determine the amount of power, favor, and victory that we see.

Let me give you a look at "out of order." This is a more in-depth look at the progression of my life from ages seventeen to thirty-four. I was living in broken order and heading to "out of order" as I was submersed in the ways of the world with all of the noise and distraction. I'll do a series of short sentences in bullet-point form to keep it as short as I can, and for simplicity's sake.

- *If I could catwalk my CR 500 down the highway through all five gears continuously without letting the front tire drop to the ground in front of everyone, I would belong.*
- *If I could drop into the "gravity cavity," as it's called, then instantly grab two more gears and a fistful of throttle without getting bucked off my machine and get to the top of the other side, I would belong.*
- *If I can finally perfect the backflip on my YZ 250 bike, I would belong.*
- *If I load the two bikes up for the ride home in my brand-new Chevy short box, crack a Red Bull and vodka, and crank the Eminem through my four twelve-inch thunderous Phoenix Gold subwoofers, I would belong.*
- *Better grab a shower, because routine activity after a day of riding is to head down to the bar and grab more throttle— Crown Royal throttle. I wonder how I will get home tonight? Ah, it doesn't matter . . . I never remember, anyway.*
- *I woke up in the drunk tank again, so now I know how I'm getting home.*
- *Winter has arrived. If I shave the heads on my 800 Mountain Cat performance sled and get an extra 17hp out of it, I may get it to the top of Tunnel Mountain with the elite few who would ever achieve such a task. I would belong.*
- *Another day of mountain riding is over, so I should grab a shower and hit the hot tub at the hotel. We ran out of Bud*

Lights on the mountain while we were riding, so let's mix a few dozen crowns and welcome in the all-night cranker. An all-out brawl in the bar that night has left me in jail—again!

- *What a hangover. How do I get back to the mountain lodge? The police will drive me.*
- *If I sleeve up my arms from shoulder to wrist with tattoos and buy a "Rocker C" Harley Davidson custom chopper, I would belong.*
- *And if I obsessively hit the gym every day with performance enhancers pumping through my veins, I would belong.*
- *If I buy a new F-150 Platinum Ford pickup truck and put a ten-inch Rize lift kit on it with twenty-four-inch KMC slides, I would belong.*
- *If I take that $80,000 jazzed-up truck and go oil field operating, I could make 175k a year. Alberta is great! I would definitely belong.*
- *Maybe if I spent $70,000 on making a 610-horsepower Super Snake Cobra convertible rocket launcher sports car, I would belong.*
- *Here we go . . .*
- *If I go to Moxies Bar and Grill to meet the boys for a Crown and Diet Coke or, better yet, a few dozen of them, I would belong.*
- *My second impaired-driving charge going home. I belong . . . I guess.*
- *If I could grab a jet to Vegas with an $1,800 UFC ticket in my back pocket, I would belong. While I'm there, I could buy a few $1,200 rounds of drinks for the company with us, and I would belong.*
- *Then I could jump in a limo with my boys and Joe Rogan from Fear Factor and the top UFC fighter at the time, Tito Ortiz, and head to the Pink Flamingo and bypass the two thousand people waiting in the line to access the VIP room. I would belong.*
- *If I could grab a jet to the Grand Cayman Islands and take a pit stop in Miami, I could get a skull tattoo at the famous Miami*

Ink, and afterward, I could ride Ogis chopper down Washington Avenue on a Friday night, and then I would belong.

- *Then I will head down to the bar they own and double-fist Crown and Diet Cokes with the most famous tattoo artists on the planet for Facebook pictures. I would belong.*
- *Then I would continue on to the Grand Cayman for the real wrecker assuming I don't pass out trying to get back to the airport and I can make the plane. I did!*
- *And I'm sure just a few of these adventures will certainly attract the likings of a few female companions to accompany me along the way. So I belong. But I guess I should grow up now.*
- *If I keep the jacked-up F-150 and retain the high-earning oil field income and get a new house to bring maturity to the situation, I will belong because I'm older now.*
- *And if I "shack up" with a woman in my new house with my annually updated F-150 and steadily increase my income from my oil field job, I will belong.*
- *I will flip a few houses, keep the truck updated every year, and do my best to provide while I'm "shacked up." I will belong.*
- *It's the oilmen's golf tournament this weekend. If I can break eighty on the first day, I don't have to worry about playing well tomorrow. Everyone will know that I can play well from today's round. That's good, because we will be so piled up by the time we do the long drive competition tonight that it won't matter tomorrow if I can manage to show up at the first tee box still inebriated from a forty-drink campaign and two hours' sleep. I belong.*
- *I'm older now, but that doesn't mean I can't grab a jet to Vegas or anywhere on the planet to go on weekend crankers, hit all the popular UFCs, the Stanley Cups, the Super Bowls, and all the exquisite and elite golf destinations this planet has to offer. Because I belong.*
- *But if I don't take the trips, I can play host to the greatest sports events finales in the basement of my new home, with*

the pimped out seventy-inch big-screen TV and the elite sound surround system and seating for sixteen. I belong.

- *Dual beer fridges help matters out. I will belong.*
- *Then we can head downtown for the extended party, which leads to the twice-extended party back at the house after last call, huddled around the coffee table. Wipe down the coffee table after. I will belong.*
- *I will belong if I can wake up by 11:00 a.m. with this boulder mountain of a headache crushing my skull. I need to get the boat hooked up to the truck and grab last night's crew to go wakeboarding on the lake for the day, because the sun is smoking and the lake is rocking.*
- *First, I have to deal with this hangover. Wait a minute. I'm not hungover. I'm still drunk. The hangover will come later. I certainly can't have that. I have backflips to do on the wakeboard all day on the lake. I better have a few shots of Jägermeister to avoid the hangover and grab a forty-eight pack of "I am Canadian" for the boat on the way out. Don't forget the ice. So I will belong.*
- *This is the good life, so I should get married now and really grow up. She can drive now, because I've already had two DUIs. Now this is the responsible way.*
- *Well, that marriage didn't work out. Arrange the divorce papers.*
- *Well, I'm single again, so the parties can go back to how they originally were. Date some women on-off-on-off-on-off. The freedom is nice. The uncommitted pleasures are too.*
- *Wait a minute. There is something different about this one. She's the one—again. She's divorced as well. And she has kids. Let's play house. Happy family. They will love Mexico at Christmas.*
- *Well, another few air miles under the belt. Weird, that didn't work out either. She's gone, and she took everything with her. It's for the better I guess.*

- *Months later, and one night, I will grab a forty pounder of Crown Royal, a rope, and a chair, and head down to the basement.*

The only decision left is climb up on the chair sober and then kick the chair out from under my feet—or drink the forty pounder of whiskey to go out in a blaze of cowardly glory—to be left hanging.

Let's call this my "last night."

That's just a very small portion of my worldly résumé—a glimpse into this seventeen-year time frame after leaving my mom and dad's home at seventeen years of age. I spent all those years trying to justify and rationalize that I was living in good order. This was noise and distraction at its best. This noise is by design.

I want to spend the next couple of chapters bringing some practical revelation into our lives about the spiritual realities that exist in terms of wounding and the source of the wounding and how our lives play out in conjunction with the order we choose after the wounds. Do we really understand the source of all these wounds and the spiritual force trying to keep us from the kingdom life (order) that God wants us to be living? I truly think that a large amount of believers wake up each day and think whatever happens, happens. Roll the mystery dice to see what life will bring me today. Again, is that the whole story? Hardly. The results of our days are going to be largely in part due to what we know and what we don't know. We need to understand the resistance that we face to live kingdom lives.

If we are not living and surrounded by the right order, we become broken and "out of order," whether we will admit it or not—even as believers. Again, if we live in the wrong order, we spend our lives masking and covering up, and masking and covering up until we die. We never actually find the kingdom life that we wish to live. This is not how God intended us to live. He wants us to be living with His power. For the remainder of this book, I will refer to any power, manifestation presence, victories, favor, freedoms, intense relationship with God as "kingdom life" to sum it up in two words.

The kingdom life is access to God's power in every form we can imagine, as discussed all through the book and up to this point.

Each and every decision that we choose to live by will simply be this: God's order (the light) or the world's order (the darkness) led by Satan himself. This is where we win or lose the battle. Making decisions in God's order accesses the power to live the kingdom life. Making decisions in the order of the world is where we stay stuck in our misery and our struggles.

> As for you, you were dead in your transgressions and sins, in which you used to live when you followed the ways of this world and of the ruler of the kingdom of the air, the spirit who is now at work in those who are disobedient. All of us also lived among them at one time, gratifying the cravings of our flesh and following its desires and thoughts. Like the rest, we were by nature deserving of wrath. (Ephesians 2:1–3)

We need to realize that the order of the world is the noise that Satan wants to distract us with. The noise is going to be subtle, even though it's loud. It will be barely visible and very attractive to us. It's designed to consume us which will separate us from God and His power. When I say the world's order, or Satan's order, I don't mean that we are a bunch of demonic, Satan worshippers by any means. Not even close. It means that Satan wants to consume our hearts with the desires of the world and the lusts of the flesh. He knows how to get us separated from God and His power.

Now, and after my "last night," my aim every day is to choose God's order to the best of my ability, because I am only interested in pursuing *the total freedom* that is available in Christ. I am not interested in no power or partial freedom from the dead life of my past. I don't want to go near that life ever again. I suppose we could walk in "some" of God's order to try and blend the two, but then we will end up with very little favor and blended results. Blended results don't interest me, so I believe in harnessing the full operation of God's order as a "target" or the standard to shoot for. So, as previously mentioned, the degree to which we understand this order and actually _apply_ and _commit_ to this order will determine the amount of kingdom life moments we will receive. The next few chapters may be basic to most believers. I want to cover these points in any case. I don't want to assume that every single person that may hold this book is a believer.

THE WORLD'S ORDER (SATAN'S ORDER)

TWO TRUTHS

Before we go any further into understanding _order_, we need to understand two truths. The first truth is easier for our minds to understand. The second truth takes an intimate relationship with God to understand at any level, and even then, it sometimes baffles us.

Truth 1: God gives all His children free will choice. It's called love. There is no love in forced obedience, only tyranny. So God would _never_ force us to choose Him or His ways. He wants a relationship with us through a free will choice, yielded by love—because God is love.

Truth 2: Bad things can happen to good people. That includes individuals who walk in God's order, as well as individuals who don't choose to operate in God's order. This is because we live in a fallen world. Ironically, the reason the world is fallen is that the first humans on the earth made a decision to choose a lie from Satan. A fleshly desire that looked good and enjoyable. God gave us free will to choose our decisions. These decisions need to be guided by God's order. Once again, as a result of this first choice, we live in a fallen world where Satan works to inflict evil on all people.

That being said, God is love, and because of His love, He gave us a rescue plan. God sent His Son to give us another chance at true life. His name is Jesus. We must choose Jesus and His order because we have an enemy looking to take everything from us. Satan wants revenge on God by destroying God's people, even people who chose to follow Jesus. We will never fully understand why bad things happen to good people, and it's generally one of the toughest truths to understand logically as a believer. I choose to yield to the understanding of why unfortunate things happen to great people, because I'm not God. I choose this decision in faith, which comes by spending time with God through relationship. Also, like we mentioned earlier, this comes by understanding that every storm that is designed by Satan's hands must pass through God's hands before they can reach us. This is God's sovereign plan that becomes very difficult to accept in some of the more extreme cases of trial.

LIGHT OR DARKNESS

Wounds and storms are different, but it matters what we do after a wound or in a storm. A wound can happen, and a storm can be happening. Both are a form of trial, and they both can end with victory or defeat. We have discussed the purpose of storms in chapter 6. Let's talk about a one-time hit, which would usually be considered as a wound. The results of a wound can be the same as the result of a storm if not handled the right way.

An open wound has one of two options: light can enter, or darkness can enter. Light is the power that will heal the wound, and darkness will keep the wound open and continue to make the wound bigger. When the wounds grow bigger and bigger, this can bring on a season of what feels like a storm. We will either choose to let the light in, or we will let the darkness into our lives. We will either power up or have the power sucked out of us. We will either choose God's ways, or we will choose the world's ways, which Satan designed to destroy us. Anything other than God's way is a lie from the pit of hell. I was there every day, and I tried every method known to man to escape the brokenness that strangled me. I tried all the self-help programs along the way, all the social suggestions to "make us happy" and all the "new age" methods and meditations at some point along the road. It was all a mask and cover-up—bandages and patches.

Satan's tactic is to wound God's people and then tell them the first aid they need is anything other than relationship with God, or

His order. Every wound is designed to break us. All *untreated* brokenness ultimately leads to one result over time: heavy weight and bondage, which is "out of order." Again, if we live in broken order, we can only pretend, deny, mask, and cover up the fact that we are still broken. This is where the rubber meets the road, power or not. Also, by *no* means do I suggest anyone who follows God's order is of any higher value than a person who doesn't. That is an absolutely ludicrous presumption, and there is just no truth in it. There is a powerful life available for us when we actually live in God's order instead of the world's order, and that's all this is about.

Let's break down the path to *out of order* and expose the source of it.

The Bible says God doesn't tempt us or bring us evil:

> When tempted, no one should say "God is tempting me." For God cannot be tempted by evil, nor does He tempt anyone; but each person is tempted when they are dragged away by their own evil desire and enticed. Then, after desire has conceived, it gives birth to sin, and sin, when it is full grown, gives birth to death. (James 1:13)

That verse says God doesn't tempt us with the things that will bring us to a place of defeat. We make decisions that bring us there. We also have an enemy tempting us continuously to choose the wrong order with his noise. We must understand the difference between the dark and the light as it applies here. Let's start with the dark. Darkness suggests the world's ways to live and how to medicate our wounds. Satan has designed these ways for us to live "out of order" since day one of human existence. I'm not going to use a thousand Bible verses, but I will use enough to help us understand. This is real stuff. The enemy is Satan. And Satan and his assistants are real. They have one plan: to destroy God's children—you and me. Their only mission is to get us to live *out of order*—to deny God's order. Satan's noise doesn't have to be loud to pull us off the path or get us distracted either. That's why the noise can be so tricky to discern.

The Bible says,

> Be alert and of sober mind. Your enemy the devil prowls around like a roaring lion looking for someone to devour. (1 Peter 5:8.)

> The thief comes only to steal and kill and devour. (John 10:10)

> When they came to Jesus, they found the man from whom the demons had gone out, sitting at Jesus' feet, dressed and in his right mind. (Luke 8:35)

The enemy is plural, and the enemy is "they." Who are they? They are demonic spirits that roam the earth looking for gateways into people's lives to steal, kill, and destroy us; to distract us with the ways of the world; to consume us with the wrong noise. They are fallen angels who were cast out of heaven with Satan, God's most exhilarating angel, at the beginning of time. It was a failed rebellion. The Bible explains it.

> The great dragon was hurled down—that ancient serpent called the devil, or Satan, who leads the whole world astray. He was hurled to the Earth, and his angels with him. (Revelation 12:9)

Satan was cast out of heaven because of his pride, and then he and his associates had one thing left to achieve: revenge toward God. Now his sole mission is to lead the whole earth astray with noise, like he did in my case. Satan wanted to sit on God's throne. He wanted to be God. There was a great war in heaven with Michael the Archangel and the other angels of God against Lucifer (Satan) and the angels he deceived to team up with him. We all know who won the war. Satan, along with his entourage of countless demonic angel "spirits," was cast out of heaven to the earth in this massive expulsion. Now Satan and his ambassadors are trying to kill, steal, and destroy as much of God's creation as they can until the return of Jesus Christ. That's all he has left. Satan knows that he is defeated in the overall picture. Satan started with God's first people, Adam and Eve.

Satan's first job started with Eve. It went down like this:

> Now the serpent was craftier than any of the wild animals the Lord God had made. He said to the woman, "Did God really say, 'you must not eat from any tree in the garden?'" The woman said to the serpent, "We may eat fruit from the trees in the garden, but God did say, 'you must not eat fruit from the tree in the middle of the garden, and you must not touch it or you will die.'" "You will certainly not die," the serpent said to the woman. "For God knows that when you eat from it your eyes will be opened, and you will be like God, knowing good and evil." When the woman saw that the fruit of the tree was good for food and pleasing to the eye, and also desirable for gaining wisdom, she took some and ate it. She also gave some to her husband, who was with her, and he ate it. (Genesis 3:1–6)

Satan uses crafty tactics to trick God's people. His noise won't be obvious to us all the time. Following his lies actually cause us to wound ourselves and others around us even more, and then he whispers more lies on how to repair the wound the world's way instead of God's way. Obviously, lies are not truth, but it's the only truth we will know when we live apart from the truth in God's order.

"Ways of the world" are Satan's "demonic" stealth tactics. When I say "demonic," I want to be clear. I don't mean that people suffering in the wrong order are possessed or demonic monsters. It just means that there are demons constantly roaming the earth looking to persuade us with demonic influence or distraction. This is his noise. They are looking for people to influence and lead astray. It becomes a demonic influence, a "stronghold," when we can't do anything to break free from it and when it starts separating us from God. In worse cases, it can start tearing our lives to pieces.

The Lord said to Satan, "where have you come from?"
Satan answered the Lord "From roaming the Earth,
going back and forth on it." (Job 1:8)

Satan and his helpers are looking to inhabit and influence <u>our</u> <u>thoughts through the spirit realm.</u> <u>It all starts with manipulating our</u> <u>thinking.</u> This leads to action. The action causes us to live in the wrong order. Separation, division, and isolation eventually lead us to defeat. Satan wants us to choose the desires of the flesh, and the ways of the world in a subtle manner, instead of choosing God's ways. Sometimes, when we follow the world's order, the brokenness can get so bad in some cases that we can lose our desire to live. Or we can live in a deep depression. When this persuasion is something we can't stop, something that pulls us into the deep darkness we can't get out of, it's demonic persuasion. So I refer to the ways of the world and Satan's influence as demonic. It's a spiritual stronghold. This means we can't break free of the grip. I have been there, and I understand the stronghold entirely.

Let's look at Satan's tactics to try and wound us and to see how he uses these wounds to inflict more wounds. This is a "cause and effect" principle at work when examining these tactics. Satan will obviously try and wound people with new wounds; but he also likes to try and multiply, using the existing wounds as well. Until we live in the correct order, the wounds get bigger. It becomes a snowball effect or a "cause and effect" wounding process. I want to explain the advancement of wounds in stages and, very specifically, to show us how these wounds can lead us down the path of defeat. We must be aware of the resistance to overcome and live powerful kingdom lives.

9 satan's strategy

LET'S BREAK DOWN SATAN'S strategy step by step:

Wound—A wound is whatever trauma or traumas we have experienced, whether very recently or years ago. This wound was engineered by Satan. Everything good is from God. Everything bad is from Satan. As mature believers, we must understand God's sovereignty in this process again and how it applies. God doesn't design the storms; Satan does. They can't get to us unless God allows them to. If God allows them, then He has provided a victorious way out as well. We need God's order to thrive through what He allows to come our way. God will allow storms to come to believers and nonbelievers alike. If we hold firm in the faith, these storms will be a setup to advance us as believers. If we don't, we will find defeat and nonstop struggle. God gives believers and nonbelievers equal opportunity to respond to wounds and storms.

Lies—Satan generally whispers three lies into our ear about the trauma that we believe to be true.

First, he whispers *a lie about the wound*. He lies about ourselves (that the wound is our own fault), or he whispers lies about the person or situation that wounded us. The lie is <u>bait</u> to keep us offended or injured, and it's designed to keep our perception obscured. In most cases, the lie tells us there is no actual wound affecting the way we make decisions or live, which is denial. In some cases, the lie keeps us from forgiving or moving on in a healthy way, which in turns keeps us injured or in bondage.

The second lie tells us *how we should medicate* the wound the world's way, and not God's way. This will be the noise and distraction. This will keep us from the kingdom life. This will keep us broken and only advance the brokenness through the viscous cycle of cause and effect.

The third lie tells us there is *no hope to overcome the wound*— that there is no victory ahead, and we will always suffer from this wound. With no hope, there is no victory.

Agreement—We agree with the lies because we don't know the difference. We don't even realize there is an enemy whispering in our ears. And without the light, we can't know the difference between a lie and truth. So it's very natural to agree with the lie, which is the darkness that continues to keep the wound open.

Commitment—We believe this "agreement lie" as long as we have an open wound. We don't know the difference. We actually make a vow with it like in a marriage commitment. We often victimize ourselves with it through commitment because we don't know any other way to free ourselves. Subconsciously, it becomes our identity. We actually start surviving off the pain. We pack the lie or the pain around like a gunny sack. We won't know the difference until we find the light—the truth in God's order. Without the light of Jesus, the darkness gets worse. We stay married to the *wound* through a *commitment* of *agreement* to the *lie*.

False identity—Because of the wound, the lie, the agreement, and the commitment, the lies of the enemy continue to multiply in our minds like compound interest. Then we believe we are something different than what God intended us to be. We have a false self or a false identity. We truly don't know who we are or what we are supposed to be, and as a result, we live in prison with no escape. This prison keeps us from fulfilling our mission and living kingdom lives.

False remedy—Because we are inebriated with this sense of false self, and all the pain that accompanies it, we desperately seek a key to free us from this prison. If we are not living in the correct order, we choose the world's order. This order is Satan's noise, and his remedies are designed to trick us. These are usually the quick fixes that feel good in the flesh, in the moment. They will have no healing results. This is Satan's last lie, which starts the cycle all over again (cause-and-affect wounding), bringing the start of more wounds, and thus increasing the snowball effect and the feeling of meaningless purpose. Satan's strategy is like an unconscious clinic for false treatment. My life was a perfect display of Satan's clinic for many years. Let's choose a different clinic.

SATAN'S ORDER: THE WAYS OF THE WORLD

From seventeen to thirty-four years old, I was consumed with the ways of the world. It always felt great in the moment. I was attempting to lick my wounds living in the wrong order, which led to "out of order." I had no idea, and I couldn't see past the deception. I couldn't spend my way out, I couldn't drink my way out, I couldn't sleep my way out, I couldn't marry my way out, I couldn't fly my way out, I couldn't work my way out, I couldn't explore my way out. There was no escape.

It was total annihilation without God's order. The purpose of this book is to discuss *kingdom living*, not temporary patches or seasons of what we feel is relief through *distraction*. This book is about *set-apart* victory and living. This book is for the ones struggling to find the kingdom life. It's for those people trying to sort out the confusion in their spiritual walks. It's for the ones who will stop covering up, those who are ready to press in with God to find the victorious life. If we are apart from the order of Jesus Christ and we try to medicate our wounds the world's way, we make choices we should never make. We follow the patterns of the world, which Satan wants us to believe will fix the struggle. The problem is God has something entirely different to say about living in the ways of the world:

> *You adulterous people, don't you know that friend-ship with the world means enmity against God? Therefore, anyone who chooses to be a friend of the world becomes an enemy of God. (James 4:4)*

If we aren't living in God's order, then we can only be living in the world's order, which is designed by Satan himself. Or we can go back and forth. Having this knowledge and really understanding it are crucial because now we may have two issues. Why? Look back and read the last verse again. Or let me give you a short version: a friend of the world is an enemy of God.

First, we have an enemy working overtime to come take our lives a step at a time. That's a fact; that is Satan as discussed in the last two chapters. There are going to be storms from Satan that God allows to pass through His hands to us. We know that. God will give us the way out of these storms through His order and with His power. These are a setup for us to advance one way or another. But then there will be less obvious storms, which are distractions from the Devil. They will destroy us just the same over time. Satan will use subtle and constant infiltration of temptations to try and get us separated from God and His order. I think God will leave the "distraction" up to us to handle through decision. We will be able to make a freewill decision when it comes to noise, distraction, and the ways of the world that feel good in the flesh. So our first issue is Satan's attempts to get us offtrack.

Second, when we are living in the wrong order, we are outside of God's protection. God is making a definite point for those who know about Him and then choose to habitually live the world's way. If we live by the patterns of the world crafted by Satan, we are sitting ducks, completely vulnerable without any sort of protection from God. This is not kingdom life. That being said, this verse should be read with wisdom and understanding in context with the rest of the Bible. We don't want to take advantage of the two-thirds grace. Let's follow in obedience.

The fact is God is love, and He loves every one of His children. He is very patient with us. He doesn't want any person to be an enemy. We make ourselves enemies. If we choose the world's order, it doesn't mean God will hurt us. Satan will attempt that over time. If we live in the ways of the world, it means we are not under God's covering and His hedge of protection. God doesn't resist us if we don't resist Him. God doesn't put a wedge in the way of us getting His protection. We do! God gave us free will to choose His covering, protection, and power.

As we read God's Word and have a relationship with Him, we realize God is an all-merciful and an all-forgiving, patient God. God knows this will be a journey of learning His ways. That being said, His promises remain the same. The promises are attached to His principles. Principle is action to get to the promise. Let's do our absolute best to follow His principles. We will all make many mistakes along the journey, and God knew this right from the start. That's why He promised us forgiveness and many more chances through His Son, Jesus Christ. All this aside, let's not be unaware of Satan's intentions. Let's choose to respond to God and His order as He calls us toward kingdom life. Whether we are believers or not, we will all have encounters of some sort with God like I had on my "last night." In fact, we will have the chance to hear God in many different ways before and after our salvation moments. We can have encounters like I did that night or through another believer sharing or through a book like this. These are all ways God speaks to us. Some of these encounters will be for nonbelievers to come to life, and the rest of the nudges will direct us toward the victorious and purpose-filled life. In any case, let's do our best to respond with *yes* so we can live kingdom lives filled with power in the body of Christ, for God's glory.

You, Lord, brought me up from the realm of the dead, You spared me from going down to the pit.

—*Psalm 30:3*

10after my last night

IN SIX SHORT YEARS since my "last night," God has rescued me from the grip of death that was on my life. I can't even find words to describe the gratitude I have in my heart toward God for this freedom. You can say all the things you want about monetary type of success, but nothing compares to this. I live a power-filled victorious life now. I am sold out for Jesus and the way He wants us to live. That being said, I've also endured tragedy as bad as or worse than before my "last night." It's completely different now. God never promised the absence of loss or tragedy in our lives. He promised the power to pass through it. He promised that we would come out better on the other side, whether it be now or eternally, if we actually followed the way He wants us to live.

We can't just believe to see new levels; we must actually follow Him in obedience to see these new levels. This is going to take action. Knowing about His power and pressing in to experience it are two entirely different things. I now see God's faithfulness in this promise. I have the scars to prove it. Scars are the evidence of victory. Scars are healed wounds. We display our scars to show God's power to the world. My life was spared on my "last night." After that night, the healing came day by day as I continued to press into His order and the principles attached to His order. During this journey, I have discovered that "knowing" about Him and "doing" in Him bring two different results. One brings results, and the other doesn't.

We will never see the fruits of God's eternal promises without these trials. But by persevering through these trials in God's order and seeing through to victory, we prove the promises made in the Bible. We experience moments of encounter, time and time again. When I reflect back, the magnitude of restoration in my life since my "last night" is mind-blowing. God has literally taken the ashes of my old life and created beauty as He promises in His Word. Today, I am rooted in a wonderful church, serving God multiple times a week. The new order in my life is God, family, people, and work.

There are no words to explain the enrichment of friends that the mighty King has put into my life. I have not had a drink since before my "last night." I have been delivered. All the diagnosis and symptoms of ADD, ADHD, manic depression, bipolar disorder, suicide, and multiple personality disorder are gone—just absolutely gone, and I'm free. I take no medications whatsoever.

Financially, God has breathed life into the business I operate. It is incredible to have enough to be a blessing to others for the first time in my life. A year and a half after that night, God brought total restoration with my mom and dad and a little later with the rest of my family. For me, it's like we never lost a single day. That's the freedom in the healing hand of God and His order. Shortly after that, God revealed the wounds that Satan capitalized on for thirty-four years of my life, starting before I was born and lasting for about a year after I was born. It was no one's fault, and nobody knew. I could write a separate book entirely on victorious kingdom life moments since my "last night." Maybe another day. I will, however, mention a few in the following chapters as they relate to the topics we will be discussing. There is truly only one place to find *real purpose* and power in this life. It's in the order and principles of Jesus Christ.

Perhaps you are a believer of many years, or perhaps you have never taken the step of faith before. Perhaps you struggle to find the victorious life after your salvation moment. In either case, the remainder of our journey is not a set of rules; it is a set of principles in the order of Christ. It's where we find kingdom power. I believe there will be a purpose in these principles for the seasoned believer or, of course, a nonbeliever as well. These experiences are an order to live by, broken up into individual sections. I actively try to live within these principles every day to ensure I walk victoriously. <u>It's within this very order, that we find His power</u>. Our faith brought together with our steps of obedience. In other words, our faith and our deeds brought together in the form of worship. These experiences are available for anyone to discover and build on.

Many of these principles in His order will be nothing new for us to hear. That being said, knowing and doing are different. Let's not be deceived. Just because we know about these experiences doesn't mean that we are actually doing them. We need to press into our worship with Him to discover the victorious power that is readily available for each and every one of us. I realize that our steps with God in the order of Christ is progress, not perfection. Not all of it happens overnight, and it happens at a different pace for everyone. Rome wasn't built in a day. I get it. However, the next section is a guide to new-level kingdom living. So yes, the measure of dedication does matter in relationship to the amount of victory we will experience. We just finished discussing this in previous chapters. This is our "faith and deeds" pulled together with our "belief." This is the B to Z part of our walk.

It's not about perfecting in the short-term and then backing off once we start finding small nuggets of victory. *It is the amount of long-term commitment that resides in our hearts for these experiences with Him. This will determine our level of success as we approach Him.* Nobody will be perfect with these experiences, and nor do we need to be. Each one of us can be "all in" in our hearts. God blesses all-in heart positions no matter how good the results. The all-in heart position will be the fight it takes for us to maintain the victory and avoid having it stripped away from us.

> But with sincerity of heart and reverence for the Lord. Whatever you do, work at it with all your heart, as working for the Lord, not for human masters, since you know that you will receive an inheritance from the Lord as a reward. (Colossians 3:22–24)

This scripture is not referring to eternal life. We can't work for our eternal life. It is, however, referring to power and favor we can have here on earth, and eternally, by positioning our hearts right, in our deeds with Him. So this is my point: we need to stay fully committed and all-in with these principles in our hearts, because our success can be revoked if we don't. We can lose our freedom and power if we stray away and choose the wrong order. If that happens, we can end up in the same spot or a worse position than where we started. Let's ask the Lord to light a fire in our hearts. Let's make a decision to walk away from all the distraction so that we can experience His glory. Let's seek first the kingdom to bring new-level power into our lives and into the body of Christ.

SECTION 3

11 choose the light

SO WHAT'S NEXT, AND how do we get our hearts in the right position to see the kingdom life take root in our lives? For many of us, we may have already taken the first few steps in the chapters coming up in our walks. This may be familiar territory already. I'm sure there is still a few golden nuggets we can grab along the way. I will start right at the very beginning because I can't assume everyone who may read this book will have accepted Jesus as their Lord and Savior. Ironically, this may even include people in our churches.

Believe it or not, I talked to a guy the other day who was in this position. He had actually been going to church for years. He was in such a world of struggle. He wasn't seeing any victory or change in his life whatsoever, even after years and years of going to church. The strangest thought came to my head. I asked him if he had ever asked Jesus to come into his heart as his Lord and Savior. He couldn't recall taking that very specific step. He assumed that this was automatic because He was in church. I was surprised to say the least. We took this step of faith together, and everything started changing for him within weeks after that moment. I wondered how many others may be in the same position after that. One would assume that a person has taken this step if they were attending church for several years. I guess we won't assume, and that's why I'll start at the very beginning. Please be patient as we continue on.

Kingdom life requires postures of submission. Submission is letting go of the control. Let's yield the control of our lives to the one who knows the way. I know that statement hurts to hear. It hurts because Satan has lied to us our whole lives and engrained self-control into our thoughts and into our minds. We must lose our lives in order to surrender our lives. This is where we will find life and real power. Many will believe, but few will surrender or surrender very little. The answers we are looking for lie within whom we surrender our lives to and to what extent.

> When Jesus spoke again to the people, He said, "I am the light of the world. Whoever follows Me will never walk in darkness, but will have the light of life." (John 8:12)

I choose the light and the love of Jesus and His order. The darkness is Satan and the ways of the world. The ways of the world were the only way I knew how to live for thirty-four years. I didn't know the difference. I heard about God. I think multitudes have heard about God. It's so mundane if it's not heard truthfully. So many different extremes and so much hypocrisy. I had never heard about the correct way to live in the order of Jesus Christ, in terms of *relationship* with Him, with His power, rather than dead and powerless religion. Or, at least, I didn't understand it.

I quickly learned that Satan has also blurred people's vision about "religion" and the Church. It is not about religion, and it *never* will be as far as I'm concerned. It's about relationship with Him and responding to the order He wants us to live in. Our Father loves us. A personal relationship is what God wants with us, His children. Darkness cannot, and will not, mix with light. That's a fact; it's impossible for darkness to remain if we position our hearts to be in a relationship with Him. You don't have to be a scientist or a pastor to see this. I'm neither. Go into a room at night and turn on the light switch. If your power is on and there is a bulb in the socket, the light has to disperse the darkness. The two cannot mix. Well, it's the same with Jesus. When we allow Jesus and His order into the broken cracks of our lives, the darkness is repelled. When the darkness disperses, the victory starts to set in.

RELATIONSHIP WITH CHRIST

The light of Jesus Christ has several colors or beams that make up this spectrum of light. In order to receive the entire measure of light that needs to come into our hearts, we will need to embrace the whole spectrum so that the full measure of power and victory can come with it. The rest of this book identifies several of the beams that make up the spectrum of Christ's light, which is His order. Each beam of light is a principle within an experience, as previously mentioned, that will bring power.

The first beam of light that needs to come into our hearts in a general manner, for now, is surrender to Jesus. The Bible says that no one can come to God without going through the process of inviting His Son, Jesus Christ, into their hearts as the Lord and Savior of their lives. If we want to operate in God's order, this is the very first step. Jesus Christ is God in the flesh and in the Spirit. Jesus was sent to the earth by God the Father as a rescue plan for His people after sin took place. Jesus is God, and God is Jesus and the Spirit—all in one.

Jesus walked this earth for thirty-three years as a real man in the flesh and blood, and then He died on the Cross for our sins. Three days later, Jesus was resurrected from the dead as our Lord and Savior, and now we have access to God through Him. The Holy Spirit is also God and Jesus all in one. The three are all one as the Godhead. We will understand this in more depth, as we go, if we haven't surrendered our lives to Jesus as our Lord and Savior yet. The understanding comes when we start travelling in a personal relationship with Him and through His Word in the Bible.

> *Jesus answered, "I am the way and the truth and the life. No one comes to the Father (God) except through Me." (John 14:6)*

After we decide to surrender the control of our lives to Jesus, we have to open the door of our hearts and ask Jesus to actually come in. He won't force Himself in. Surrender is the first step, but we need to know what we are surrendering to. By asking Jesus into our hearts, we agree to surrender our lives in *a general manner for now*, with more specific areas of surrender coming up in the next chapters. General surrender is the mandatory step taken to discover that there is a different order to live by. Surrendering our lives and then entering into a relationship with Christ most often go hand in hand—but they didn't in my case. As mentioned in chapter 1, I surrendered and then left my old life behind for a power source I was not yet familiar with. I asked Jesus to take over my life many days later. But just because it didn't happen that way for me doesn't mean it can't work that way for the rest. All I knew at the time of surrender was that I was leaving the old life behind no matter what the cost and no matter what the results were going to be. This was His two-thirds grace and power working in me at the time. I still had to say yes to Him.

Once we have decided to surrender our lives, we need to open the door of our hearts and ask Jesus to come in. Ask—that's all we have to do because He has been waiting for us with joyful anticipation.

> Here I am! I stand at the door and knock. If anyone hears My voice and opens the door, I will come in and eat with that person, and they with Me. (Revelation 3:20)

These are the words Jesus uses to say: "I'm waiting here for you to invite Me into your life. I will never force My way in, but I delight in you, and I want to give you a new life."

I believe most often we will hear God's voice and His invitation through fellow believers. He will use other believers to access our hearts, and I'm speaking through experience. That's why there is so much strength within the body of believers. It's possible, as you are reading this book, that God is talking to you through me in these pages if you haven't made this decision yet. Some people think that if we are to meet God, there must be this marvelous supernatural experience where we see a vision or hear a loud voice, and then we will fall to the ground and follow Jesus from that moment on. I've heard of this experience; it's possible for sure but rare. My experience was close. The experience of meeting Jesus right now doesn't become any less significant if we don't have an unusually supernatural type of encounter.

God loves us. He also loves us through His people. If you have not made this decision, this is God's love being sent out through me. There is no need to delay an encounter with Jesus any longer. Jesus is waiting for you to ask Him into your broken heart right now through my words to you. There are no coincidences in God's world. There are just two incidences coming together. God's love through my words and you are the two incidences coming together. He's waiting to give you your freedom. The Bible says anyone who hears My voice and invites Me in has access to My freedom. Not some people. *Not* right-standing people or people who go to church or people who are not addicted or whatever you think disqualifies you. We have discussed this thoroughly already. Remember the thief on the cross? He says *anyone*, no matter what you have done or think you have done. "Whoever hears My voice and invites Me in can have the privilege to My freedom through My Son Jesus Christ."

> *For God so loved the world that He gave His one and only Son, that whoever believes in Him shall not perish but have eternal life. (John 3:16)*

Again.

> *Anyone who believes in Him will never be put to shame. For there is no difference between Jew and gentile—the same Lord is Lord of all and richly blesses all who call on Him, for, everyone who calls on the name of the Lord will be saved. (Romans 10:11–13)*

No one is restricted from access to Jesus and His freedom. His access is available to anyone. All is all. God doesn't lie. God says *all*, and He means all to whoever believes. So if you believe this with your heart and you want Jesus to come into your life, God says that anyone can come to the Father through His Son, Jesus Christ, and receive what's in this book and, more importantly, what's in His book, the Bible—freedom and eternal life with Him.

> *Very truly I tell you, the one who believes has eternal life. I am the bread of life. (John 6:47)*

Here is an invitation to make the most important decision you will ever make. Take some time to really think this through. It is a chance to start your new life today—to leave the darkness and struggle behind. This is not the easiest path to choose; it's just not. It won't be the most popular journey either. It will, however, be the only eternally rewarding and victorious path to the freedom you are looking for. Take time to consider this decision thoroughly.

If you have made the decision to ask Jesus into your heart for the rest of your life as your Lord and Savior and you don't know how to do it, simply say what's written below:

Jesus, I believe in You. I believe in Your power. I believe in Your freedom. Please forgive me for all of my sins. Please forgive me for not yielding to You and letting You into my heart earlier. I confess You as Lord and Savior of my life. I believe You came for me and that You died for me and that You rose again three days later so that I could have eternal life and freedom. Please come into my heart and take control of my life. I surrender everything to You right now, in Jesus's name. Amen.

Close your eyes and take a moment with Jesus. Enjoy this.

If you have made the decision to invite Jesus Christ into your heart as your Lord and Savior, then welcome! You have just let the healing light of Christ into the cracks of your broken heart and have taken the first step to receiving the purpose-filled kingdom life. You have accepted the invitation to receive eternal life and eternal healing. Your life will never be the same. It just won't be. Take some time and thank Jesus for His love.

For the Lord your God is the one who goes with you to fight for you against your enemies to give you victory. (Deuteronomy 20:4)

If you have surrendered your life to God through His Son, Jesus, there are specific areas of surrender and detailed experiences and principles coming up. Again, the focus should be on the all-in heart position with God, more than achieving results. Let God focus on the results as we position our heart to surrender in these areas. That's the whole point of the surrendering to Him. It's yielding to Him and allowing His power to change us. To point us toward kingdom life. If you have not yet made this decision, I pray that you will mindfully consider God's love for you. I hope that you will continue on reading. You don't have to make this decision right this moment to keep reading.

12 managing our decision

THE MOST IMPORTANT PART of growing our relationship with Jesus and pursuing
the kingdom life is *managing our decision*.
Kingdom life is not automatic just because we
believe. Managing our decision will determine
how often kingdom life moments happen in
our lives and how intense they get. The path
to victory doesn't end with the first decision.
Once again, we have an enemy who wants to
take our decisions away from us more than
anything. This is another part that doesn't get

talked about very often when discussing the journey in Christ's order, so let's talk about it.

Contrary to anyone's thoughts, Satan's tactics are real. We need to talk about them again, because we don't want to be walking blind and be easily deceived. Believing in Jesus Christ as our Lord and Savior doesn't mean Satan goes away. As we talked about earlier in this book, his efforts to keep us discouraged will only increase because of the decision we made. The decision to invite Jesus into our lives was the last thing on earth Satan wanted to see happen. He didn't want us to have any <u>real</u> freedom *without* Jesus in our lives, so he certainly doesn't want us to have it now. Satan already knows he is defeated, so he wants to try and confuse us in this journey. He will tell us more lies, and he will try and tell us that this power isn't possible. He will try and tell us that His set-apart favor isn't real. He will say more things like Jesus isn't real and our choice won't change anything. He tries to manipulate our thoughts to keep us pressed down. Satan doesn't just lie down like a dead dog when we invite Jesus into our lives. We must manage our new decisions and positions to stay strong in the pursuit of the kingdom life.

The upcoming principles and worship experiences in the order of Christ are meant to build up the body of Christ as a whole for His glory. They are readily available so that we can tap into kingdom life here on earth. They are also the weapons to fight back and the armor we need to persevere as we journey.

One of the most important concepts we will need to understand for the rest of our lives with Jesus is this: *we have to move first*. If we are going to pursue His power and the kingdom life, it's going to take first steps by us—and then more "first steps" after that. I still take those "first steps" every day so God will move in my life the way I never could. The first step is <u>managing our decisions</u>. The decision to say yes to God.

Possibly, there may be some of us who have just taken the most important step of our lives by asking Jesus into our hearts through surrender. Let's talk about the next steps that are just as crucial as the "first" first steps to pursue the victorious kingdom life. The next chapters are for seasoned believers and for new believers alike. As believers, perhaps we are stuck, or we feel defeated. Perhaps we are not accessing the power in the kingdom of God because we haven't been active in the order of Christ for some time, even though we believe. Or maybe we have grown weary? Sure, we know about all these upcoming experiences in God's order. But are we actually active and pressing into them with our hearts wide open? Do we even realize that the very power and breakthrough we are looking for exists within His order? Or maybe the next lessons and worship experiences to come just seem like a bunch of religious jargon? No offense, but if we can relate to any of these statements, perhaps this is the reason we can't seem to find the breakthrough and the victorious lives we hear about from a far-off distance.

God invites us to press into these worship experiences for our own good. Belief doesn't mean we are working in His order. It's time to get serious and realize that the power and the victorious kingdom life actually exists in His order and within the principles of action associated with His promises. Faith, if not accompanied with deeds, will be a dead walk. It doesn't mean that we don't believe; it means that there will be very little power. The sooner we accept this, the faster we will find victory in our lives. Salvation is free; the power is not. If you have made it this far, you are likely one of the believers who will find kingdom life and favor right around the corner. Let's rise up and be a body of Christ that embraces this power for His glory! Father, give us something to talk about!

I have been crucified with Christ and no longer live, but Christ lives in me. The life I now live in the body, I live by faith in the Son of God, who loves me and gave Himself for me.

—Galatians 2:20

THE ORDER OF MELCHIZEDEK

13 raise the white flag

SURRENDER EVERYTHING AND DIE TO SELF

EVENTUALLY, WE HAVE TO surrender our old lives, like I did on my "last night," to walk in victory and to live the kingdom life. After we make the most important decision to receive God's love and surrender our lives to Jesus in a general manner, we now have to look at "specific" measures of surrender. Surrender *will* bring power in a radical way.

Put to death, therefore, whatever belongs to your earthly nature: sexual immorality, impurity, lust, evil desires and greed, which is idolatry. (Colossians 3:5)

Surrender is this: die to ourselves, die to our pride, die to the world, die to our old identities, and die to the desires of our flesh. I know. Intense. But we will not see intense kingdom power and favor without intense action. We have to say, "It's done. It's over no matter what the cost. I'm leaving my old life behind." We need to raise our white flags of surrender. Our white flags of living in the world, so to speak. This is the spiritual baptism—the sanctification process that will start bringing kingdom power into our lives.

Whoever finds their life will lose it, and whoever loses their life for My sake will find it. (Matthew 10:39)

What are we trying to hold onto from our old lives that is blocking the way for us? Look at the Israelites again. The Lord wanted to take His people to the promised land of Canaan. After the Exodus out of Egypt, the Lord took His people through the Red Sea and all the way up to Jericho. The Lord told them to march around the city for seven days. On the seventh day, they were to circle the city seven more times on that day and then shout. They did as they were instructed, and then the walls of Jericho came crashing down. The Lord's people were moving forward with success. Upon taking over Jericho and looking ahead to more land, Joshua gave instructions to his fighting men to go spy out the county of Ai, east of Bethel.

The spies told Joshua that the battle would be easy because there were very few opponents in the land they wanted to take. Joshua only sent up three thousand men. What happened? They got chased out. Joshua tore his clothes, and the Lord told Joshua that his people had sinned by taking the "devoted" items from the city of Jericho when He handed it over to the Israelites just days before. This was a new life for the people after four hundred years of slavery in Egypt. The Lord wanted to bring His people to a favored and promised land, and yet these people would hold onto old ways of living. This blocked their success.

The Bible says,

> This is why the Israelites cannot stand against their enemies; they turn their backs and run because they have been made liable to destruction. I will not be with you anymore unless you destroy whatever among you is devoted to destruction. *(Joshua 7:12)*

What part of our old lives are we trying to bring into our new lives? We can't bring the old into the new. This is a conversion that will cause a conflict. Our flesh will want to battle with the Spirit all day long as we choose a different order. We have spent so long letting the world build who we were.

> But do not use your freedom to indulge the flesh. So I say, walk by the Spirit, and you will not gratify the desires of the flesh. For the flesh desires what is contrary to the Spirit, and the Spirit what is contrary to the flesh. <u>They are in conflict with each other, so that you are not to do whatever you want</u>. *(Galatians 5:13, 16–17)*

Of course, like always, we can't earn or behave right for salvation, so these instructions are for something else—power and purpose. The world won't change to fit our conversion. We must do the changing. During the conversion, we have to intentionally ask God for the strength to continue in this new order, even if we don't know what that looks like or how we will get through it. We will. We know this because God is faithful to His Word. Surrender in my life isn't perfect, and it never will be. It will always be in a state of progress, not perfection, with an all-in heart position to move closer to that goal. It's a journey with God, and He will show us the answers to come if we do the surrender part. It's what He does.

The glory of God to come in our lives will not compare to the short-term pain of dying to our old lives right now. We have to let go and surrender anything and everything that Satan uses to keep us in the prison of our old lives—reputation, activities, places and locations, friends, and even family in some cases (if their influence is contrary to how God wants us to be living in His order). The Bible says that the company we keep *does* matter—in a *huge way!*

> Do not be misled: "Bad company corrupts good character." Come back to your senses as you ought, and stop sinning; for there are some who are ignorant of God—I say this to your shame. (1 Corinthians 15:33–34)

This is carrying our crosses. First Corinthians was written by the apostle Paul in Ephesus. He was talking to believers, not unbelievers who don't know the difference! We need to surrender to the idea that there is a better and different order, even if we don't know what that order looks like this very minute. We will not see the kingdom-powered lives living apart from the Lord's order.

DIE TO PRIDE

> God opposes the proud but gives favor to the humble. Submit yourselves, then, to God. Resist the devil, and he will flee from you. Come near to God and He will come near to you.
> —James 4:6–8

One of the first steps of a more specific surrender is that we must die to our pride. We must check our pride minute by minute because this isn't a one-time deal. It's a habitual process. We don't want to lose the hedge of protection that God offers us by being in pride. God opposes the proud. Pride comes before the fall. What is pride as defined in the Bible? The scriptures have so much to say about pride, and none of it is positive. I realize that pride is not always viewed in a negative way. For example, "I was proud of them" is a phrase to express accomplishment or joy and acclamation.

However, when the Bible talks about pride, it's for a very different purpose. Pride is the root of all sin from selfishness. Almost every failure will come from selfishness birthed from pride. The first sin ever committed was from pride. Eve wanted to control her own destiny, so she ate the forbidden fruit that Satan tempted her with. Where was Adam to protect her? A different story for a different day.

Biblical pride makes us blind. It makes us oblivious to danger. It gives us this foolish feeling of independence away from God. I know this posture all too well. That is what got me to my "last night." It's agreeing with the voice of Satan that is whispering, "We don't need anyone or anything. We can make our own decisions. Our destiny is what we make it. We are a good people, and we are good to go on our own merit." Very often, this pride carries into our new journey after our salvation moment. Pride will suck the kingdom power right out of us. Dying to pride is saying, "God, I'm done with pride. Please give me the strength to let go of the control of my life to You."

If God "opposes the proud" as read in James 4:6, then what does "He gives favor to the humble" mean? His favor is limitless because God is limitless. The more we surrender our own wills to God, the more He will move in our lives. But not until we do. His actions are limited until we yield control. This isn't because God doesn't have the ability to do anything He wants. This is because He gives us free will to choose Him. He won't force His ways or His favor on us. There is power when we surrender our wills to His ways. God says, "If you will hand Me the keys to your life, I will open the most amazing doors you never could have opened in your own strength."

Once we surrender the control of our lives to the order of Christ, it doesn't mean we become nonfunctioning robots with no responsibilities of our own. Relationship with Jesus, and operating in His order, is a partnership under submission to Him and His ways instead of our own. We still play a huge role in the outcomes of *many* circumstances in our lives during this journey. God helps those who help themselves, so we can't expect to give up and roll over and play dead and expect to see supernatural works of His goodness in our lives. We do this by balancing our faith with our deeds at work in excellence.

DIE TO THE WORLD

Do not conform to the patterns of this world, but be transformed by the renewing of your mind. Then you will be able to test and approve what God's will is— His good, pleasing and perfect will. (Romans 12:2)

He says it again in James:

You adulterous people, don't you know that a friend-ship with the world means enmity against God? Therefore, anyone who chooses to be a friend of the world becomes an enemy of God. (James 4:4)

He says it again in 1 John:

Do not love the world or anything in the world. If any-one loves the world, love for the Father is not in them. For everything in the world—the lust of the flesh, the lust of the eyes, and the pride of life—comes not from the Father but from the world. The world and its desires pass away, but whoever does the will of God lives forever. (1 John 2:15–17)

Let's leave the old ways behind, regardless of what the pain feels like right this moment, as we prepare to journey with God. Let's absolutely walk away from our old, sin-filled lives and environments no matter what the cost. We cannot hold onto any part of our old, sin-filled lives and see His favor (not all parts of our old lives will be apart from God's ways, but we are looking to let go of the parts that are).

Can both fresh water and salt water flow from the same spring? My brothers and sisters, can a fig tree bear olives, or a grapevine bear figs? Neither can a salt spring produce fresh water. (James 3:11–12)

We will feel a portion of instant power with the thought of this one decision alone. We will need to ask God for His power to con-tinue leaving the world behind us. That being said, God will reward us for our obedient desires. God gives set-apart favor to His children that will make a decision to live set-apart lives for Him.

The morning after my "last night," I woke up and replaced my old phone with a new one. I didn't even know why all this was happening. I only entered mandatory life-breathing contacts into it. Metaphorically speaking, I cleaned the house entirely. That was just the first step of many to come. Like I said, the sacrifice we think we are making now does not compare to the favor that God wants to bring into our lives if we do this.

> *I consider that our present sufferings are not worth comparing with the glory that will be revealed in us.*
> *(Romans 8:18)*

Again, knowing about God's favor and pressing in to receive God's favor—those are two different things. His favor is not automatic just because it is there to be had. These are the most important decisions we will ever make in our lives. The Bible is clear: we can't play both sides of the coin. If we attempt to play both sides or live both ways, we can expect few results. This is where we receive victory or not. God is so awesome, and He wants to give us His power and His freedom. But once again, He will not force. There is a freewill decision to be made. If we yield to His Order, He says,

> *"For I know the plans I have for you," declares the Lord, "plans to prosper you and not harm you, plans to give you a hope and a future." (Jeremiah 29:11)*

And that's *exactly* what happened in my life. A good plan began to show up. He prospered me in every area of my life when I continued to take steps to leave my old life behind. I'm not perfect by any means, but the good things in this journey are not even close to being finished! This is because I have so much more to leave behind. We are like clay being formed by the Potter's hands, and the sculpting will never be finished, because God is limitless. He won't force us to choose Him or leave our old lives behind, but He will put out His hand and say, "Take it, My child. I'm here for you now. I delight in you."

> *For the Lord takes delight in His people; He crowns the humble with victory. (Psalm 149:4)*

God loves and delights in us. He gives us these suggestions for our own good. The Lord *will* reward us for choosing His order as we die to the ways of the world. As said before, God gives us these principles to protect us, not to prohibit us. His ways are so much higher.

DIE TO OUR OLD IDENTITIES

> *Put off your old self, which belongs to your former manner of life and is corrupt through deceitful desires, and to be renewed in the spirit of your minds, and to put on the new self, created after the likeness of God in true and righteousness and holiness. (Ephesians 4:22–24)*

This means we have to die to our worldly reputations and our worldly statuses. Again, there are no options. If we hold onto our worldly statuses and our old reputations, it will be absolutely impossible to leave our old lives behind. If we don't leave our old, worldly lives behind, there will be no power. The Bible tells us that we shouldn't put new wine into old wineskins. Let's not drag our old lives into our new lives. This includes things and thoughts. The two don't mix. They will keep us entangled and trapped. Ultimately, it will lead us back to the same spot that kept us pressed down.

I believe that the lies from Satan concerning status, reputation, and work are what kept me from seeing the truth all those years. I thought status was my identity, my security, and my self-worth. In fact, I thought the harder I pushed to build up these areas of my life, the less isolated and the less broken I would feel. In reality, I was in pursuit of my own glorious kingdom. I'm here to tell you that is just another lie right from the pit of hell. Life was empty, lonely, and jam-packed with counterfeit lies back then. There was absolutely no significance in that life.

The energy that it took to maintain status and reputation in my personal and work life was incredibly draining, and it was all for nothing. It cost a lot of money as well. Satan teaches us that our statuses and reputations *are* the most important things in our lives. It's who we are and everything we ever worked for—-our "identities" that is. Blah blaah blaaah. This train of thinking is a lie and a joke if I ever saw one. Let's die to it. We need to "burn the plows so to speak."

> We are not trying to please people but God, who tests our hearts. You know we never use flattery, nor did we put on a mask to cover up greed—God is our witness. We were not looking for praise from people, not from you or anyone else, even though as apostles of Christ we could have asserted our authority. (1 Thessalonians 2:4–6)

Whose identity are we seeking after? We need to take on Christ's identity to really see His power show up and show out in our lives. Look at Elisha, for instance. Elijah the Prophet would come to Elisha in the field while Elisha was plowing. Elijah threw his cloak onto Elisha. This was a sign to follow him for the Lord's purposes.

The Bible says,

> So Elijah went from there and found Elisha son of Shaphat. He was plowing with twelve yoke of oxen, and he himself was driving the twelfth pair. Elijah went up to him and threw his cloak around him. Elisha then left his oxen and ran after Elijah. "Let me kiss my father and mother goodbye," he said, "and then I will come with you."
>
> "Go back," Elijah replied. "What have I done to you?"
>
> So Elisha left him and went back. He took his yoke of oxen and slaughtered them. He "burned the plowing equipment" to cook the meat and gave it to the people, and they ate. Then he set out to follow Elijah and become his servant. (1 Kings 19:19–21)

That's one of the most radical stories to show us how we are to leave our old lives behind. We can't bring the old "*worldly*" lives into our new lives with God. This wasn't even sin or bad habits that Elisha was agreeing to let go of to walk into his new destiny with God. This was his living! This was his business. He would "burn the plows" to take proactive steps to make absolutely sure that he wouldn't be tempted to mix the old with the new. This was because God was calling him into a new life. He was a hundred-percent "all-in."

Again, what do we need to leave behind so that we can walk into the fullest of our destinies with God? We can't let our businesses and careers be at the center of our lives, even though we get to make a living and we get to run businesses and have careers. We are very busy people; I get it. That being said, we will either work to glorify God, or we will work and run our businesses to glorify ourselves. The heart position in the two different postures is so much different. I'm not suggesting everyone quit their jobs and leave their businesses by any means. It just means we need to put God at the very center of every one of our endeavors and at the very core of our hearts as number one. We will need to let go of certain areas of our lives completely, when God asks, to see His power and glory in our lives.

To be honest, status and reputation mean virtually nothing when we are dead, and it doesn't mean a whole bunch while we are alive. This is the ultimate lie that keeps us ensnared by the enemy with his "worldly" teachings. Accomplishments are good, don't get me wrong. No one wants us to accomplish our dreams and our goals more than God himself. He put these goals and dreams in our hearts to begin with. In fact, the Bible says God has bigger aspirations and plans for our lives than we do. Read Jeremiah 29:11 again. That being said, these goals and dreams should never become our identities or become bigger than God himself in our hearts. There will be no kingdom life in these postures.

Our accomplishments should give glory to God in alignment with His purpose and the eternal picture according to His plan. The reason our goals and dreams should never become bigger than

God is because God Himself says that we shall have no other gods above Him. When we make our lives and our accomplishments more important than God's purpose in our lives, they become the other "gods." Also, when we rely on status or identity to feel complete and then they fail, then what? We are left feeling lost, broken, and without a real identity. I try to live for Christ's purpose now, and my biggest concern is how I can glorify God and let people know I'm free because of His power. I want people to know that I am His. I want my identity to be known as a believer of the King of kings. Once again, we should be very much interested in accomplishments and challenges and forward movement. That's all still very important.

God wants this for us more than we even do for ourselves. Now I do it for God's glory and not for my own identity, status, and reputation, because that was fatal. When we are focused on giving God the glory for what *He* brings us in the first place, He advances us to the next level in His timing. This is kingdom life. Let's die to our status and reputations, and take on God's identity. God will release His power and favor to us when we put our identities in Him.

DIE TO THE DESIRES OF THE FLESH

The desires of the flesh are all the wrong appetites Satan has taught us to crave from the first day of our lives to the present moment. They are not God's desires for us.

> *As for you, you were dead in your transgressions and sins, in which you used to live when you followed the ways of this world and of the ruler of the kingdom of the air, the spirit who is now at work in those who are disobedient. All of us also lived among them at one time, gratifying the cravings of our flesh and following its desires and thoughts. Like the rest, we were by nature deserving of wrath. (Ephesians 2:1–3)*

Have you ever noticed the standards in society are getting more extreme, less reserved, and more provocative? Ask your grandparents. This isn't society's natural path of progression or its way to adapt with the "new times." It's not a "coincidence." It's Satan's stronghold on society, and it's not God's original plan for us. Yes, He could stop it, but free will . . . God will not force His way.

The trends in society are Satan's barely visible strategy to make things worse and worse by the day. There are more than four hundred million pornographic sites on the Internet. This is 36 percent of all the websites on the web. Movies are allowing more smut every year with lower age restrictions to get in. Clothing is slinkier than ever. War and terror are at an all-time high in our world. DUIs are natural today, and booze is the way. Pot is legal now, and you barely get your hands slapped for having it. Besides, it will be legal everywhere very shortly. Sexual activity is starting much younger, and sexual promiscuity is much more convenient. Swipe right for a good time. The evidence is all there. These tactics by the enemy are designed to slowly but surely tear us to pieces. This stops any type of kingdom living to say the least.

The Bible says,

> For if you live according to the flesh, you will die; but if by the Spirit you put to death the misdeeds of the body, you will live. (Romans 8:13)

We must turn from our past and the desires that pleased our flesh. They are designed to destroy us, and they are designed to keep us away from God's power. They feel great at the time, but they leave nuclear carnage behind us. Again, I was there. I'm certain that nobody loved to be drunk more than I did. It was a desire of my flesh, and it also masked the pain. And yes, sex is desirable, no doubt. Our flesh loves it. But we are not to be living drunk and having sex outside of the order of Christ. These are just two examples in an endless list that we may need to let go. There will be no kingdom life by *choosing* to live in our old lives.

Jesus wants us to desire the things He does, and there is good reason for this. Jesus is whole, and He wants us to be whole. Being whole brings peace and joy and the victorious life for His glory. So let's put off the ungodly thoughts, habits, and behaviors. Let's put on the desires and character of our King. This, again, is not optional. Dabbling in "a little bit" just doesn't cut it. If we continue to dabble in the old order, we will not even come close to seeing the kingdom-of-God type of power and favor in our lives. Remember, we are talking about victorious kingdom-power-filled lives here. Not natural and powerless saved lives. One is so much more set apart than the next. God is looking for people who will live they set-apart life for Him. It can't be partial as the Bible says,

> You cannot drink the cup of the Lord and the cup of the demons too; you cannot have a part in both the Lords table and the table of demons. (1 Corinthians 10:21)

It's pretty black-and-white when it comes to kingdom power and favor. We have a choice to make. We cannot have both; it's not possible. That's if we want to see serious power and favor in our lives. There are repercussions to our choices. We have to make a choice to flee from temptations, which are traps set to destroy us and lead us back to defeat. They are designed to keep us stuck, contrary to how we feel. We must avoid them at all costs to enjoy the power that God wants to give us.

> Submit yourselves, then, to God. Resist the devil, and he will flee from you. (James 4:7)

Do not flirt with temptation, because we eventually lose every time. Many believers think they have set healthy boundaries—boundaries that hinge on the old order but don't actually cross over the fence, so to speak. On one side of the fence is God's order, and on the other side of the fence is the world's order. "I can go up to the fence, but I will never cross to the other side." That's pride. Who are we in our flesh to think we can keep putting temptations at arm's length and not eventually fail? The Holy Spirit won't lead us to the fence; our flesh will.

I say let's stay away from the fence entirely. Living by the desires of the flesh and our old worldly ways will suck the kingdom power right out of the body of Christ as a whole. We need to be a set-apart people to experience His power. When we blend in with the world, there will be no access to His power. We are to live in the world, but we are not to be "of" the world, as the scriptures say. God is asking us to take a different position. When we are set apart for Him, we will see His power in our lives. That is an absolute fact. Let's tweak our scopes to aim at a different target: God's target.

> *Now to Him who is able to do immeasurably more than all we ask or imagine, according to His power that is at work within us, to Him be glory in the Church and in Christ Jesus throughout all generations, for ever and ever! Amen.*
>
> *—Ephesians 3:20–21*

THE ORDER OF MELCHIZEDEK

14 the body of Christ, power in numbers

BODY OF CHRIST

IN MY SHORT TIME walking with God, I've realized something pretty important: we likely won't see that much of God's glory if we walk alone. As we continue with this topic, I want to be clear. I'm talking about thriving with Christ, not just surviving. I'm talking about the calling on our lives. This will have nothing to do with being saved or not. If we are not all that concerned with God's calling on our lives, then we may be offended or not much interested in hearing this next part.

This isn't "opinion." God's people did life together all throughout the scriptures. Nothing has changed today.

> He is before all things, and in Him all things hold together. And He is the head of the body, the church. (Colossians 1:17–18)

"We are the temple for the Holy Spirit now, not the Church." Say what? This posture claims that we are God's temple as a bailout to dissolve the purpose of going to church today, to congregate with God and His people. This is an obscure posture and is once again taking one part of scripture and isolating it. Sure, we are absolutely the temple for the Holy Spirit to dwell in. But it doesn't end there. It's not one or the other. It's both. It doesn't mean that the Church is forsaken because of this one point alone. We need to bring *all* the scriptures together in our response back to Jesus. Three points that are all different, but all very useful, are these:

First, we are the temple for the Holy Spirit to live in.

Second, the Holy Spirit is also around us in an omnipresent form. This is the kingdom of God. The omnipresent power of the Holy Spirit can—and will—be witnessed in an outward and manifested form, as well.

Third, God's house and the reason we go to it is for *many more* reasons than just the topic of where the Holy Spirit will dwell. The Holy Spirit will be in us, and it will also be in God's house (Church). That being said, there are so many other reasons in the order of Christ to congregate in God's house—outside of the point of where the Holy Spirit will dwell. After the Holy Spirit has "dwelled," that doesn't mean we *quit* everything. That's like going to a job interview, then receiving the job and then never showing up for work.

If we are, in fact, believers, walking alone in this journey is prideful to be frank. Why is it prideful? It's prideful because, in effect, we are saying, "We can build our own homes alone. We don't need anyone, and we don't need the Church. We have everything figured out, and we know what's best for our lives." Again, this discernment is a hundred-percent opposite to the teachings of Christ, so it can't be truth. This is what keeps us pressed down. This is where we will live in constant struggle. God is *very* specific about the care and attention He wants on His house and on the body of Christ—outside the topic of where the Holy Spirit will dwell.

The Bible says,

> Then the word of the Lord came through the prophet Haggai: "Is it a time for you yourselves to be living in your paneled houses, while this house remains a ruin?" Now this is what the Lord Almighty says: "Give careful thought to your ways. You have planted much, but harvested little. You eat, but never have enough. You drink, but never have your fill. You put on clothes, but are not warm. You earn wages, only to put them in a purse with holes in it." This is what the Lord Almighty says: "Give careful thought to your ways. Go up into the mountains and bring down timber and build My house, so that I may take pleasure in it and be honored," says the Lord. "You expected much, but see, it turned out to be little. What you brought home, I blew away. Why?" declares the Lord Almighty. "Because of My house, which remains a ruin, while each of you is busy with your own house. Therefore, because of you the heavens have withheld their dew and the Earth its crops. I called for a drought on the fields and the mountains, on the grain, the new wine, the olive oil and everything else the ground produces, on people and livestock, and on all the labor of your hands." (Haggai 1:3–11)

Some believers may say, "Oh, that was Old Testament. It's not like that after Jesus died for us and the Holy Spirit came." Really? *Jesus* said *Himself* in the *New Testament*:

> And I tell you that you are Peter, and on this rock I WILL BUILD MY CHURCH, and the gates of Hades will not overcome it. (Matthew 16:18)

The Church, and congregating together, is mentioned many times in the New Testament. Ever notice how stuck people stay when they avoid the body of Christ and His house? When we are able but detach ourselves from the body of Christ, we tend to get spiritually dry and low in faith. We default back to the world's way of determining life choices.

> *These are the people who divide you, who follow*
> *mere natural instincts and do not have the Spirit.*
> *(Jude 1:18–19)*

And again,

> *They are from the world and therefore speak from the*
> *viewpoint of the world, and the world listens to them.*
> *(1 John 4:5)*

"Well, things will do this, because things are doing that. The economy is heading this way, so I guess we will have to move that way. Well, the doctor said this, so I guess I have that." What? There's no faith or hope in that. We get like this because we are not walking with other believers in the faith, and we have no other way to gauge life. I understand that God gave us brains to make adjustments to changing circumstances along the way; that's life. Doctors reports are real, I get it. But when Jesus was on earth, He put a lot of work into creating unity and the body of Christ for a purpose. It was for edification, and that brought sanctification. It was for kingdom purposes. It was to help the lost and brokenhearted. It was for the power that comes in numbers. It was to multiply His power for His glory.

Often enough, we get so consumed with our own lives that we forget to build up God's house and His people. Many have built up God's house for seasons of their lives, then quit after receiving His abundances. We detach from the body because we are comfortable in this abundance. Through deception, we figure that we are self-made people. We forget that the abundance and provision came from God in the first place. Then after God is faithful and gives us the abundance, we think we don't need God's house or His people anymore, because we are set up pretty nice. Let's think again. The same God who gives can take away. Sooner or later, we watch this abundance dwindle or be "blown away," as the scripture said. This happens when we give more thought to our lives than to God's house and His people. This isn't God's best for us, and there will be no power in this posture.

I have met several people who say they believe in God, yet they are completely detached from the body of Christ. They are without any connection to other believers or local church. It's pretty bizarre, really, to have one without the other. I believe it's absolutely impossible to see _all_ the riches of God's amazingness without being plugged in with His people and His house. We may survive, sure, but who wants to just merely survive? This is a book about tapping into His power for the sake of the Gospel. We are talking about thriving in the purpose of God's calling on our lives. We aren't talking about living comfortable "worldly" lives apart from God's purpose. We must see the difference.

Isolation from the body of Christ means we won't be interested in participating in a part of the purpose that God has called us to live out. And it is the biggest purpose really. It means we have actually decided that we know what's best for our lives by shutting out believers. "I'll live out God's purpose in my life, but just not in the church or with other believers." This isn't a submissive posture. How are we obedient to Christ by avoiding most of His people? How "anti" Christ is that when we look directly at Jesus and His ministry? This wasn't Christ's message at all. It's directly opposite, and that's why it is "anti." Are we actually "submitted" in any way at this point? Who are we to decide how we live our lives, or with whom, if we are really listening to God? This is where we find the power—or not. This is where we start seeing supernatural things start to happen, versus only natural things from day to day.

I understand there is a large population of people in the body of Christ and in the churches leading people away from the truth in God's Word. There always has been, and there always will be. The Bible tells us there would be people trying to muck with God's truth in every generation. That's all the more reason we need to be there. Let's not be surprised or offended. This isn't something new. It's funny how the most "mature-looking" believers will get offended the most. Weird.

> I know that after I leave, savage wolves will come in among you and will not spare the flock. Even from your own number men will arise and distort the truth in order to draw away disciples after them. So be on your guard! Remember that for three years I never stopped warning each of you night and day with tears. (Acts 20:29–31)

We know that various groups of power would infiltrate the body of Christ and our churches. They will try and evolve the truth to fit the devil's plan with society. These powers will try and water down the Gospel to nothing more than a bunch of "good" worldly principles to live by. This is the devil's work. These are "anti-obedience" messages without actually saying that they are. This will make some of our churches more of a social club setting than houses of God. Some of these people would even be the leaders of our churches. These leaders will try and establish man-made systems to obtain power for themselves by keeping people away from God's power that comes through truth in obedience. Obedience isn't popular, so they sell the ways of the world and all the attractions of it which are. Politicians, movements, groups, and governments will try and control, influence, and manipulate the Word of God into a universal "belief." This is scriptural. The believers that will stand firm in truth will need God's power in these times. We will need kingdom power. We will need to be Spirit-led believers working in His gifts. We will need to let the Spirit of God build the church, instead of trying to force it like salesman and women with man-made efforts and systems. We will need His power and His gifts to discern man-made operations and efforts. Some of these operations will be designed to try and multiply "people" for the sake of business and monetary reasons in the church, instead of the real truth in God's Word.

Even if we see this happening, it's all the more reason for us to stay and stand firm in the truth. It won't be easy to be set apart in the body of Christ. Of course, we know that Jesus wasn't concerned about easy. He Himself proved that. There will, however, be a reward for standing in the actual truth and being set apart—even in the body of believers. We are called to truth in obedience, done in love, regardless of the persecution, even within the body of Christ. Poison in the churches is no reason for us to leave them. We were not called to avoid the body of Christ if we find false disciples trying to lead the sheep astray. We were called to be courageous to try and keep the flock together and strong.

Every part of Christ's teachings tells us to congregate and to come together inside and outside of church. This was the instruction from Jesus Himself all through the Gospels. Jesus and His apostles lived this out by example. They congregated with each other while they headed out to the nations. And not without persecution. Jesus said that it is the sick that need a doctor. This will include individuals in the body of Christ. Being involved with God's church is the very nucleus of knowing Jesus. Perhaps we aren't reaching out to anyone whatsoever for the purpose of the Gospel, let alone the church. The good news? We can start, or we can start again.

Some people may say, "What if, for some reason, it just wasn't hypothetically possible for someone to go to a church. A real and legitimate reason. Are you trying to say that I can't live a kingdom life then?" Absolutely not.

I say, "God alone knows our capabilities every second of the day. Our abilities are all different and very unique. He will adjust His power and provision accordingly to meet us in our circumstances." That is why God is so amazing. Let's not be a bunch of religious and mechanical-sounding nut bars here. All of our deeds done in obedience are done in worship because we love the Lord and we want to glorify Him. God is an awesome and merciful God. He knows the truth in every matter. <u>Furthermore, that last sentence applies for each and every one of these experiences we will discuss in this book</u>. God knows the exact capabilities of each and every one of us at any given point in our days, and His grace will be adjusted accordingly to meet us in our abilities. God alone knows the real truth in our abilities at any given time.

The Bible says *we are* the body of Christ—each one of us. He is the head, and we are the body, the arms, the legs, and the feet that support each other during this journey. We actually need to come together to make a body! Individual pieces don't make a body; they just make individual pieces. This is another spectrum of the light that we must let into our lives in order to find advancement. If we don't want to grow ourselves, maybe we have made the decision that we are already complete and finished people. We think we have everything figured out. At this point, we won't be interested in being involved with others in the body of Christ.

God wants His people in teams because we are powerful in numbers. We overcome with numbers better than we do alone. We are meant to build each other up during this journey by uniting together.

> *Whatever happens, conduct yourselves in a manner worthy of the Gospel of Christ. Then, whether I come and see you or only hear about you in my absence, I will know that you stand firm in the one Spirit, <u>striving together</u> as one for the faith of the Gospel without being frightened in any way by those who oppose you. (Philippians 1:27–28)*

Why do we think Jesus selected twelve apostles to walk with Him? Why do we think Jesus sent the crew out in numbers of two and not one? Why do we think Jesus spent so much time building the Church? It wasn't for "religion" or so that they could have a "building" to go to. It was for supernatural strength through unity to multiply before Jesus returns. It's no different for us. When we engage and put ourselves in the body of Christ and really *belong*, supernatural and miraculous things start to manifest all the time. I have seen it over and over.

> Again, truly I tell you that if two of you on earth agree about anything they ask for, it will be done for them by My father in heaven. For where two or three gather in My name, there I am with them. *(Matthew 18:19)*

Jesus was explaining there is power in numbers; He wants us to join hands and go at this together. He said we can overcome the world's obstacles way better together through the "supernatural" than alone in the "natural." If we do the natural, God said He will add the super—if we go at it unified. There is a purpose to us gathering together, worshipping together, serving together, entertaining together, and praying together. I have seen the firstfruits of this power in my life so many times it's undeniable. Let me give you one example.

I run a home construction company for a living. I am very blessed because of God's provision in my life. That being said, new home construction at the level we are at is very exhausting every day. Things started getting heavy again. I had been in the church for about two years, and things were going great in my life, except for the heavy weight of the business. The stress of the business had been heavy since day one, really, but it was getting to the point where I just couldn't handle another day. It was the "unbearable" type of weight, and if you run a business, I'm sure you can relate. I prayed and prayed, day after day, for a breakthrough that would allow this weight to be lifted to some sort of bearable level. After years of struggle, I still wasn't seeing any change, and quite frankly, it was still going the opposite direction.

The stress got so unbearable I was convinced I couldn't get through another day. I thought that I was going to be forced to throw the towel in. I started wondering if I was even called to business in the first place. I couldn't understand this part of my life at the time.

I couldn't just quit because there were several projects still on the go, so I really felt hopeless and trapped.

This went on day after day without me telling anyone in the church or the people in my life. I didn't want to burden anyone with my problems, and besides, everyone appeared to be so tickled pink watching the success of the business. Who wanted to tell people I couldn't handle another minute of running it? Talk about total pride again! That's why I say this is a journey of progression, and not perfection.

Anyway, the agony continued, and it got worse and worse almost to the point of a nervous breakdown. How could this be happening? I was still praying and believing and trusting, and yet I wasn't seeing any relief.

Finally, I attended a business leaders meeting at the church that I had been neglecting to attend for the longest time. Let me emphasize the "neglecting to attend" part. The church has a ministry specifically designed to support business leaders, and yet I said, "Ah, I don't need them." In my worst time!

Anyhow, I was exhausted beyond measure that day when I went into the meeting. I was completely spent. To be honest, I didn't want to be there. When we got to the prayer time portion of the gathering, the pastor asked, "Does anyone need prayer?" I was in such a stressful spot; I didn't even have enough energy to plead my case.

All of a sudden, I felt a nudge from the person standing behind me. It was the type of nudge that said, "Get off your butt, and tell them the situation you're in, and ask for help." Apparently, the struggle wasn't as private as I thought it was. After several minutes of resisting and with tears in my eyes, I surrendered my pride and mustered enough energy to say, "I'm done. Absolutely done, and I'm likely going to throw the towel in, but I don't know how yet." The look around the room was bewilderment. The mask I put on to hide the stress each week was amazing. Once again, pride. The pastor and the prayer team huddled around me to pray about the situation. Some other business leaders prayed for me as well.

One week later, after years and years of stress, the miracle appeared. The relief came right out of the church body from a guy I didn't even know attended our church. This gentleman had been in the church for over a year and a half (we have a big church).

God supernaturally provided the *perfect* fit to take up the job details I couldn't handle any longer. He rearranged my entire business setup through visions and company structure with a new employee who completely fit my needs. The company and my position have never been the same, and it all happened one week after the prayer meeting. It was like an angel appeared. This fella approached me and asked me if he could have a little bit of my time later on in the week to get some advice on setting up a small business of his own. His request for my time was completely unrelated to the needs in my business. The next day, we sat and chatted for a few hours, and there it was. He was the miracle.

What's my point? After looking back, I am absolutely convinced God wasn't going to bring the relief I needed until I humbled myself and attended a meeting specifically designed for this purpose. Attending and confessing, that is.

Why? It wasn't because God didn't want me to have the breakthrough; it's because He wants us to band together and team up in unity. Power in numbers! "Where two or three gather in My name . . ." If all of our prayers were automatically answered one on one with God, we wouldn't need each other or help each other with anything. That isn't God's design for our lives. God wants us to love one another through compassion and support. That includes people inside the church and outside of it. This is kingdom living.

IT TAKES TIME

I have to say that the conviction for engaging with the body of Christ didn't happen with me at first. When I surrendered my life to Christ, the last place I wanted to be was in church. I thought Christians were lame and boring, and so were all things church. I thought there was nothing I needed from church, so why bother going? Besides, how could church be enjoyable? What a total lie again from Satan. I have two immediate points on this thought:

First, I go to an amazing Bible-based church in Alberta. It's fun, and so are the people. We need to get the misperception of boring out of our heads. I've done the most amazing things with the people of my church, inside and outside of the walls of the church building. If the first church doesn't feel right, try the next one. Keep going until you find a home that works. Don't be a church hopper, but be patient in finding a home to get rooted in. I have been to many great churches all over the world since my journey began. I guarantee there is one out there for you.

Second, it's not what the church can do for us; it's what we can do for the church. This is the entire point of what God writes in the Haggai verse. This is what brings the kingdom life. I encourage you to read Rick Warren's book *The Purpose Driven Life*, especially the section on getting rooted in the church. God doesn't want us to be sponges, and no one wants to be categorized as a "taker" only. Belonging to a group in the body of Christ is a give-and-take relationship with its people. What we put in is what we will get out. So let's not go into the situation with the attitude of, "What can I get out of it?" The results we receive will happen naturally upon getting involved. God will take care of our houses if we will take care of His. The key here is to go in expecting to worship Him with His people— to be engaged as a part of His order.

PRESSING IN

Engaging in the body of Christ is one part of the spectrum of light we need to advance with God in His powerful kingdom here on earth. It's the same old saying again. "We move first. Then God will move more." When we take a small step toward Him, He takes way bigger steps toward us. That's why God is so amazing. That being said, He won't force us to take the steps. Why would God take care of our homes and our lives if we aren't one bit concerned about His people or His house?

God will bless the people that get *rooted* in His house. It's hard to experience all of the freedom in Christ's order if we are not in the body at all or if we are just "one day a week only" fans. To be honest, "one day a week only" fans won't get to see the power of God show up and show out that often. There is no power in those numbers. That is why we see so many pressed-down believers. We show up once a week for an hour and a half, then walk out the door doing very little in the order of Christ until we show up again the next week. There is no power in that.

Let's press into the activities and get as involved as we can. Again, it's not what the church can do for us; it's what we can do for the church. This is the part that makes us belong and helps bring purpose in our lives. This is a part which brings healing and freedom and victory into our lives. God blesses those who press in, serve, and help others in His house.

The Bible says,

Blessed are those who dwell in your house. (Psalm 84:4)

If we can't attend a church, there are lots of other options that I will discuss later on. The important thing right now is to understand it is crucial to belong to some sort of group within the body of Christ if we are going to thrive and experience kingdom-life moments. I have seen the hand of God move so frequently being in the strength of God's people, inside and outside of the walls of the church.

QUICK TO FORGIVE

While on the topic of church, I think we can all agree nothing is perfect. Neither is God's house. Every single person has been offended outside of the church by someone, and it's no different inside. Things are going to happen. We will be offended a time or two if we stay committed. That's a given. Let's show some character. We will not advance with bitterness in our hearts. Offense is poison. We don't want to be bitter people; we want to be better people.

Character isn't who we are in the good times, because anyone can be good in the good times. That's called personality. Character is who we are in the rough times. We can get offended multiple times a week in the bank or at a hockey game or in the grocery store or driving on the streets. Yet we still return to those venues almost every time. So why do we so easily leave church if we get offended? It's because, like mentioned earlier in this book, Satan whispers a lie into our ears to try and separate us from the body. He wants to use the wound or offense so that he can get us travelling alone again.

The lying whisper *generally* makes the offense seem <u>way worse</u> than it actually is because the stakes are *way* higher. We are talking about Satan's number one plan here—to separate us from God and His people and His order. Satan doesn't much care if we go back to the bank or the hockey game. The stakes for victory aren't nearly what they would be in the body of Christ. Satan drops a lie into our minds, which says, "Everyone should be perfect in church, and this is the one place I shouldn't get offended."

I say, "Let's get over it." If we can be strong and forgive somebody if an offense has occurred, that is true character. God rewards character. I have forgiven people on lots of occasions, and I'm certain that someone has extended grace to me a time or two—or three or fifty times, as well. If Jesus can forgive us, we must forgive others. No options here. If we leave the church and try and walk alone, we will hinder the good works God wants for us, and we will forfeit the power that comes with unity. Also, we will want the covering from our pastors and leaders.

Even though we know that the general population makes mistakes, let's not forget pastors and leaders can make mistakes too. We don't attend churches or groups because of the leaders and their messages *only*. We go there to glorify God as a part of His order, and we praise and worship Him in unity. We go to God's house to reach out to the brokenhearted because God tells us to do so in His Word. There are broken people walking through the doors of God's house every day, and it's up to us to help bring them back to life through the experiences God has gotten us through. We are community. We work missions. We band together to help the nations. We go to God's house in selflessness, not selfishness. I understand that pastors have had affairs and businessmen have cheated others out of money. I understand that people have been hurt and offended. I get it. We must forgive minor and major issues and press in. Jesus says we won't be forgiven if we don't forgive others, so let's not forget to extend a good portion of grace to our pastors and leaders. They have an incredible responsibility each week presenting the Word of God to us.

> Do not judge, and you will not be judged, do not condemn, and you will not be condemned. Forgive, and you will be forgiven. (Luke 6:37)

Again,

> But whoever has forgiven little loves little. (Luke 7:47)

We must forgive offenses and move on. We will block His power if we don't.

LET'S BATTLE TOGETHER

Look at power in numbers this way. We are always stronger as many rather than just one. You can't win the Stanley Cup if you are the only player on the team. It's impossible. And certainly, if you are the only linebacker on the team, you will never wear a Super Bowl ring. It's the same way in the church. We are united warriors standing against Satan's tactics. We stand together to overcome the assault.

The Bible says God gives us full armor to battle against Satan.

> Therefore, put on the full armor of God, so that when the day of evil comes, you may be able to stand your ground, and after you have done everything, to stand. Stand firm then, with the belt of truth buckled around your waist, with the breastplate of righteousness in place, and with your feet fitted with the readiness

that comes from the Gospel of peace. In addition to this, take up the shield of faith, with which you can extinguish all the flaming arrows of the evil one. (Ephesians 6:13)

Okay, that's good so far. It sounds like we are all armored up to go battle against the enemy at this point. We are gladiators. Hold on. Wait a minute. All this armor is good, but gladiator armor is all front-side armor and protection. Who is going to protect my back side from the enemy? The Bible says, "The glory of God protects our back sides." I believe brothers and sisters in the body of Christ protect our backsides as <u>part of God's glory</u>. We watch each other's back sides, like the gladiators did in battle. They stood back-to-back with their swords opposite each other to take on the enemy, because they knew that nothing could come in from behind them when they battled this way. That's how we roll in the church or in our groups within the body of Christ. We protect each other's back sides when we can't see the enemy coming at moments in our lives. We stand united back-to-back so Satan can't sneak in from behind and secretly take us down. That's what will happen if we attempt to travel without the body of Christ. The damage will not happen all at once, but it will happen if we're alone. That's where the deception is. The damage will come slowly so that we don't know it is actually happening. It is by design.

COMPATIBILITY AND OVERALL PURPOSE

As we wrap up this section on the body of Christ and power in numbers, I have a few more thoughts to share about people in the church and the warriors who battle with us. Not every single person in the church is going to be our best friend or battle with us. Let's be reasonable. We have all sorts of different personalities, age groups, interests, and occupations. During my journey, it took a little while for me to see whom I connected with and whom I didn't so much. It's okay if we aren't compatible with every single person in the church. That's not the point. We will find the people to mold with eventually.

On the other hand, let's try and avoid being cliquey and gluing ourselves to certain individuals only. Let's try to keep open minds. There are a lot of needs in other people's lives. It's not about "me." It's about the broken-down people who walk through the doors all the time. We never know what amazing things can happen when we take a step of faith and approach someone who looks completely opposite to ourselves. I'm speaking from experience.

> Do not forget to show hospitality to strangers, for by so doing some people have shown hospitality to angels without knowing it. (Hebrews 13:2)

Church is not just a place to have some good friends; there are people who will need to hear the stories of how God brought us through the storms that are now approaching them. This is how we multiply and live the kingdom life.

RELIABILITY AND LONGEVITY

There are a lot of compassionate people in the house of God. I spent thirty-four years without these types of reliable relationships in my life. Outside of church, I found it tough to authentically mesh with people who would walk with me through my struggles for more than one day at a time and actually understand them. I'm not saying that supportive or compassionate people are exclusive to the body of Christ by any means. I'm just saying there seems to be concentrations of experienced people who have travelled the same roads before us in the church and in groups of believers. A big purpose in being there is to help others, so the body of Christ is certainly going to contain the support we need to advance.

Lastly, the Church or groups in the body of Christ will always exist! The body of Christ isn't the latest trend or the next fashion to come and go. It's forever. There will always be churches and groups which form the body of Christ somewhere. Even in the worst times of the world, they will never disappear. They will exist in big and small buildings, in people's homes, and public and private spots. My point is this: the body of Christ is dependable, no matter what. The Church is not going anywhere. We can always count on it because tens of thousands of churches or hideouts will never just vanish and be gone. Not on this side of eternity. Jesus speaks of the Church's longevity. Mentioned again:

And I tell you that you are Peter, and on this rock I will build My Church, and the gates of hell will not overcome it. (Matthew 16:18)

There is strength and power in numbers. Like it or not, we will need to be committed to the body of Christ to live out the fullness of our purposes in Him. This is one area where we will need to "plug in" to access new levels of power and victory.

Let the message of Christ dwell among you richly as you teach and admonish one another with all wisdom through psalms, hymns, and songs from the Spirit, singing to God with gratitude in your hearts.

—Colossians 3:16

THE ORDER OF MELCHIZEDEK

15 fellowship

BEING ROOTED IN A church, with the body of Christ, is very important as we have just discussed. It's a place where we go to praise and worship God regularly and welcome the brokenhearted. We usually get a great message for the week, and we are very blessed to hear the Word of God. As we push ahead, there are various activities outside of the church building that keep us engaged and growing with God as well. We need more than just a morning service each week to live a kingdom life. The more we plug in, according to our abilities, the more we will experience His glory; it's just the way it is. Faith without works is powerless. We need to live the "God-first" life to experience new-level living.

I want to talk about another way to engage with the body of Christ that is just as important. It's called fellowship. Fellowship is when we get together with other believers to engage with one another. Fellowship is generally centered around Christ and the Gospel and experiences in our lives. We have healthy relationships in church, of course, but if we *can't* attend a church for any reason, it's okay, because there are several different ways to get the fellowship "light" that is required as a part of the order of Christ to access more power.

Most churches provide "branches" from the church, which are "small groups" or "Bible studies." These fellowship groups are an extension of the church family divided up into smaller, more intimate groups. They gather regularly at people's homes, hospitals, assisted-living homes, public places, or even prisons. Yes, I said prisons. Nobody has to be alone in prison. Kingdom life can and will happen in prison.

> On the first day of the week we came together to break bread. Paul spoke to the people and, because he intended to leave the next day, kept on talking until midnight. There were many lamps in the upstairs room where we were meeting. (Acts 20:7–8)

Small groups are very powerful because we get to engage with people we trust at a much more intimate level. This is an amazing way to give and receive support at a local level without all the distraction. The amount of victory that can come into our lives in a small group environment is amazing. Some small groups watch a recorded curriculum from a trusted teacher and then follow up with a question-and-answer session. If there isn't a curriculum to follow, that's just fine as well. Some groups will gather to break down Bible verses for strength and understanding. We share life experiences, victories, and struggles. We pray together and do life together. It's power in numbers again. My small group has seen victory after victory through prayer and sharing together. This is where we get the real meat and potatoes in our spiritual journey with God. The more time we spend in God's presence, the more power we will experience. Pastors in the church can't serve a heavy meal every service because newcomers might be arriving for the very first time. New people need some milk at first. That being said, most pastors are very good at balancing the milk with the meat and potatoes in the church services. But as we grow with God and desire a deeper level of kingdom life, we will require more solid food each week. By joining a small group, we will find the meat and potatoes we require in our spiritual diets. If you come to my house on Thursday nights, your diet will also include some sort of fabulous arrangement of treats and snacks to pick away at as well.

But seriously, we have seen incredible breakthroughs, healing, and growth through the branches of our church's small groups. Plugging in to our small group family during the week gives us more access to the power we will need between services. An hour at church just isn't going to cut it. Remember, Jesus said, "Where two or three gather in my name . . . I will be with them." Iron sharpens iron, which is why we team up and fellowship together during the week. We need it to stay strong. Special things start to happen when we gather regularly. Nobody can tell me any different after this experience.

A SPLIT SECOND

It was about 8:00 p.m. on a spring night in 2012 when I heard a knock at the door. I answered the door to see a police officer standing there.

He said, "Ryan Shaw?"

I said, "Yes."

He said, "You've been served."

He handed me an envelope.

He turned around, walked to his cruiser, and then drove away.

I stood there in shock.

At that point, I was only four months into my new relationship with Christ. I was just a baby. What could this possibly be? I went inside to unpack the envelope. I unpacked what is called "disclosure" in Canada or "discovery" in the US. This is the evidence from an investigation for the charges that are pending against that person. Apparently, an investigation had happened. I was being criminally charged in conjunction with a minor traffic stop that I barely even remembered from three months prior. In that incident, I received a speeding ticket. I drove away and never gave it another thought. I won't get into all the details, because that would be five chapters alone.

Criminal charges were being brought forth in relation to the traffic stop on the highway three months prior. It was a complete manipulation of details and a fabricated case. A total abuse of power. The results of the charge would be a criminal record with a one-thousand-dollar fine if I complied without a challenge. Another criminal record? I was devastated. Are you serious? How could this be happening? How could this police officer do this to me?

Time for another lawyer, I guess. There was no way I was having these criminal charges and the fine for this type of manipulation. My lawyer agreed that this was an absolute manipulation of power. He told me that he would go to the crown prosecutor and handle my "issue" in three to four months. My court appearance to face the charges wasn't for nine months if I elected to challenge. In the meantime, I was to wait. Day to day, the stress and worry were building up as I waited for my lawyer to go to the Supreme Court to quash these charges before my actual court date. I couldn't help but think of the worst-case scenario. I just couldn't understand how this could be happening to me after such an extreme change in lifestyle after my "last night." The grace and restoration I felt in just four months with the Lord felt like years. In fact, it felt like my past was completely erased. How could I be dealing with stuff like this again? I had already received two DUIs in the past, giving me two criminal records already. I brought this matter to my small group Bible study.

We prayed many times, week to week, as the date approached for my lawyer to meet with the prosecutor for the first time. I couldn't imagine walking through this all alone.

Finally, the day came, and I headed to Supreme Court with my lawyer. He told me that the matter would be over within ten minutes. I waited in the lobby as he went into the prosecutor's chambers. About ten minutes later, he came out of the chambers. He was as white as a ghost. He came over to me and said that the crown had just increased the charges because we were challenging, and there was nothing he could do. They increased what was a criminal record and a thousand-dollar fine to a "summary" charge with ten years maximum and a two-thousand-dollar fine. I was out of my mind.

I asked him, "How could this happen? That's why I hired you!"

He told me that we got a "nasty" prosecutor that day and that he would make another appointment in two to three months. This would give us some time to let them cool down. This would highly increase our chances to get a more reasonable prosecutor on a different day to negotiate a deal or, better yet, to get the charges dropped completely, as expected.

Again, I went to my small group to ask for prayer and support during this time. I had to wait three more months as the stress accumulated. This was serious now. "Summary" charges are a serious matter. Any guilty verdict whatsoever means prison time of some sort no matter what, my lawyer said. All things aside, he told me to relax because there was absolutely no evidence to support these charges. His counsel wasn't helping after what had just happened in court that day.

Three months later, we finally got to court, and the same process happened all over again. He came out of the chambers and said the prosecutor increased the charges again. What? This time it was *worse*. The prosecutor increased the charge to an "indictment" charge that holds a maximum amount of fourteen years in prison—with the fine! Indictment charges are for the worst of crimes. Murder, rape, grand theft auto, etc. You could imagine the state I was in now. He told me he would delay the court date and reschedule to meet the prosecutor again in a few months. He assured me of the results the next time. He told me that he had never seen anything like this in the thirty years that he had been a lawyer. Go figure.

Devastation was an understatement at this point. Now I was *really* requesting prayer and support from my small group family. I was stressed right out of my brains. There was so much on the line. Most people in my life suggested that I needed a new lawyer. I agreed. I made some calls to guys who "know guys" and finally got the number to one of the most powerful criminal lawyers in Canada. I made an appointment two days later and met with him.

He told me that this charge had become very serious, but there was no evidence. He told me that he could quash these charges with just a phone call. I thought, "Oh yeah, baby, now we are talking." He said we would still have to show up at court but our appearance would just be a formality and everything would go as planned. I was so relieved in that moment. The new lawyer told me that he would charge me a $17,000 retainer up front and then another $17,000 when he got the results I was looking for. He reminded me of how "results oriented" he was. He told me to sleep on it and to call him directly in the morning if I wanted to proceed. Thirty-four thousand dollars ($34,000) is a lot of money, but it was peanuts in comparison to the results that could come if this went sideways with my other lawyer. I had a made up mind as I left his office, and I told him that I would call him in the morning with measures to retain him for his services.

As I was driving home with a made-up mind, the Holy Spirit whispered a thought in my head that I will never forget.

He said, "If you hire this new lawyer, you are going to prison."

It came over me like a shockwave. I was so weak that I had to pull over and park on the side of the highway heading home.

He said, "When are you going to quit trusting in man and trust in Me to overcome? You are not buying your way out of this. Use the lawyer you have and trust in Me."

I couldn't believe what I was hearing. I said, "Lord! I will go to prison!"

There was no more talking. He went silent. I had no idea what this meant or what to do next. I was just as devastated as before. What a roller coaster of emotions. That night was our small group session again. I was under such immense pressure. Many were anxious to hear about my news from earlier in the day. I had told them *everything* that had happened from the very start and right up to that minute. The room was quiet. I was in tears. The whole group surrounded me to pray. What happened next would forever change me. My buddy Larry, who had put his faith in Jesus shortly after me, put his hand on my shoulder. He said, "You will go to court with your first lawyer and not fight the charges. You will go in guilty, take the charges, and come out as if nothing ever happened."

That was all he said. I was so shocked I opened my eyes to look at him. I wanted to say, "Are you out of your mind? That's impossible! If I go in guilty, I have to go to prison no matter what. Even if I get the minimum charges. The lawyer already told me that. I would lose everything. I will lose my business, my home. Everything!"

Just as I had these thoughts, an intense blast of peace came over me. It was only for a split second. I can't explain it. Larry doesn't even know why he said that to this day. It just came over him. I had made up my mind right in that moment. I wouldn't hire the new lawyer, and I wouldn't fight it with my existing lawyer. No more fight. I was going to take a guilty plea to my court date. Everyone thought I was crazy, including me.

The next day, I phoned my original lawyer to tell him the new plan. He told me that this was legal suicide. He told me that I would go to jail no matter what. I told him I didn't care. My mind was made up. I specifically told him I was going to leave it in the Lord's hands and all the reasons why. This lawyer was a believer, and he still thought I was out of my mind. This was an extremely radical moment in my life, to say the least.

Months later, the court date came. I'm not going to say that I went into Supreme Court in total peace, because I didn't. I was terrified—but I didn't care. My mind was made up. Whenever the fear got unbearable, I would think back to that split-second blast of intense peace after Larry prophesied. If I hadn't received that split-second blast of peace, I would have thought Larry was off his rocker. After that split second, there was no more peace after that. The Holy Spirit was quiet again. My whole life depended on trusting in that split-second, mind-blowing peace from months earlier.

I was told that if we got the woman judge, my day wouldn't go well. I got the woman judge. She called my case and asked me to approach the bench. After all the legal mumbo jumbo, she asked my lawyer, "How does your client plea?"

He said, "Guilty, your honor."

She said, "Do you have anything to say, Mr. Shaw?"

All I said was, "Have mercy on me, please."

Just then and completely out of nowhere, my lawyer became very urgent and said, "Your honor, I'm sorry, we would like to put in a new request! We would like to request twice the fine, with six months of house arrest for the guilty plea."

She rolled her eyes and said, "Excuse me?"

He repeated the question just the same as the first time.

After what seemed like forever, of course, she said, "Mr. Shaw, what do you do for a living?" I said I was the owner of a new home construction company. I told her that I was the only operator in the whole company. She asked me what a normal day looked like in my life. I told her that I drive from town to town every day, making multiple stops from 7:00 a.m. in the morning until 9:00 p.m. at night on some days.

She looked up and said, "Not anymore. I'll agree to the house arrest terms. I'll grant six month's house arrest. Mr. Shaw, your home will be a prison for the next six months. You will not be doing what you just told me, in terms of the work you just explained. This isn't your lucky day if you own a business and you are the only operator in it. You will be at the mercy of a parole officer in two days. Your days of driving around are over. If you think I'm hard, wait until you meet with him. He's way less tolerant and has more authority than me when it comes to your outcome. If you breach a single detail of your house arrest parole agreement, you will find yourself behind bars in federal prison. Your lawyer will process the paperwork out front. Case dismissed."

Are you kidding me? There was relief mixed with fear. I won't be behind bars, but I will lose my company. I have eleven homes under construction. If I can't check them and meet with the subcontractors and clients every single day, I will lose everything and get sued for all that I was worth. The pressure was incredible.

After court, I went home and processed my future for hours—my company, my home, and my upcoming meeting with the parole officer. I met with my small group the next night and told them the outcome. We all prayed about the matter.

Then, as calm as could be, a buddy piped up and said, "Let's pray for a miracle with the parole officer. It's not over yet. God's still in control."

Imagine what I was thinking right about then. To be honest, I felt defeated. But what did I have to lose? We all agreed that we would believe for some kind of miracle irrespective of the circumstances ahead.

Two days later, I arrived to meet my new parole officer. His name was Calvin. He led me into his office and said, "Have a seat." I was as nervous, or maybe even more, than when I was sitting in court. My entire future was in this man's hands. He opened the file and read it for about two minutes, flipping back and forth through the pages. Finally, he looked up and said, "So you build new homes for a living?"

I said, "Yes, that's right."

He said, "What's the name of your company?"

I told him the name. He said, "Oh, I've heard of your company." To come next was kingdom power. He said, "I built a home with the company across the street." He opened the blinds and pointed across the road to the competitors. He said, "I would never do that again."

For the next hour and a half, we talked about new home construction. That discussion led into my new faith. That discussion lasted another hour. Calvin was a believer. He was just rocked by my conversion moment on my "last night." After over two hours of talking, we still hadn't talked about *anything* to do with my case.

Finally, he closed my file and said, "This is garbage. You are free to go. There will be no conditions to your parole. Not one. Call me once a month to let me know you're alive until your 'house arrest' term is over. I need to cover my butt with the courts. There will be no actual house arrest or restrictions associated with it. I have the authority to make this call. You are free to carry on as normal."

I burst out into tears and hugged him and thanked him. He let me out of his office, and that was it. Prophecy and prayer fulfilled. Peter was at the gate! I couldn't believe what just happened. I had just had the most powerful kingdom moment of my life. I went into Supreme Court pleading guilty to an "indictment" charge facing a maximum of fourteen years and walked away as if nothing ever happened—just as prophesied.

Coincidence? This wasn't coincidence; this was evidence. I know this was a long story, but this was one of the most mind-blowing kingdom experiences that I've had in my short walk in God's order. I've had many since. I've reflected back to this season in my life many times. It is scary to think of the alternate outcome. What if I wasn't fellowshipping with my small group? What if we weren't gathered together in prayer? What if I wasn't there to hear that prophecy, for that split-second blast of peace, for a confirmation. Would I be in jail today, or would God have shown me a path to victory another way? I don't know for sure, but that's not a chance that I'm willing to take. I'm going to do the things that I have the power to do as a starting point. I'll stick to His order and what He suggests we do within it. Then His power can take over from there.

After my lawyer handled all the paperwork in court that day, he told me that I would never step foot on American soil ever again, especially after 9/11. I had this new indictment charge and two DUI charges on my record. Since that court day, I've been on American soil over twenty times, and I've never gotten so much as a second look going through customs. Not even once. In fact, my very first time back onto American soil was two weeks after the "house arrest" term was over. I drove into the United States <u>by accident</u> at Niagara Falls. I didn't even have my passport with me. All I had was my driver's license. Since when does this happen after the towers came down in New York? And since when does this happen at all nowadays even with a clean record? I think God was showing me something *very* specific again—evidence of a prophecy fulfilled and a reminder that He was in complete control. This was new-level faith for all of us from that moment on. This was His kingdom power being released through fellowship, because He says we are powerful in numbers. This was God's powerful favor.

CONFESS

I'm a results-oriented guy. I can't sit still for long without seeing results, or else I start taking more action. Sometimes it's a gift, and sometimes it's not. Although everyone might not be so results driven, we all want to see results. When we find a good Bible-based church home or small group, we want to press in and engage—but we need to be patient to find some good people to connect with. When we connect with people who are willing to walk through some of the storms with us, <u>let's tell them what the storm actually is!</u> Like mentioned above. This is the "confess" part. We need to be vulnerable, because vulnerability in the order of Christ is a huge part of the spectrum of light. This is what brings kingdom power.

It is essential that we share and confess our struggles and storms with one another. Too many of us are attending church or small group bodies without confessing our struggles because of pride. We don't want to look weak, or we want to present the image that everything is going well. "Hey, I'm going to church now, and I'm blessed, and I want everyone to see I have it all together now." Hardly. Read the part about my business storm again. Let's not keep it to ourselves for two years like I did. Let's not struggle in the misery for any longer than we have to. Lesson learned for me. Let's not be afraid to tell others about our storms when we fellowship. <u>There is power in confession</u>. Confession is humility, and humility is powerful. Look at what the Bible says about confession.

> *Therefore, confess your sins to each other and pray*
> *for each other so that you may be healed. The prayer*
> *of a righteous person is powerful and effective.*
> *(James 5:16)*

Confession is powerful in numbers. It is good to confess struggles in sin, but it doesn't have to be just sin that is confessed. Being vulnerable with our brothers and sisters will accelerate the healing process and bring the victorious life moments in a very effective manner. This is because it disarms the enemy. Satan hates it when we team up together. Power in unity overcomes his influence. When we team up together, we pray these storms out of existence. Remember, we are gladiators working together, and God loves it. When God sees brothers and sisters teaming up, He says, "Okay, I like it. Now I can release My power in and through these people. They are humbly walking with each other through life."

Speaking of humility again, let's remind ourselves what the Bible says about the reward we will receive for the humility when we are vulnerable enough to confess our weaknesses.

The Bible says,

> *God opposes the proud but shows favor to the hum-*
> *ble. (1 Peter 5:5)*

God mentions humility two times in three consecutive pages of the Bible at the end of James and in the start of 1 Peter. Weird. Humility is talked about elsewhere in the Bible on several different occasions as well. Humility is where we see kingdom power, especially through confession in fellowship groups.

Again, it's like the business testimony or the court case I shared earlier. I confessed my storm and the weakness I felt—and then God activated His blessing. The miracles came through His kingdom power to help me through those storms. Lots of people may say, "Oh, that was just a coincidence. It could have happened to anyone. It could have happened on your own." Generally, those are the people who are still waiting for their breakthroughs. They may wait forever. I know, for certain, God articulated those victorious moments.

We need to have a made-up mind about this and follow through. That's if we want kingdom life moments. If we don't want these moments, then we don't need to have made-up minds about this. Salvation is free; the power is not. We need to be active in the order of Christ to see His power. We can't sit around and do nothing and expect to have victorious kingdom life moments. There will be a cost. The more we press in, the more we will experience His power. Frequency in our efforts will determine the amount of power that we will experience. We don't do all of these experiences as a bunch of religious duties. We do them because we love God, and there is power in His order. Also, we intensify our relationships with Him during the process.

If we are in the body of Christ and we can't find *any* freedom for a *prolonged* period of time, it's likely because we haven't told someone what our storm is. It's a direct roadblock. Victory isn't very likely to take place if we don't confess our struggles or the storms that we are battling. Confession isn't weakness or a burden. It's power. But Satan wants us to think otherwise. His goal is to get us alone in the storm because isolation always keeps us pressed down. Satan and the world want us to think confession is embarrassing. Or that interdependency with one another is weak or that our problems make us less than others. News flash: we all have struggles that aren't all that unique from the guy or gal sitting across the table. Interdependency and confession and humility unleash God's power.

SERVING

Another form of worship in the order of Christ is serving in the church. Serving people anywhere is God's plan for us, no matter where we are serving. Serving is another supernatural way God activates His blessing and healing in our lives. Again, if we do the natural, God will do the *supernatural*. Belonging to the house of God, or His Church, does not mean showing up once a week and then rushing out the back door just as the service is closing. Not even close. It's our home. What do we do in our own homes? We participate to keep it running. It's vital. The church doesn't run magically. It takes people like you and me to volunteer. Serving connects us to people in such an authentic way. We can't help feeling a sense of belonging and purpose. Belonging brings the kingdom power into our lives. There is little fruit in just attending. To belong in a church means we are getting our hands dirty and helping out. There is nothing more fulfilling than belonging to a church and serving with it. Wait until you see the power that the Lord unleashes when we serve in His house.

Blessed are those who dwell in your house. (Psalm 84:4)

The amazing part? Usually the freedom or the victory taking place in people's lives is completely unrelated to the actual serving itself. The blessing takes place after we take the first step toward God in serving in His Church—or in any group, really. God loves a selfless heart, and because serving is selflessness, God rewards people for putting their own needs aside and helping others instead. In our natural thinking, it would appear the more we put our own desires aside, the less we achieve for ourselves. But just the opposite is true. Service to others, inside or outside the church walls, brings meaningful fulfilment and purpose to our lives—a purpose bigger than ourselves. The purpose and the fulfilment provide freedom in a way that money, possessions, or self-centered pursuits can never bring.

As the Bible says,

> For if you give, you will get! Your gift will return to you in full and overflowing measure, pressed down, shaken together to make room for more, and running over. Whatever measure you use to give, large or small, will be used to measure what is given back to you. (Luke 6:38)

This is how the supernatural release of power comes into our lives. Some of the most unusual breakthroughs in people's lives come through serving. When we combine all of these forms of worship together, there is absolutely no question that our lives will change.

SCANDALOUS GRACE

A young man we know started coming to our church about a year ago. He had previously never set foot in a church in his life. He chose our church through the love of another brother who invited him on several occasions until he finally felt the conviction to attend.

Week after week, this young man attended church services regularly, with all of his addictions still following behind him. Alcohol, cocaine, and all the other substances you could think of accompanied him. Many weeks later, the young man showed up at our Wednesday night Bible study, and he looked like a completely different guy. He looked so free and so healthy. I asked him about the new freedom he was wearing, and his answer was this:

> My buddy who invited me to church asked me to volunteer with the bus ministry. So I decided to help out with him. But you would never guess what happened! I woke up the next morning, and all of my addictions for alcohol and cocaine were gone! I have no desire to use!

We have sure witnessed a remarkable amount of healing and breakthrough for people who have stepped out in faith and started serving. This is just one story of many, of how God has released His kingdom power and His freedom in areas of our lives when they don't seem to be connected to the actual serving we do. In other words, being addicted to cocaine had nothing to do with the bus ministry, yet he was released from his addictions one day after serving. Through service, we give others the things they lack, and we find the purpose and fulfilment in our own lives. It's a part of God's order. God rewards us for this service as is written in the scriptures.

The Bible says,

> And if you spend yourselves on behalf of the hungry and satisfy the needs of the oppressed, then your light will rise in the darkness, and your night will become like the noonday. (Isaiah 58:10–12)

It's remarkable how much victory we experience when we are serving others. On many occasions, we can feel it instantly. If we are serving others while we have lack in our own lives, the lack in others is usually the same or greater than our own lack. When the other people's lack is greater than our own lack, the pain of our own lack tends to feel relieved right on the spot. I know this, again, from experience. But one way or another, whether the relief comes in a month or the very next day—like in the case of the young gentleman I just mentioned—Jesus promises victory in His order.

There is no service too small or too petty either. There are countless needs in our churches and in this world. One need is just as important as the next, so let's not focus on status. Like we talked about, God rewards humility. I feel some of the greatest releases from the enemy's strongholds when I do some of the smallest jobs or give some of the smallest gifts that go unrecognized inside or outside of the church. I believe these releases are God's kingdom power for humility, according to His Word in the Bible as we have already read. The key to remember is it's not necessary for us to put on a full-time volunteer show or for us to be the biggest philanthropist to get a great blessing from God.

Be careful not to practice your righteousness in front of others to be seen by them. If you do, you will have no reward from your Father in heaven. (Matthew 6:1–2)

The focus here is to serve within our means and within the gifts God has given us. Again, we are trying to live in God's righteous order. We aren't living to . . . look righteous. Our deeds should be motivated by the heart of compassion that Jesus has put in us to help others, not selfish ambition and the need for recognition.

Truly I tell you, this poor widow put in more than all the others. All these people gave their gifts out of their wealth; but she out of her poverty put in all she had to live on. (Luke 21:1–4)

This scripture applies to serving as well. Some of the smallest acts of service will be recognized and rewarded by God the most as we are serving others. All service, whether big or small, is equal. Deeds bring His kingdom power into our lives. It's that simple. This is bringing our faith together with our deeds.

Again I tell you, it is easier for a camel to go through the eye of a needle than for someone who is rich to enter the kingdom of God.

—Matthew 19:24

THE ORDER OF MELCHIZEDEK

16 tithing

LIKE MENTIONED IN CHAPTER 5, this text does not mean wealthy people won't go to heaven. More often than not, money becomes a consuming idol that can tear our lives to pieces if we don't have very sound foundations in Christ. This will most certainly move us away from God's power. Where do 90 percent of people fail? Believe it or not, in abundance. No matter what that abundance is, really. As soon as we get the relief or the breakthrough that we so desperately need, we pull away from God and His principles. We begin to feel self-sufficient and don't rely on God at that point. We become distracted by the lusts of the world and the desires of the flesh with all the temptation in abundance. It will be extremely difficult to experience power in the kingdom of God if we don't understand the purpose in money and abundance.

"Money will never buy us happiness."

Of course it won't. That's not what it was designed for. This is false humility again for a few different reasons. Maybe because we fear that we lack, have fallen short, or don't trust God in His purposes for it. That statement is an absolutely irrelevant comment in a believer's life. Or at least it should be. This shows us that we are still in a posture of "self." Why? That's because we are still consumed and talking about "our own" happiness. This posture is not of Christ. That's why we throw out a comment like that in terms of wealth and abundance. We make this comment because we don't realize that having abundance or the ability to create wealth is not just about ourselves. When are we really going to read our Bibles and actually understand and apply the Word? It's all His to begin with! We are not trying to buy happiness. We are trying to live for God and His purposes, instead of living like we are our own gods. When a believer makes these comments, this basis is off point, and we have completely missed the mark in God's overall purpose. Maybe that's because we aren't one bit concerned about God's purpose? Maybe we think that we are the source? Maybe we think we are our own providers? Victory and favor are only going to come when we take God's purposes and principles seriously. Radical power is going to take radical revelation and obedience.

The Bible says,

> Wealth and honor come from You; You are the ruler of all things. In Your hands are strength and power to exalt and give strength to all. Now, our God, we give You thanks, and praise Your glorious name. "But who am I, and who are my people, that we should be able to give as generously as this? Everything comes from You, and we have given only what comes from Your

hand. We are foreigners and strangers in Your sight, as were all our ancestors. Our days on Earth are like a shadow, without hope. Lord our God, all this abundance that we have provided for building You a temple for Your Holy Name comes from Your hand, and all of it belongs to You. I know, my God, that You test the heart and are pleased with integrity. All these things I have given willingly and with honest intent. And now I have seen with joy how willingly Your people who are here have given to You." (1 Chronicles 29:12–17)

Tithing is another form of worship in the order of Christ that brings victory and kingdom living into our lives. A tithe is considered 10 percent of what comes into our bank accounts. God asks us to give the first 10 percent of our increase, every time, to His house. The full 10 percent too. Not 10 percent after bills, the mortgage, groceries, and a spa—or when the finances are so built up that we won't really notice a dent in our accounts. Perhaps we should jump back to Haggai 1:3–11 again. This is a verse that relates to us directly in terms of our financial responsibilities and outcomes. When we build up God's house and His people, God will build our homes in return. That's if we trust God and His Word. He tells us the repercussions of our decisions in that verse and in many others. Money is generally a sensitive topic in the body of Christ, but I can easily and openly discuss the topic of giving a *portion* of our finances back to God because

A) I have the same responsibilities as everyone else when it comes to finances,
B) I don't know you,
C) I don't know your church, or
D) I don't own a church. Nobody does. A regulatory committee of many handle the finances in a church, so I am just going to speak without bias and say it how it is, because it's the truth.

Tithing is structure, and it is for a purpose bigger than just ourselves. Tithing is a form of trust and another act of <u>worship</u> in our relationship with God. We can't forget that His power is in His order. When we look past ourselves and past our own current circumstances toward something bigger than "ourselves," then things start changing; they just do. Besides, looking at it from the logical side, how do we think the church provides for its pastors and its leaders who are so graciously giving of their time to us each week, outside of the weekly services? How do we think the church fuels the buses to pick up the less fortunate people for church service every week? Who do we think pays for the mortgage on the property the church sits on? Who do we think pays to keep the lights on and keep the heat running in the building? Who do we think . . .? I think we get the point. The church isn't there to steal our money (I'm not going to entertain the 4 percent of churches that may have embezzled money in this conversation). Church is a real place with grown-up bills and responsibilities. We may think, "Well, that's not our problem." But let's think again. We need to understand the bigger picture and the calling on our lives instead of the current situation that has us pressed down. This includes our finances. <u>Only when we see God's order being bigger than our current order *will* we see kingdom life take root.</u>

> As the heavens are higher than the earth, so are My ways higher than your ways and My thoughts than your thoughts. (Isaiah 55:9)

Part of belonging to God's community is giving a portion of our money, much like we would in our own homes. There are real bills and real needs to keep our churches running. If we have ever been a part of seeing someone come to life through the church, we can't deny the purpose of it. That being said, God's promises for us are so awesome; there is always a flip side to every coin. There is always a promise associated with the principle. God says if we will give a portion of our money to the house, then He will reward us. He calls this the harvest.

> Bring the whole tithe into the storehouse, that there may be food in My house. 'Test Me in this,' says the

Lord almighty, and see if I will not throw open the floodgates of heaven and pour out so much blessing that there will not be room enough to store it.
(Malachi 3:10)

THE HARVEST

God promises us a harvest if we plant seed in the form of tithes and offerings. In fact, He says, "Test Me in this!" It's the only place in the Bible He says to test Him. And then He says in return, "I will open the floodgates of heaven on you because of it." I could write a whole book alone on the goodness of God in my finances since I started tithing. The results have been supernatural (which is the natural way of Christ's order). It's amazing to have enough to be a blessing to others for the first time in my life. Increase like this did not start happening until after I started tithing. It was like a definite before and after picture. Six years later, the same miraculous things keep happening. Let me give you one example:

THE FLOODGATES OF HEAVEN

I had been a junior-level homebuilder for about two years before I started in a church and learned the tithing principle. Sales were a grueling task. To actually sign a new client was like finding a needle in a haystack. It seemed like such a rare experience that I wondered if the business would ever take off. After being in church and tithing for about three months, I received one of the most bizarre phone calls I've ever received. Even to this day. At 6:30 a.m. Here's how the call went:

"Good morning, it's Ryan speaking."

"Hi, Ryan, this is Darrel speaking."

I said, "Hi, Darrel, how can I help you?"

He continued, "My family and I are in the vehicle right now. We are driving to the airport. We are flying off to Mexico in about four hours. The reason we are calling is we are building a new home right away, and we want to get started as soon as possible. We have heard about you and your company, and we have selected your company to build our home. The blueprints are on the kitchen island of our existing home out on an acreage. The front door is open. We never lock the front door out there. I'd like you to pick up the blueprints and build me a quote as soon as you can. E-mail me the quote, and I will look it over here on vacation. If the quote is close to what we expect, we will start the process and sign the contract via e-mail while we are away."

I couldn't believe what had just happened. I had never even seen this guy before. Never even heard of him—and yet that's what happened. I *really* needed a new contract at that particular moment. I did what he asked. We signed the contract over e-mail the next day, and we started the process. The icing on the cake? That was the most lucrative contract that I ever had signed in my company up until that point. God gave me a kingdom-life moment that I will never forget. I have never had a call that way since. God made this moment *so* obvious to show me that it was <u>His hand at work</u>. I was a new believer. If He didn't make it that obvious, I would of never knew that it was Him providing like that.

The Bible says,

> He did this so that all the peoples of the earth might
> know that the hand of the Lord is powerful and so that
> you might always fear the Lord your God. (Joshua 4:24)

Although I never had another call quite that radical, the sales started trickling in on a regular basis just as we needed them from that point on. The abundance started immediately after I learned the tithing principle. Again, some may say, "That was just a total coincidence. That could have happened to anyone. You were just lucky." Isn't it funny how the people who are generally making these comments are the ones who are usually struggling to advance? Or maybe they have shut the doors on their businesses because they couldn't make it? This was a divine kingdom-life moment that started thrusting me ahead, years before the natural rate of time. I never looked back. My finances have truly never been the same. This wasn't a coincidence; it was the evidence again.

When it comes to tithing and trusting God with the finances He gives us, it's important to realize the harvest comes in His timing. God is always on time and never too late in doing <u>what's best overall, for His purposes and ours</u>. In my short journey, I've noticed this timing rarely lines up with my timing. He knows how much we can handle and how much we can't handle all at once, to keep good order. Sometimes, we may disagree with Him. Let's let God be God. I have seen instant miracles, and I have seen seasons of waiting for the miracles as I trusted God with my finances. Either way, it always comes because He is faithful. I have seen it happen so often that it's undeniable.

That being said, not everyone seems to have this experience. If we encounter someone who has been rooted in the church long enough to know the tithing principle and we see lack in their lives financially, we can trace the lack back to the same thing almost every time—withholding the tithe or being inconsistent in it. They eventually confess their lack in obedience. Again, this is not something to be critical about. We need to come together and support one another on this journey. God wants the firstfruits of what He provides for us in the first place. Obedience will bring kingdom life. Tithing is worship. Tithing is relationship with Him. Tithing is order. If we feel like there is lack in our lives while rooted in the house of God, generally one of five things is happening:

1) not tithing the full 10 percent,
2) not tithing the full 10 percent every single time,
3) a distorted understanding of lack,
4) impatience, or
5) wasting the remaining 90 percent.

I'm not trying to offend anyone; I am just talking about the truth in God's Word, since money is such a sensitive and important issue. Let's take a moment to talk about the last three points quickly as we discussed the first two already.

Understanding lack: If we have regular food, clothing, and shelter, we don't really lack. It's just that simple. Especially in Western culture. If we have these three things alone, it's a rich life. We need to adjust our "perception."

Patience: Let's understand that God has His timing. The provision *will* come. He is never late and always on time to do what's best for us.

We need to be patient and let God do His thing. We can't claim that we trust God if we aren't willing to part with our money. That's no faith at all as far as I'm concerned. If we trust God, then we trust Him in everything. I know this seems harsh, but financial lack is crushing in today's world. This is not God's best for us. He wants us to build His house, and then He will build ours in return, which is the harvest. Let's find the freedom in God's promises sooner rather than later. Let's trust the Lord and be patient as we wait on His promises.

Waste: Also, if we waste His provision, He will correct us. We can't just tithe 10 percent and then blow the remaining 90 percent on frivolous lusts of the world. It's bizarre how we can buy six-dollar coffees every day and buy every little thing we put our eyes on in the mall or online and then struggle to make the mortgage. And then we claim that we are hurting in our finances or that there is lack. We are way out of balance, in reality. Most of us are way off in our spending habits, and that's why we think we lack. It's called nickel and diming. Nickel and diming is a disease, and it will destroy our finances. We need to get control of this pattern because most of us spend like this, whether we will admit it or not. We are addicted to spending, and we drain our accounts because we can't stop.

This isn't God's fault, and we will not be properly blessed until we sort out this issue in our lives. Nickel and diming will wrack up the debt slowly but surely. We need to be truthful with our actual spending habits, because God knows the truth. God doesn't want us to squander His money. God wants us to be quality spenders and givers. In fact, God is very specific with money issues in the Bible. He wants us to "multiply" the provision He gives us. There is purpose in abundance if we can learn to partner with God and take our eyes off ourselves. God wants us to keep building up and multiplying our finances to help others. Having extra is not about us and our cushy lifestyles; it's about others in need. This is His order, and this will bring His power. Heart position—it's so crucial in everything we do.

> Command those who are rich in this present world not to be arrogant nor to put their hope in wealth, which is so uncertain, but to put their hope in God, who richly provides us with everything for our enjoyment. Command them to do good, to be rich in good deeds, and to be generous and willing to share. In this way they will lay up treasure for themselves as a firm foundation for the coming age, so that they may take hold of the life that is truly life. (1 Timothy 6:17–19)

God said that there would always be the poor among us. Why is this? This is because sin took root right at the beginning of humanity. After sin took root, God knew that most of the world, even His believers, wouldn't follow His ways, especially in total obedience. For the poor, we don't condemn. We show them the goodness of God in our lives to draw them to the faith, as God told us too through love. That's why abundance in our lives is so purposeful. It's all part of His order and His master plan.

> Now He who supplies seed to the sower and bread for food will also supply and increase your store of seed and will enlarge the harvest of your righteousness. You will be enriched in every way so that you can be generous on every occasion, and through us your generosity will result in thanksgiving to God. This service that you perform is not only supplying the needs of the Lord's people but is also overflowing in many expressions of thanks to God. Because of the service by which you have proved yourselves, others will praise God for the obedience that accompanies your confession of the Gospel of Christ, and for your generosity in sharing with them and with everyone

else. And in their prayers for you their hearts will go
out to you, because of the surpassing grace God has
given you. Thanks be to God for His indescribable gift!
(2 Corinthians 9:10–15)

God didn't say, "I want my faithful and obedient followers to be poor." He said there will always be the poor among us. <u>Let's not get the two confused</u>. Sin took root with the first two people to ever walk the earth. It's no different today. Most would not trust the Lord entirely with their lives, and especially in their finances. God knew this was coming. That's why we will always see the poor living in defeat.

This wasn't God's original plan for our lives before sin took root. Also, some believers think that they have been shown to live poor for "kingdom reasons." I don't see any Biblical evidence of this. I actually think that we are just being shown to get our kingdoms in the proper order—God's kingdom or the world's kingdom. Which one are we more focused on? I believe God will ask us to lose the items that have become idols in our lives for seasons of our lives until God becomes bigger than these items. We have to be in a position to let abundance become way less important than our actual purposes in the abundance. That last sentence will only make sense when we understand the purpose in abundance.

Much like the rich young ruler mentioned in the Gospels, we have to place everything the Lord provides for us in the proper position in our hearts. If we don't, God will certainly let us know we have our priorities mixed up. Also, this doesn't mean we can't have nice things. That posture comes again from a religious spirit. I met with a guy the other day that said he always gets ragged on by other believers for driving annually updated Cadillac SUVs every year. This happens to be a good friend of mine. He and I stay accountable with our finances together as a part of God's order. If I had to guess, the same people that rag on him for driving a new vehicle every year likely don't know that he gives away 65 percent of his annual income every year to God and His people. To ever think we could have such criticism in our hearts about a vehicle as we struggle to give away 10 percent of our own finances—each year, in most cases. Oh, the things we don't know before we are quick to be critical and judge others.

We can always see where our hearts are positioned when it comes to our money. If we have a heart for God, His house, and His people, there is never an issue with our giving. The "givers" are generally the people who are leading the financial leadership meetings and being approached for wisdom in the area of business and financial stability. This is not a coincidence as there are no coincidences. God says, "Test me in this." I've watched financial miracles take place over and over with faithful givers. It's amazing. But again, it's one piece of the full spectrum of light that needs to come into our hearts to experience parts and pieces of kingdom living.

Let's face it: financial burden and lack hurt. Financial lack starts breaking down all areas of our lives. Financial issues are wounds. God doesn't want us to be strapped for cash. That's a fact. Any different teaching is wrong doctrine. He wants us to be faithful stewards of the provision He gives us, and He wants us to be taking care of His house and the poor and the needy. He doesn't want us to be idolizing money. The needs of others will always be beyond comprehension; therefore, we must multiply to meet these needs to the best of our abilities in faith. The Bible uses a parable to explain how God wants us to be good multipliers for His purposes and what He thinks if we don't. God wants us to have extra.

The parable of the bags of gold from Matthew 25:

> *Again, it will be like a man going on a journey, who called his servants and entrusted his wealth to them. To one he gave five bags of gold, to one he gave two bags of gold, and to another one bag, each according to his ability. Then he went on his journey.*
>
> *The man who received five bags of gold went at once and put his money to work and gained five bags more. So also, the one with two bags of gold gained two more. But the man who had received one bag went off, dug a hole in the master's ground and hid his master's money.*

After a long time, the master of those servants returned and settled accounts with them. The man who received five bags of gold brought the other five bags of gold. "See, I have gained five more." His master replied, "Well done, good and faithful servant! You have been faithful with a few things; I will put you in charge of many things. Come and share your master's happiness!"

The man with two bags of gold also came. "Master," he said, "you entrusted me with two bags of gold; see I have gained two more." His master replied, "Well done, good and faithful servant! You have been faithful with a few things; I will put you in charge of many things. Come and share in your master's happiness!"

Then the man who received one bag of gold came. "Master," he said, "I knew that you are a hard man, harvesting where you have not sown and gathering where you have not gathered seed. So I was afraid and went and hid your gold in the ground. See, here is what belongs to you." His master replied, "You wicked, lazy servant! So you knew that I harvest where I have not sown and gather where I have not sown seed? Well then, you should have put my money on deposit with the bankers, so that when I returned I would have received it back with interest. So take the bag of gold from him and give it to the one who has ten bags. For whoever has will be given more, and they will have an abundance. Whoever does not have, even what they have will be taken from them. And throw that worthless servant aside outside, into the darkness, where there will be weeping and gnashing of teeth."

It doesn't matter if we are a current earner or a retired investor. God wants us to multiply the provision He gives to us for His purposes and not only for ourselves. The first step to keep multiplying what He gives us is giving back to His house and His people in need. In return, God does the supernatural part of bringing more provision our way if we responsibly give back and do our part in using it constructively. We cannot expect to receive the supernatural blessing of

God's continual increase if we don't do our part with Him, by giving back to Him and His people. We may be able to increase a little bit on our own, but if we do it God's way, He promises to increase the provision in our lives way more than we could ever do by ourselves.

Remember this: Whoever sows sparingly will also reap sparingly, and whoever sows generously will also reap generously. Each of you should give what you have decided in your heart to give, not reluctantly or under compulsion, for God loves a cheerful giver. And God is able to bless you abundantly, so that in all things at all times, having all that you need, you will abound in every good work. As it is written: "They have freely scattered their gifts to the poor; their righteousness endures forever." (2 Corinthians 9:6–9)

We may say, "There are people with millions who don't do it this way with God." I say three things about that:

1) We shouldn't assume successful people who don't go to church don't give to God's people or His purposes just because it appears that they don't. I have seen many corporations that have donated massive amounts of money to ministries when it would appear that they don't.
2) Just think of how much fruit they may be able to produce in God's order.
3) There will be no eternal significance in the gifts God gave us to produce wealth without doing it unto Him and for His glory. We will all be accountable at some point with what we did with the gifts God has given us.

The whole point being made here is this: We give because God asks us to give as a part of His order regardless of all the math we want to do on this matter. If we look at the people with the gift of creating wealth, whether they follow God or not, we usually see one common theme. They are giving to a cause in need somewhere. This next part is just *my* opinion, and I want to be very clear on that. I don't think

God withholds the ability to create wealth to those who give freely, even if they don't choose to follow Him. God isn't narcissistic—and His principles work when we do them. I believe anyone operating in His order will get the blessing whether they are doing it in His name or not. That being said, we will all have to answer to God at some point on this matter, one way or another. We will all be accountable like mentioned in point number 3 above. It gives Him no Glory to earn it without acknowledging Him. End of my opinion.

And again, we may be able to produce during seasons of our lives, but it can be "blown" away at any time. The same God that provides can take it all away if He sees fit. I understand financial suffocation. I was there for a long time. We have to trust God no matter what the circumstance is. We don't wait until we have enough money or have a cushy bank account before we start giving money back to God and His house either. We will never get freedom that way. As said many times, we move first, and God will move more. Giving to God in faith before we feel ready to is how we start seeing the activation of God's power in our finances. God says, "Test Me in this." He will provide. Tithing is another form of worship in the order of Christ. We will see mind-blowing kingdom power activated in our lives when we get our hearts positioned right in the area of abundance, tithes, gifts, and offerings.

> *But since you excel in everything—in faith, in speech, in knowledge, in complete earnestness and in the love we have kindled in you—see that you also excel in this grace of giving. (2 Corinthians 8:7)*

*Devote yourselves to prayer, being
watchful and thankful.*

—Colossians 2:20

THE ORDER OF MELCHIZEDEK

17 devotion

THE NEXT SPECTRUM OF light in the order of Christ is our devotion time. What is devotion?

Devotion is the time we set aside (generally in private) every day to read the Bible and talk to God. Devotion is generally outside of the church, but it doesn't always have to be. Devotion time is very important in our growth. Time with God is absolutely necessary to "manage our decision" to have the kingdom life. Again, the frequency will change the results of our lives. The level of commitment matters. I can't stress this enough.

Devotion time is the nucleus of our entire relationship with Jesus. The Bible is the inspired Living Word of God, sharper than a double-edged sword (as it says). The Bible is the single-most important reference to anything we will *ever* know about God and His Son and the Holy Spirit.

The Bible says,

> They are not just idle words for you—they are your life. (Deuteronomy 32:47)

Along with talking to Him and praying to Him, the Bible is how we develop our relationship with God. We can build relationship with Him anywhere and at any time of the day. But setting a specific quiet time aside to read His Word is foundational for growth in the believer's walk.

> For the Word of God is alive and active. Sharper than any double-edged sword, it penetrates even to dividing soul and spirit. (Hebrews 4:12)

Every inspiration for me to write this book came from reading my Bible and devotion time with God.

ONE COLD MORNING

It was a cold winter morning of December 6, 2014. It was 6:56 a.m. I had a nice cup of coffee. I was in my prayer office in complete silence. I was reading my Bible and praying for a specific young lady who was in need.

Right there, in that exact moment, something completely unrelated came over me. Ideas, thoughts, words, and visions in my mind started pouring in. It was like God Himself stuck a memory stick in my ear and then pressed my eyeball to download the information. I started typing my thoughts. I typed for months and months every single day. Sometimes for fourteen to sixteen hours straight. I had never had such a thing like this come over me before. I didn't know if God was healing me from something, by typing out my thoughts, or what the purpose was.

One day, months later, I woke up to go down to my office to start typing again, and there was nothing. No thoughts, no ideas, just nothing. I pushed print, gathered all my papers, set them aside, and headed out to do some other things that I needed to get done. That very day, we had our small group Bible study in the evening. After our study, I started visiting with a friend of mine.

My buddy Bryan said, "I had a good day today. I went to the city to visit a friend I haven't seen in a while. It was a nice visit."

After that, he said, "As we were parting ways, we ran into one of his friends. I was introduced. Then we had another quick visit, and then we all parted ways. I drove straight to Bible study from there."

Then Bryan said, "I can't help but think that I was supposed to meet that guy right at the end of our visit for some reason. I thought about him the whole way home, but I just can't figure it out."

We both agreed that there is always a reason and that God would likely show him the reason another time.

I then asked him, "What does this guy do for a living?"

Bryan answered, "He's a Christian publisher."

Do I need to say anything more? The very same day that I was finished typing! I didn't tell anyone what I had been up to, including Bryan, in terms of all this typing I had been doing for all of those months. Two days later, we drove into the city to have a meeting, and the rest is history. That was the birth of the first book I wrote called *Loneliness*.

I realize the kingdom power in this story. Other than the obvious points in that story, I don't have an academic bone in my body! I don't care for computers or reading, and there wasn't a desire in the world to write a book one minute before 6:56 a.m. that cold morning in December of 2014. The reason I looked at the clock was I was so surprised with all this power that was coming over me. And here I am—writing again. This book came on me just as powerfully. In fact, this writing came on from the last writing. Regardless of all the reasons for these books, this was kingdom power being released both times, while in devotion moments with the Lord, in His order. Then the fruition of them came through fellowship gatherings.

The Bible is the most powerful book on the planet. Every word of it is truth and was inspired by God the Father. You don't have to take my word on this. You will see it for yourself as you press into your Bible and engage in these template experiences of God's order, instead of the world's order. Our Bibles should be our most-prized possessions. Watch the amazing things that happen when we study it every day. We shouldn't just read our Bibles like a book as we won't get that much out of it that way. We should study it intently, looking for the secrets and mysteries God wants to reveal to the ones dedicated to finding them. It's the power behind everything in our lives. Scripture is a weapon against Satan and his lies.

If reading the Bible seems a bit dry at first, keep at it because it's the spiritual food we need to thrive and advance. God will anoint us to read, if we will start, and keep pressing in. As we understand it more and more, it grows in magnificence. If we quit reading, we start to become spiritually stagnant, and we starve. We need spiritual food to become healthy and to stay healthy. There is extreme power in the Word of God. Anything we can possibly know about healing, freedom, breakthrough, and whom we are fighting against comes from the Bible. It's the answer to every question on earth as we learn it and understand it. It's the manual for our lives and how we are to live them. It's a book of romance. It's a book of love, and it's a book of correction. It's a book of teaching, and it's a book with mystery. It's a book about the past and a book about the future. It's a book on marriage, and it's a book on freedom . . .

Oops, that didn't sound right. Let me explain . . . Marriage is awesome.

My point is if we don't study it daily, we will not thrive like God intended us to.

Reading the Bible is the foundation of devotion in God's order that leads us to victory. The power is not in the "knowing"; it is in the "doing." There is obviously a big difference. We will either get serious with the scriptures, or we won't. Again, it's the combination of all of these forms of worship together that releases His kingdom power into our lives.

PRAYER

I talk to God all day long. He's my best friend. When we talk to God, it doesn't have to be "professional" or sound a specific way to be all "proper." A prayer, or talking to Jesus, can simply be a cry for help. All Jesus is looking for is an authentic heart, not some fancy and professional babbling tongue that sounds all sophisticated. In fact, there are scriptures that specifically tell us to refrain from praying like that, because that's how the Pharisees prayed. The more we talk with someone, the more we will learn about them and know their secrets, their character, their personalities, and so on. How can we have a personal relationship with Jesus Christ if we don't talk to Him? How can we live kingdom lives if there is no communication? How can we love someone if we rarely speak? Jesus loves us, and He wants to talk to us all the time. There will be no power in silence.

We can speak to Him at set times every day, or it can be at many random times a day like I do. It can be short and casual, or it can be long and intense. I talk to Him very seriously quite often, but sometimes, I just tell Him how thankful I am that He took me out of slavery and into the freedom of His promises. I tell Him my deepest secrets and admit my daily weaknesses and ask for help. I ask Him what it is that He desires from me, and I tell Him what I desire from Him. It's a multidimensional relationship. That's what healthy relationships are like.

HERE WE GO AGAIN

It was December 6, 2011, at 11:06 p.m. One evening, I was reading my Bible and talking to God. I would read for a while and then stop and talk for a bit. I went back and forth like this for well over an hour. Just as I was about to shut my Bible to go to sleep and prepare for work the next day, I got rocked again. When I looked down at my Bible, one verse stuck out like a sore thumb.

> *No one who puts a hand to the plow and looks back*
> *is fit for the service in the kingdom of God. (Luke 9:62)*

The Holy Spirit gave me that verse, and then I felt an impression as powerful as anything I had ever felt before. That impression was like a voice in my head. It said, "Go to South Africa tomorrow to be with Greg." The intensity of this moment was like the power surge that I had on my "last night."

"What? I have to work tomorrow! I have three homes due before Christmas, and I'm the *only* one in my company, Lord! What are you saying to me? Why would I go to South Africa? I have only ever met 'Greg' one time. And that was three months ago. I don't even know this guy!"

"Go to South Africa tomorrow," He said.

"What? This makes no sense. I can't. Who will finish the homes? And why would I even go? What's the whole point? I can't just pick up and go! I own a business. And why would anyone just go like this?"

"Go, Ryan. You have put your hand to the plow. <u>Now don't look back</u>."

This was crazy. There was nothing logical taking place in my head in this moment. What was going on? And get this: this was the exact same day that I been stopped for that traffic violation that had landed me in Supreme Court the next year! I was absolutely frustrated with a million questions in my head. I shut my Bible, turned off my lamp, and went to sleep. I was going to forget this ever happened. The work pressure and stress I was feeling was already enough. I didn't need this thought bouncing around in my head.

I woke up the next morning. I remembered the "moment" that took place the night before. I was sneaking around my house as if this thought wouldn't come back into my head if I snuck around all quiet. I know. Dumb, right?

Bang! There it was again. Oh, come on! "I can't!"

I jumped in the shower and then got dressed. I turned up the worship music in the house to try and push away God's voice. I got into my truck as I prepared to go to the first of eleven locations that I had constructions happening at. I was one guy with eleven homes on the go. And three were due for Christmas. The most intense time of the year for construction. As I backed out of my driveway, there it was again.

"Looking back . . . is not fit for the service in the kingdom of God."

Ugh. I was mad as I altered my route and drove to the flight center. When I got there, I realized that I was going to book a ticket to South Africa, and I hadn't even told anyone I was going! Again, I had only met Greg one time at a group lunch, three months prior. A few of us exchanged phone numbers. He was one of them. So I pressed Send. And wouldn't you know, he picked up his phone. Go figure. I explained the whole thing to him, and long story short, we agreed to hook up, and we set some details. Greg was already in South Africa and had been there for a week already. He was just as surprised as me. I guess I was going to South Africa. I guess I'll lose my business. I guess I'll lose everything. I think you get my point. This was ridiculous.

I went into the flight center and got with my travel agent. She thought I was out of my mind just as much as I thought. I had explained everything to her. I still pushed forward. I told her to find me the quickest way out of Canada possible. I told her I didn't want some stupid twelve-hour layover in Amsterdam or something. I was aggravated still, to be honest. With a reluctant attitude, she told me to wait a week or so to "plan" for something like this. I told her that wasn't an option. She told me to come back in an hour. It would take her some time to find the most cost-effective route without a day of layovers. I agreed.

I came back an hour later, and she had a travel option ready to present. It was a good one, actually. It would leave the next day at 8:00 p.m. She said, "At least this will give you one day to try and put some order in your business affairs."

This was crazy! Who would get my homes done in time for the Christmas deadlines? The other ones I can work with but not these ones. That was the thought playing through my head over and over. Anyway, I agreed with the travel route and said, "Okay, let's book it." I pulled out my credit card. Just as I was about to hand it over, I heard,

"Now. Today. Go today."

Here we go again. I asked her, "Does that same itinerary leave tonight instead of tomorrow night?" You can imagine how she looked at me next.

She said, "Not a chance," and rolled her eyes at me like the judge did. She said, "Do you know how long it took me to find this route so that you wouldn't have a bunch of layovers?"

I said, "Will you at least look, please?" She reluctantly agreed, again.

Several minutes later, her eyes went as big as golf balls. She looked up and said, "Wow! God must want you to leave tonight. The *exact* same itinerary leaves tonight, and it's a thousand and eight hundred bucks cheaper!"

I said, "Book it."

This gave me only six hours to check in for my flight at the airport. I sent Greg a text and told him the details of my arrival. I had no idea what I was doing. I spent the next six hours phoning anyone and everyone I could think of to set up some sort of schedule. I was leaving for twenty-three days. The events to come in the next six hours still lift the hairs on my arms. Jesus bumps, that is.

Without a word of a lie, all three clients who had homes due for Christmas called me before I boarded that plane. Every one of them had a different reason they couldn't take possession of their new homes for Christmas. They all apologized for the pressure they had put on me to deliver their homes for Christmas. They told me it would be more convenient to take their homes after the holiday season. I couldn't believe my ears. I shut my phone off in total peace and flew away into the night. Twenty-six hours later, I ended up getting to South Africa within an hour of when God needed me to get there. This was a time-sensitive mission. I can't get into the reasons, but it's true. Neither of our lives would be the same after the next twenty-three days. This was new-level stuff.

We will all learn ways in which we can communicate and talk with Jesus as we journey with Him. The point to focus on is that He wants to hear from us, and He wants us to ask Him anything. We need to remember to get quiet enough in our devotions to actually hear the answers. When we talk to Him, there is nothing too big, and there is nothing too small. He wants us to request big, and He wants to hear the petty things too. One of the most powerful things we can do is talk to God, and that's why it is so essential. He loves to connect with us.

Also, when we team up with other believers in prayer, it really gets interesting. It multiplies! Once again, God loves us doing things in groups—including prayer, as we talked about earlier. There is power in numbers.

> *The prayer of a righteous man is powerful and effective. (James 5:16)*

And again,

> *Again, truly I tell you that if two of you on earth agree about anything they ask for, it will be done for them by My Father in heaven. (Matthew 18:19)*

Without talking to God, it's impossible to have a relationship. And without a relationship, it's impossible to have the kingdom life here on earth. Our efforts do matter. If reading our Bibles and talking to God are rare moments for us, we can expect very few kingdom-life moments in our lives. God said that these moments will be reserved for those who carry their crosses and devote themselves to Him entirely. When we actually hear from God, we also have to execute. A set-apart kingdom life will require set-apart effort to see the fullness of His glory. Sometimes, we will need to "burn our plows" to be "fit for the service, in the kingdom of God." In other words, let go . . . and let *God* to see His power.

18 fasting

BIBLICAL FASTING IS A spiritual discipline that some Christians choose to draw closer to the Lord. Fasting is not a command. Jesus did, however, show us in His own flesh the importance of fasting when the Holy Spirit calls us to. In one case, Jesus fasted in the desert for forty days and forty nights, to show us as symbolism, how to draw the strength from the Holy Spirit, as He headed into a very tough season of trial and temptation, from the enemy.

In every one of my personal stories I've told in this book, I was doing a fast of some sort. In fact, I fasted for the first month that I started this book. I generally wouldn't be telling anyone that I'm fasting, but I'm just making a point here. Fasting will bring very powerful kingdom-life moments into our lives. Especially in conjunction with all the other worship experiences we have talked about. When Jesus was on earth, He gave His disciples limited power to do the miraculous works that some of them did. He also told them that He would have to depart in the near future. He continued telling them that something new was to come. That was the Holy Spirit. He continued to tell them that the whole dynamic of their walk would have to change after He left. In doing so, He also told them that they would also have to "prepare" differently in this walk after He left. Fasting would be a new way to prepare for their walks. When we fast, we deprive ourselves of a fleshly desire of any type. This will attract God's power to us. Paul wrote,

> But He said to me, "My grace is sufficient for you, for My power is made perfect in weakness." (2 Corinthians 12:9)

When we fast, we forfeit earthly desires to fill up with spiritual desires and His power. If we fast the correct way, we will grow closer to God, which will always boost some sort of new level in our lives. This has happened so many times in my life that I could never deny the power in these moments. When we fast, we are not to do this in a religious manner to "look" a certain way for others. Fasting must be done in an attitude of humility, with our hearts in the right position. Fasting is a private matter between us and God. In fact, the Bible speaks very specifically about this:

> But when you fast, put oil on your head and wash your face, so that it will not be obvious to men that you are fasting, but only to your Father, who is unseen; and your Father, who sees what is done in secret, will reward you. (Matthew 6:17–18)

God says He will reward us in the last verse. Our hearts and our motives for fasting must be right unto the Father. We also see that there will be power brought our way when we fast. We see proof of this when Isaiah writes,

> Is not this kind of fasting I have chosen: to loose the chains of injustice and untie the cords of the yoke, to set the oppressed free and break every yoke? Is it not to share your food with the hungry and to provide the poor wanderer with shelter—when you see the naked, to clothe him, and not to turn away from your own flesh and blood? (Isaiah 58:6–7)

This verse tells us that there will be kingdom power being executed while we fast. Fasts can last for different lengths of time. There are no "rules" when it comes to fasting. The length will be determined by the Holy Spirit if we are listening to Him. Fasting is meant to bring us into a closer union with the Holy Spirit and the Father. The Spirit is power, and with power comes breakthrough. When we draw near to God, He promises to draw nearer to us in return.

The Bible says,

> Come near to God and He will come near to you.
> (James 4:8)

Every form of worship experiences we talk about in this book are designed to bring us closer to God, which, in turn, will give us access to His power. If we forsake these experiences in obedience, then we will not experience this type of kingdom living. Don't take my word on it. Take the Bibles word on it:

> If you seek Him, He will be found by you, but if you forsake Him, He will forsake you. (2 Chronicles 15:2)

That verse sums up the entire point of this book really. There is *power* in these experiences! These aren't just ideas to ponder. We need to get serious in our relationships with our Father. We need to take the first steps to draw near to Him so that He will respond to us.

These scriptures mean if we do this, then we will get that. If we don't do this, then we won't get that. These principles aren't so that we can be mechanical robots or religious nuts. We need to put God at the center of our lives. These are real-life works in the form of worship to access His power for kingdom living. This is dialed-in relationship with our Father. Fasting separates us from the desires of the flesh and the things of the world. God will reward us for the effort to draw near to Him when we fast. New power, revelation, wisdom, discernment, breakthrough, and direction for our lives. Anything can happen when we fast with God.

"Few will enter," He said. Or in other words, few will access My power. This is because He knew that people (even believers) would be *so* consumed with the ways of the world and the desires of our flesh that few would discipline themselves to seek Him in an intense way after their salvation moment. That's why we see so many believers living the nonvictorious life. Too much distraction. Too many kid's activities, too much work, too much sport, too much television, too much . . .

God knew that few of His children would pay the cost to let these things go, to spend more time with Him after their salvation moment. That is precisely the point of all the "qualifying" and "disqualifying" verses. God's not against all these activities. He wants to give us the desires of our hearts. When we let these things go, He brings them back into our lives afterward. When they come back into our lives, they are much richer for the right reasons. It's funny how we can let a vacation go for the wrong reasons and then how God brings it back twice as good for the right reasons. This is how kingdom life works.

The problem is this: when all these activities start becoming our gods, we forsake our real Father. We can start leaving Him out of these things instead of making Him the center of these things. There will be no significance when we leave Him out. There will be so much more of a reward in all the things we do when we plan around Him and His order. We can be so consumed with life, noise, and distraction. The noise becomes so loud; we find ourselves feeling disconnected or with no direction in our walks. Is it any wonder? When we forsake the Lord, He will forsake us. That doesn't mean He's not there. It doesn't mean He moves away from us. It means we have moved away from Him. It means there will be no special privilege, power, or favor. Why would there be? "Thy kingdom come. Thy will be done." We must do the "thy will be done" part. Every single time I press into these worship experiences, I access His power in some sort of new way, and things start shifting. When I don't, it's a completely opposite experience. The devil doesn't want us to talk about deeds. He's deceived believers that deeds are "religious." He's confused believers about the deeds verses and what they are intended for. It's so bad these days that nobody will even talk about works. The word *deed* is virtually off limits.

News flash: *The power is in the obedience under submission in His order.* Look at Moses! What happened when he stuck out his staff over the water in obedience? The waters stopped and preached a whole sermon without words! God uses His power to make a point! It's not about us; it's about *Him*! What happened when Abraham took his son to the altar? What happened when Joshua marched around Jericho seven times? What happened when Rahab took the spies in? What happened when the woman poured perfume on the feet of Jesus? What happened when David grabbed a slingshot? What happened when Ruth moved to another land? What happened when Joseph . . .? Let's not even get started with Joseph. The power is in His order. Obedience, deeds, and work. We will either get this, or we won't. Not only do we have to seek Him, but we must actually execute when we hear the answer.

There will be no reward in hearing the answer and not actually follow His instructions. Sometimes, following will be very difficult. This is where we see the reward, though. The reward will always outweigh the execution of following Him. I notice that the most life-changing moments from God come in the quietest times. Sometimes, I wonder if I have even heard Him. Why is this? This is because He wants us to suppress the noise of the world to actually hear His voice. This is a dialed-in place of worship. This is the way He wants it. He has reserved the execution of His power, favor, and special privilege for those who will actually block out the noise of the world for more than fifteen minutes a day.

Often, we hear leaders telling us that we only need to open our Bibles for ten to fifteen minutes a day. To be honest, we will only get ten to fifteen minutes worth of results. In other words, we won't expect much. Why would we put so little time into the only Man who can truly shift our lives in a radical way? Would we only train for the Olympics for fifteen minutes a day? Would we only go to work for fifteen minutes a day? Again, we are *so* desperate for a real change in our lives and so unwilling to go after it with our Father. We need to be dialed-in with Him to see these shifts in our lives. This won't happen living noisy and distracted lives that are consumed with all the things in this world. I have never had a life-altering moment with God when I was distracted with the things of the world. It's always been in a very committed or quiet time with God. In a time when all of these worship experiences were working together.

If I was busy doing my own thing all the time, I would have never recognized His signals to move or act. This isn't just me. I model my life very closely around what I see others doing in terms of worship with our Father. The ones living a victorious life are always pressed in with God. They are sold out for Jesus in every part of their day. They are consumed with His purpose and callings on their lives. They have brought Jesus into the very center of every part of their days, whether it be at work or in leisure or on vacation. Jesus is there in the center every time. Even when they are busy. Jesus can be the center of our busy. These are not opposites.

> We do not want you to become lazy, but to imitate those who through faith and patience inherit what has been promised. (Hebrews 6:12)

Salvation is free; the power is not. The Lord knew that a disciplined believer would be a rare find. He took inventory of the people on the earth and saw very few people trying. And because of that, He wrote,

> For who is he who will devote himself to be close to Me? *(Jeremiah 30:21)*

He wrote that because there were very few. Next are a few that would merge their belief with their deeds. This is the Hall of Faith for the elite of the elite in the Bible. These people were sold out for God and His order. They weren't people that would seek God for fifteen minutes a day and then go about their worldly lives. They weren't perfect people either. They did, however, position their hearts in a radical place of commitment.

FAITH IN ACTION

> Now faith is confidence in what we hope for and assurance about what we do not see. This is what the ancients were commended for.
>
> By faith we understand that the universe was formed at God's command, so that what is seen was not made out of what was visible.
>
> By faith Abel brought God a better offering than Cain did. By faith he was commended as righteous, when God spoke well of his offerings. And by faith Abel still speaks, even though he is dead.
>
> By faith Enoch was taken from this life, so that he did not experience death: "He could not be found, because God had taken him away." For before he was taken, he was commended as one who pleased God. And without faith it is impossible to please God, because anyone who comes to Him must believe that He exists and that <u>He rewards those who earnestly seek Him.</u>
>
> By faith Noah, when warned about things not yet seen, in <u>holy fear</u> built an ark to save his family. By his faith he condemned the world and became heir of the righteousness that is in keeping with faith.
>
> By faith Abraham, when called to go to a place he would later receive as his inheritance, obeyed and went, even though he did not know where he was

going. By faith he made his home in the promised land like a stranger in a foreign country; he lived in tents, as did Isaac and Jacob, who were heirs with him of the same promise. For he was looking forward to the city with foundations, whose architect and builder is God. And by faith even Sarah, who was past childbearing age, was enabled to bear children because she considered Him faithful who had made the promise. And so from this one man, and he as good as dead, came descendants as numerous as the stars in the sky and as countless as the sand on the seashore.

All these people were still living by faith when they died. They did not receive the things promised; they only saw them and welcomed them from a distance, admitting that they were foreigners and strangers on Earth. People who say such things show that they are looking for a country of their own. If they had been thinking of the country they had left; they would have had opportunity to return. Instead, they were longing for a better country—a heavenly one. Therefore, God is not ashamed to be called their God, for He has prepared a city for them.

By faith Abraham, when God tested him, offered Isaac as a sacrifice. He who had embraced the promises was about to sacrifice his one and only son, even though God had said to him, "It is through Isaac that your offspring will be reckoned." Abraham reasoned that God could even raise the dead, and so in a manner of speaking he did receive Isaac back from death.

By faith Isaac blessed Jacob and Esau in regard to their future.

By faith Jacob, when he was dying, blessed each of Joseph's sons, and worshiped as he leaned on the top of his staff.

By faith Joseph, when his end was near, spoke about the exodus of the Israelites from Egypt and gave instructions concerning the burial of his bones.

By faith Moses' parents hid him for three months after he was born, because they saw he was no ordinary child, and they were not afraid of the king's edict.

By faith Moses, when he had grown up, refused to be known as the son of Pharaoh's daughter. He chose to be mistreated along with the people of God rather than to enjoy the fleeting pleasures of sin. He regarded disgrace for the sake of Christ as of greater value than the treasures of Egypt, because he was looking ahead to his reward. By faith he left Egypt, not fearing the king's anger; he persevered because he saw Him who is invisible. By faith he kept the Passover and the application of blood, so that the destroyer of the firstborn would not touch the firstborn of Israel.

By faith the people passed through the Red Sea as on dry land; but when the Egyptians tried to do so, they were drowned.

By faith the walls of Jericho fell, after the army had marched around them for seven days.

By faith the prostitute Rahab, because she welcomed the spies, was not killed with those who were disobedient. And what more shall I say? I do not have time to tell about Gideon, Barak, Samson and Jephthah, about David and Samuel and the prophets, who through faith conquered kingdoms, administered justice, and gained what was promised; who shut the mouths of lions, quenched the fury of the flames, and escaped the edge of the sword; whose weakness was turned to strength; and who became powerful in battle and routed foreign armies. Women received back their dead, raised to life again. There were others who were tortured, refusing to be released so that they might gain an even better resurrection. Some faced jeers and flogging, and even chains and imprisonment. They were put to death by stoning; they were sawed in two; they were killed by the sword. They went about in sheepskins and goatskins, destitute, persecuted and mistreated—the world was not worthy of them. They wandered in deserts and mountains, living in caves and in holes in the ground.

These were all commended for their faith, yet none of them received what had been promised, since God had planned something better for us so that

only together with us would they be made perfect.
(Hebrews 11:1–40)

Even after all these miracles because of deeds done in faith, God said that they had not received the *full* promise yet. Something even better was still to come! We see in this famous scripture that victory doesn't come by belief (faith) alone. It comes through belief at work. Again we need to see that faith has two parts. The first part is to believe. The second part is to believe in His promises and then execute in obedience after that—bringing our belief together with our deeds.

> *You foolish person, do you want evidence that faith without deeds is useless? Was not our father Abraham considered righteous for <u>what he did</u> when he offered his son Isaac on the altar? You see that <u>his faith and his actions were working together</u> and his <u>faith was made complete by what he did</u>. And the scripture was fulfilled and says, "Abraham believed in God, and it was credited to him as righteousness," and he was called God's friend. You see that a person is considered righteous <u>by what they do and</u> <u>not by faith alone</u>. (James 2:20–24)*

These people were obedient enough to put their faith into action to bring God's glorious power into their lives. When we put the deeds to work in faith, sin drops off our lives, miracles start happening, and things start to shift. That is a fact. This is kingdom living at its best. This is the victorious life. This is what will attract the nonbeliever to our Savior. This is what will bring the nonvictorious believer back to life. Again, we can speak all of the words in the world, but it will be God's power, and the shifts in our lives from His power, mixed with our words, that will shake the nations. Jesus didn't put His power on display to show off. He did it to shake people's faith. It was to lay proof of the evidence of His existence. The power is waiting for each and every one of us. Let's be a generation of believers that will actually press in with God and make Him the center of every part of our lives.

> Be diligent in these matters; give yourself wholly to them, so that everyone may see your progress. Watch your life and doctrine closely. Persevere in them, because if you do, you will save both yourself and your hearers. (1 Timothy 4:15–16)

Worship the Lord your God, and His blessing will be on your food and water. I will take away sickness from among you.

—*Exodus 23:25*

THE ORDER OF MELCHIZEDEK

19 praise and worship

ALTHOUGH I CONSIDER EVERY form of worship absolutely essential, I consider praise and worship to be top on the list of significance in our relationships with God. Picture all of the experiences mentioned from the surrender section, all the way down to the fasting section, as planted seed. The release of God's power or the growing of this seed will require praise and worship for the seed to grow to a harvest. Praise and worship is a <u>posture that works simultaneously with all other forms of works and deeds in relationship with</u>

Him. Praise and worship is absolutely essential to access His power. Or again, to see the harvest grow into blessing of *any* type.

Praise and worship is where a lot believers fall short, even though they are doing some of the other works. Our works become religious acts without praise and worship in our hearts. This comes from unresolved negative thoughts that we have allowed to be deposited into our minds by the enemy. We stay stuck in these thoughts which creates negative weight. The negative weight will stop the praise if we don't deal with it. We need to reconcile these thoughts and turn them around, regardless of our circumstances, so that we can get our hearts in a posture of praise and worship. We need to get rid of our negative attitudes and old ways of thinking. The devil has trained us this way from the very beginning, and then we drag these attitudes into our new lives with Christ.

Many believers don't realize the power that is activated in praise and worship times—publicly or privately. This is why large portions of our church congregations walk in late for church services. Sometimes, even some of the pastors come into the sanctuary after the worship is done, to start their messages. We don't realize the power in the worship portion of our service before the pastor's message. Worship is where we draw the power of the Holy Spirit around us, from the omnipresent form into a powerful, manifested form. Most times, members are out in the foyer drinking coffee and visiting while worship is happening in the sanctuary. We are oblivious to what is supposed to be taking place in the service during worship. Or we come late every time. I think this is a spiritual stronghold on the body of Christ, designed by the enemy, to keep us from the power that comes with worship. Especially where two or three are gathered.

Praise and worship brings completion to all of our works. <u>Our belief brought together with our deeds needs to be capped off with praise to activate the growth.</u> God doesn't answer complaints. He answers praise and worship. Complainers are a dime a dozen. We need to be a cut above—a set-apart group of believers. It's hard to imagine, but even if we do all of the worship experiences mentioned previously but have grumbling spirits or complaining words coming out of our mouths, God's blessing will be blocked. This is because praise and worship is faith. There is no faith in complaining. There is no faith when we are not praising Him either. For the harvest to be released to the fullest, we must walk with an attitude of gratitude toward Him, no matter what the circumstances are. We can plant and water the seed, but only God can make it grow. I truly believe that God will make it grow when we have praise coming out of our mouths.

The Bible says,

> I planted the seed, Apollos watered it, but God has been making it grow. So neither the one who plants nor the one who waters is anything, but only God, who makes things grow. (1 Corinthians 3:6–7)

As we read God's Word in the Bible, we begin to realize God will not cause the harvest to grow or rather the blessing to be activated to its <u>fullest</u> if we have negative thoughts, grumbling, or complaining spirits.

> Do everything without grumbling or arguing, so that you may become blameless and pure, "children of God without fault in a warped and crooked generation." Then you will shine among them like stars in the sky as you hold firmly to the word of life. (Philippians 2:14–16)

It's not in our best interest to wait for the blessing to come before we praise God, because it likely won't come until we adjust our attitudes. We want to praise God when life is good, but we must especially learn to praise God in the storm. Praise precedes the victory and negative thoughts limit what God will do for us. God is not moved by our problems; He is moved by our praise. I'm not saying that God is not compassionate about our problems by any means whatsoever. I'm just saying that God wants to see that we believe His promises are larger than any of our problems as we approach Him in faith, praise, and worship.

> *Rejoice in the Lord always. I will say it again: Rejoice! Let your gentleness be evident to all. The Lord is near. Do not be anxious about anything, but in every situation, by prayer and petition, with thanksgiving, present your requests to God. (Philippians 4:4–6)*

When we praise God, He takes our tough situations and turns them to good for our advancement. Nothing attracts the favor of the Lord more than when we praise Him through the discouragement of a tough situation. It's one of the hardest things we will ever do. If we have praise and gratitude in our hearts for the Lord, then all of the seed we planted will be remembered by the Lord in due time. He will activate the great harvest we have been waiting for. The Bible says,

> *Then those who feared the Lord talked with each other, and the Lord listened and heard. A scroll of remembrance was written in His presence concerning those who feared the Lord and honored His name. (Malachi 3:16)*

The Bible says a book of remembrance is being written of those who fear the Lord. Fearing the Lord includes praise and worshipping God. It's reverence. It's honor. When we praise the Lord, our names are being remembered and written down in the record books. In our time of need, the Lord will reference His book with His angels and say, "I know that guy . . . His name is written all over My book. Let's give him the harvest. It's time, and he needs it."

Again, this is where most believers forfeit the breakthrough. We get so close, then hit a storm, then stop praising God or start grumbling. We need to remember God's sovereignty in these storms like we talked about in chapter 6.

> *Rejoice always, pray continually, give thanks in all circumstances; for this is God's will for you in Christ Jesus. (1 Thessalonians 5:16–17)*

We need to have an attitude of gratitude no matter what is happening around us, as hard as it may be. Any one of us can praise Him when times are good. That's easy. It's a real test of faith to praise God in a storm. If we praise God through the rough times, He will give us double for our trouble. The Bible says,

> *After Job had prayed for his friends, the Lord restored his fortunes and gave him twice as much as he had before. (Job 42:10)*

In the tough times, we need to turn up the praise. It brings completion to our works and deeds. It's like pushing Send at the end of a long e-mail. Without pushing Send at the end of the e-mail, all the works would be pointless. Let's thank God and continually praise Him no matter what the circumstances are, and the favor will come.

> *I will extol the Lord at all times; His praise will always be on my lips. I will glory in the Lord; let the afflicted hear and rejoice. Glorify the Lord with me: let us exalt His name together. I sought the Lord and He answered me; He delivered me from all my fears. (Psalm 34:1)*

Thankful praise comes in many different forms such as singing to Him, prayer, and speaking about His greatness to others. It is the simple words which come out of our mouths all day long about how grateful we are for God's goodness in our lives. This is ministry, really. Praise isn't focusing or talking about the things we think we lack. Praise is an attitude of gratitude, even when it doesn't make logical sense. When we praise Him, dreams, goals and ambitions will come to pass. Supernatural doors will open, and kingdom-life moments will start appearing. We will see His power being harvested.

> *Yes, and I will continue to rejoice, for I know that through your prayers and God's provision of the Spirit of Jesus Christ what has happened to me will turn out for my deliverance. (Philippians 1:19)*

I like to start each morning with a coffee and a boatload of praise to turbo-boost the start of my day. I thank God for causing my dreams to come to pass, and I thank Him for all past and present blessings. Then I continue to thank Him in advance for the blessings that haven't quite arrived yet. The praise is what will release the blessing from the seed already planted. I like to speak life into my future in faith. I use His Word to do it. I continue by saying a number of these praise declarations out loud. The Bible says our words matter:

> *The tongue has the power of life and death, and those who love it will eat its fruit. (Proverbs 18:21)*

Thank You, Jesus, for the prepared blessing You have for me.

> *For the Lord your God is bringing you into a good land—a land with brooks, streams, and deep springs gushing out into the valleys and hills; a land with wheat and barley, vines and fig trees, pomegranates, olive oil and honey; a land where bread will not be scarce and you will lack nothing; a land where the rocks are iron and you can dig copper out of the hills. (Deuteronomy 8:7–9)*

Thank You, Jesus, for the supernatural increase and promotion You have waiting for me.

> *And Jesus grew in wisdom and stature, and in favor with God and man. (Luke 2:52)*

Thank You, Jesus, for an explosion of unexpected finances and provisions You are about to release into my life.

> *Bring the whole tithe into the storehouse, that there may be food in My house. "Test Me in this," says the Lord Almighty, "and see if I will not throw open the floodgates of heaven and pour out so much blessing that there will not be room enough to store it. (Malachi 3:10)*

Thank You, Jesus, that I am framed with Your favor all day long according to Your word.

> Surely, Lord, You bless the righteous; You surround them with Your favor as with a shield. *(Psalm 5:12)*

Thank You, Jesus, that I prosper at anything I put my hands to today.

> "For I know the plans I have for you," declares the Lord, "plans to prosper you and not to harm you, plans to give you hope and a future. *(Jeremiah 29:11)*

Thank You, Jesus, for the divine encounters You have prepared for me with influential people which will cause favor to come to pass on my life today.

> Joseph found favor in his eyes and became his attendant. Potiphar put him in charge of his household, and he entrusted to his care everything he owned. *(Genesis 39:4)*

Thank You, Jesus, that I am weighed down with heavy favor from You today.

> The Lord make His face shine on you and be gracious to you. *(Numbers 6:25)*

Thank You, Jesus, that You have caused people to be attracted to me today, wanting to give me unexplained favor for no particular reason.

> When the turn came for Esther (the young woman Mordecai had adopted, the daughter of his uncle Abihail) to go to the king, she asked for nothing other than what Hegai, the king's eunuch who was in charge of the harem, suggested. And Esther won the favor of everyone who saw her. She was taken to King Xerxes in the royal residence in the tenth month,

the month of Tebeth, in the seventh year of his reign.
(Esther 2:15–16)

Thank You, Jesus, that You are thrusting me ahead years before the natural rate of time.

Isaac planted crops in that land and the same year reaped a hundredfold, because the Lord blessed him. (Genesis 26:12)

Thank You, Jesus, that You take evil that was plotted against me and turn it for good in my life.

You prepare a table before me in the presence of my enemies. You anoint my head with oil; my cup over-flows. Surely Your goodness and love will follow me all the days of my life, and I will dwell in the house of the Lord forever. (Psalm 23:5–6)

Thank You, Jesus, that I live in divine health all of the days of my life.

Dear friend, I pray that you may enjoy good health and that all may go well with you, even as your soul is getting along well. (3 John 1:2)

Thank You, Jesus, that You are blessing me more in the latter days of my life than in the prior days.

The Lord blessed the latter part of Job's life more than the former part. He had fourteen thousand sheep, six thousand camels, a thousand yoke of oxen and a thousand donkeys. (Job 42:12)

Thank You, Jesus, that I can be a blessing to others today because of the goodness You bestow on my life.

Remember this: Whoever sows sparingly will also reap sparingly, and whoever sows generously will also reap generously. (2 Corinthians 9:6)

Prepare my heart today, Lord, to be concerned with what concerns You as I go about my day today.

> Not looking to your own interests but each of you to the interests of the others. (Philippians 2:4)

These are praise declarations I pronounce out loud regardless of the circumstances I am in or how things may look in that current moment.

I want to encourage us all to press into this part our relationships with Christ in His order. This is where victory is birthed and the seed is activated to live the kingdom-powered life.

THE THREE RYANS

It was 10:07 p.m. on January 6, 2012. This was eight days after getting home from South Africa. I was back to work and playing catch-up. My buddy Ryan had been asking me to join him on a five-day trip to Arizona for the last few months before I was summoned to go overseas. Earlier that day, he asked me one more time. I told him that there was no possible way I could go with all of this catch-up at work. As evening approached, I was feeling very overwhelmed with the workload. I decided that I would shut down work-related issues for the night to get some praise and worship in. To be honest, I felt too tired and just wanted to go to bed. Instead, I decided I would be determined to push into God so that I could draw from His power.

I shut down my computer, went upstairs, and put some music on. I dimmed the lights to set the mood and closed my eyes and let the music play. The fireplace was on, and it was a very relaxing setting. I was overcome with emotion as I was just lying there. Then I got into a moment that is usually not me, to be honest. I stood up and lifted my arms to the sky and just absorbed. I wasn't saying or doing anything. I was just standing there all alone in the house with arms lifted high, and I was soaking it all in. Then I started praising the Lord out loud. I was thanking Him for His goodness and for

His presence in my life. I was overcome with praise and worship for about twenty minutes. Then there it was again:

"Go to Phoenix with Ryan in the morning—and call your mother right now."

You know the story. "Come on, Lord, I *just* got home!"

It was the exact same thing all over again.

I hadn't talked to my mother on the phone for years. I had created seventeen years of relational distinction between my folks and me. This part of my life was not put back together yet. I had an inkling that my folks may be somewhere in Arizona. I had received a group e-mail, months earlier, about their whereabouts. I wasn't sure if they were still there or back home already. I had never been to Arizona before.

I dialed my mom's local phone number, but there was no answer. I dialed her US number, and she picked up. I had never called this number before. It was a wonderful moment. We talked for a while, and then I told her that I was coming to Arizona in the morning. She asked me where I was going. I told her Phoenix and that I was coming with a buddy of mine named Ryan. She told me that she was fifteen minutes east of Phoenix. What were the odds . . . I was thinking? Only fifteen minutes away in all of Arizona. I couldn't believe it. We agreed to spend some time together when I arrived. I told her I would call her after getting settled in. I was very emotional at this point. We talked some more, and then we hung up our phones. The next five days would be the start of a miraculous reconciliation between my mom and dad after seventeen years of pain. We are still very strong today. Although this ended up being the most magnificent part of the story for me, that's not where it ends.

After I hung up the phone with my mother, I had booked my flight into Phoenix that night. My flight wouldn't be with Ryan, as he was booked months earlier. It was too late for that. We agreed I would fly in separately and meet at the hotel. When I booked my flight, the lady said there was only one seat left on the flight. She said it was a middle seat on a completely full plane. Yuck. Anyway, I booked it. I sent Ryan a text message to tell him my flight was booked and that I would see him at the hotel in Phoenix. Don't forget. I was leaving work behind again. Now I'm rolling my eyes.

Upon arriving at the airport and checking in the next morning, the terminal lady said there had been a change in the seating plans. She told me that I was reserved for an aisle seat now. In the emergency row. Awesome! Aisle seat and extra leg room too. Well . . . praise the Lord! Things were looking good already. When I got on the plane to be seated, I was pleasantly surprised with the beautiful young lady sitting to my left in the window seat.

She looked right up at me and said, "Hi, I'm Jen!"

She caught me off guard.

I said, "Hi, I'm in love!"

I mean, "Hi, my name is Ryan!"

She greeted me with a very unusual enthusiasm. It never quite happens like that, if at all. Especially the pretty ones (just saying the truth). They usually keep to themselves or say very little. In any case, we both buckled in as the plane prepared to depart. It turns out that nobody ever sat in the middle seat between us. What are the odds again? On a completely full flight. This was *excellent*. Just me and the beauty and all sorts of leg and elbow room for the next three hours of my life.

Okay, this is where it started to get really interesting. Jen was *all* chat. I mean, I had never had a beauty like this engage me with such enthusiasm before. Not sober, anyway. We talked about this and that and other things. I told her about my walk with God, and she was very interested in hearing more. We were about fifteen minutes after takeoff, and she said, "Are you staying in Phoenix?" I told her I was.

She said, "What brings you to Phoenix?"

I said, "Well, it's kind of a weird story, actually. Last night, I was just listening to some worship music and talking to God. I absolutely, without a doubt, felt God tell me to come to Phoenix with a buddy, Ryan. Then He told me to call my mom."

I told her that I was hoping for a miracle in my family life by being obedient to God's voice last night. I told her that I had no business being away again, because I just arrived home from an overseas trip.

She said, "Wow, that's why I'm going to Phoenix too!"

She said, "Okay, this is getting way too weird."

I said, "What do you mean?"

She said, "Where do I start? The very reason I'm going to Phoenix is I think God is telling me to go to make peace with my stepfather. I talk to God the same time every night. When I was talking to God a few nights ago in the evening, I got the same message as you did."

"And furthermore," she said, "you look exactly like one of my very best friends that died last year. You *even* talk like him. The way you sound, the way you talk about God, and even the way you look. He was a Christian too. He was always trying to encourage me to accept Jesus into my life."

"And guess what his name is—Ryan!" she said.

"This is just crazy," she added.

She became overcome by tears at that point.

I told her I was sorry about her loss with Ryan. I also told her how my seating arrangement got changed at the terminal, just before I got on the plane.

We were both a little overcome by this articulation of events at this point.

She began to tell me that she struggles with belief, but she does talk to God the same time every single night. She didn't really know who she was talking to.

I thought that was interesting, so I asked her why she picked a certain time of night to talk to God and only once a day.

She said, "I talk to God every night at 10:07 p.m. because that was Ryan's recorded time of death."

More tears came to my eyes, and the gears in my head starting turning at that point.

Then it came to me.

I said, "*Wow.*"

Instantly, I had a surge of energy shoot through me, and the hairs on my arms stood up. I had Jesus bumps again.

I pulled out my phone and looked at my "outgoing" calls in the history.

What came next shook us both.

The call history showed us both that I had called my mom on her US landline at 10:07 p.m. the night before.

We both became overcome by some serious emotion. She felt an absolute conviction that God was giving her a message about the reality of His existence. She said, "God sent me a replica of my Ryan to tell me that He is real. You look like him, sound like him—everything."

She was in a puddle of tears at this point. I was very emotional as well. We talked about Jesus Christ, belief, and all topics related for the next two and a half hours. We didn't stop even once. The plane landed, and we hugged and went on our separate ways. I never saw her again. Talk about a divine moment, articulated by the hand of God since the beginning of time. It birthed at 10:07 p.m., January 6, 2012. The story doesn't end there.

Early on in the trip, my folks and I had finally come together in a remarkable reunion. I rented a motorcycle, and they had one of their own. We toured all through the desert and had an absolutely wonderful time together. They took me to all their favorite spots, which included a historical old town site. Upon touring the old town, I discovered a church. I sat on the steps of the old church and asked my mom to take a picture of me in front of it. It was a Thursday.

I sent this picture back to a few guys in Canada who were going to continue with small group at my house that evening. I gave one of the guys the code to get into the house so that they could continue with the study and fellowship.

That evening, Vance, who was leading the study, decided he would play a joke on me from my own home. As a joke, they emptied out the entire pantry of my kitchen onto the island. It was a huge mess. Knowing my OCD tendencies, they all gathered around the huge mess and took a group picture. They sent me the picture that night. The text that accompanied the picture said, "Have a great trip. This is us having church back home."

When I saw the picture, my thoughts at that point? Ha-haaa (sarcastically).

I told them to enjoy the evening, and that was the last I heard from them.

Anyway, I finished out the trip in Arizona three days later and returned home to Canada. After returning home, I received a call from Vance. He was ecstatic. I asked him what was going on. He reminded me of the picture that I had sent him from the church in Arizona. Then he reminded me of the group photo that they sent back to me from the kitchen of my home. He then proceeded to tell me that the picture that they had sent back to me, <u>in response to the one that I had sent</u>, just ended a year-and-a-half criminal court case for one of our small group members who had been falsely accused of assault and sending hate messages to someone.

It turns out that another hate mail had been sent out from this particular guy's work computer in another town fifteen minutes away, three seconds before they took that group picture around my kitchen island. He was in the picture. It was absolutely impossible for our small group member to be in two places at the same time, and Vance had the proof in the picture. For whatever reason, the authorities could prove that this last hate mail had been sent through an actual computer e-mail account and not a mobile device. Vance and our small group member later built a defense case around this one picture, and all charges were dropped.

I hung up the phone and just reflected on the amazingness of God, the entire trip to Arizona, and how it birthed. Five days before, I stood in the living room of my home. All alone, in praise and worship. When I didn't even feel like it. Then I heard the still small voice whisper, "Go to Arizona with Ryan, and call your mom." One second before that moment, I thought I would go to bed and then wake up for work, as usual. Little did I know.

Reconciliation with my folks, the divine moment with Jen and a court case being quashed would all happen. I won't even begin talking about the lobsters in Scottsdale. This is kingdom life birthed in a praise and worship moment. This is . . . the victorious life! This is "Thy Kingdom Come." Thank you, Father.

*We are destroying speculations
and every lofty thing raised up against
the knowledge of God, and we are
taking every thought captive to the
obedience in Christ.*

—2 Corinthians 10:5

THE ORDER OF MELCHIZEDEK

20 managing our thought life

WITH ALL THE NOISE, distraction, and stress in the world today, sometimes it can be difficult discerning the thoughts and feelings that are filling up our minds. I want to talk about managing our thought-lives. Managing our thought-lives from day to day is critical, because the enemy is working overtime to plant lies into our minds. He's also using the noise and distractions of the world to pollute our thoughts.

The mind is the first place Satan will flash pictures and deceptions of how we should live our lives (his order) and what we should expect for results. Are we even aware of this? Are we even aware that Satan's most effective weapon of mass destruction will be the assault and warfare against our thoughts? Did we even know he can mess with our thoughts or how this is possible? This is possible through the spiritual realm. This is called spiritual warfare. This can work one of two ways.

THE STRATEGY

In the first attack, Satan tries to deceive us into thinking we <u>can</u> overcome storms, trials, and tribulations his way. He wants to lead us into living some sort of "kingdom type" of life in his order, as mentioned throughout this book. This will be Satan's kingdom, which is the ways of the world.

And in the second attack, he tries to plant polar opposite seeds of doubt to make us believe we can't succeed in the healthy and prosperous things God has designed for us in the kingdom of God. Satan wants us to be double-minded. It's estimated that we will have over sixty thousand thoughts a day. How do we discern through all these thoughts to know who is actually speaking?

> *A double-minded man is unstable in all his ways.*
> (James 1:8)

All through this book, we have discussed salvation, power, and the two kingdoms, and what they mean. We have also talked about the ways of the world, which is a third kingdom that Satan is trying to set up in our <u>minds</u> to destroy us. With thought comes action. Satan wants to plant thoughts in our heads so that we take his action. He wants to get us offtrack, to live confused lives. His ways are Gucci glasses we look through (the ways of the world). Looking through these figurative Gucci glasses will look good at first. The problem with the Gucci glasses is that the lenses are broken. Furthermore, we won't even know we are looking through these glasses or that the lenses are broken. They are designed to slowly and subtly pull us away from God. This will bring destruction in our lives.

Understanding that Satan is truly speaking into our thought-lives is an absolutely essential revelation to recognize each and every day. We won't live victorious kingdom lives if we aren't aware this is happening, or we don't care enough to take it serious enough to fight back. The purpose in these lies is to keep us *living destructively*.

A CLOSER LOOK AT THE SECOND ATTACK

In this second strategy, Satan tries to manipulate our thought-lives by dropping seeds of fear, doubt, worry, and untruth about what will happen in our lives from day to day, and what we should expect for results. I'm talking about Satan attempting to *stop* any successful progress in our lives by means of negative thoughts of *failure* for the *good* things in the kingdom-of-God life. These lies will be completely opposite to the first strategy of lies previously mentioned (ways of the world lies).

In the first strategy, he wants us to believe that his lies will help us through the storms and our struggles. In the second strategy, he wants to hinder any true success in our lives. He attempts this by dropping negative seeds and lies into our minds from the minute we wake up until the minute we go to bed about kingdom life living. This is a full-out assault on our minds.

Both strategies, if successful for him, will accomplish the same result. Satan wants to steal *any* hope of success God has intended for us. Without hope in God's good promises, there is nothing left, and there will be no access to the kingdom power without the faith and hope in God's order.

Consequently, the Bible says we have a responsibility for the choices that affect this outcome. The Bible is very clear about our part in managing our thought-lives. The Bible says if we believe God's Word and His promises, then we will prosper and succeed in His timing here on earth to live kingdom lives. Only by believing and standing with God in His promises can we overcome the lies of the devil. We overcome by faith in His Word and by managing our thought-lives.

It means we habitually shut out the *continuous lies* of the enemy, and we stay rooted in God's promises and His order by "taking captive our thoughts" so that we can be *all* that Christ designed us to be.

The Bible says,

> We demolish arguments and every pretension that sets itself up against the knowledge of God, and we take captive every thought to make it obedient to Christ. (2 Corinthians 10:5)

How do we make our thoughts obedient to Christ in His order?

By knowing His Word and believing in His promises for our lives through faith. As mentioned earlier, the Bible says,

> They are not just idle words for you—they are your life. (Deuteronomy 32:47)

God gives us this council in His Word because He knows the enemy is lying to us continuously, and we need truth to overcome. Why doesn't God just deal with Satan's lies for us? God allowed free will through love, and that includes giving us the ability to choose our own thoughts and what we want to believe. He also gives us strength and protection through His Word by giving us the weapons to fight back and overcome.

> I write to you, young men, because you are strong, and the Word of God lives in you, and you have overcome the evil one. (1 John 2:14)

These weapons include taking captive our thoughts or managing our thought-lives. God didn't design us to be robots, so He gives us the power and strength to fight back through the power of His Spirit and the knowledge of His Word.

THE COUNTERATTACK

Satan uses a continual infiltration of negative thoughts into our minds to get us feeling defeated. Such thoughts may include things like

I'm too short. I'm too tall. I'm too ugly. I'm too heavy. I'm too skinny. I don't have enough money. I don't have the skills it takes. I will never be able to accomplish that. I'll always be alone. My family suffered from this disease, so I will end up with that disease. My family was this, so I will be that. My marriage is this, so it will end up like that. The doctors said this, so I'm going to have that. The economy is doing this, so I guess my finances will do that.

The list is utterly endless. Any of these thoughts sound familiar? These thoughts are designed to completely halt us in any area of success God has planned for us. They will keep us pressed down and defeated. When we are defeated, we won't live the kingdom lives that God wants us to live.

In order to overcome these lies, we need to have the ability to know the source of these thoughts and understand that there is actually a spiritual war against our minds. With this awareness, we can be on the offensive every day instead of sitting back on the defensive waiting for something to happen. We need to come out of the gate armored up and prepared for battle, so to speak.

The Bible says,

Put on the full armor of God, so that you can take your stand against the devil's schemes. For our struggle is not against flesh and blood, but against the rulers, against the authorities, against the powers of this dark world and against the spiritual forces of evil in the heavenly realms. Therefore, put on the full armor of God, so that when the day of evil comes, you may be able to stand your ground, and after you have done everything, to stand. Stand firm then, with the belt of truth buckled around your waist, with the breastplate of righteousness in place, and with your feet fitted with the readiness that comes from the Gospel of peace. In addition to all this, take up the shield of faith, with which you can extinguish all the flaming arrows of the evil one. Take the helmet of salvation and the sword of the Spirit, which is the Word of God. And pray in the Spirit on all occasions with all kinds of prayers and requests. With this in mind, be alert and always keep on praying for all the Lord's people. (Ephesians 6:11–18)

God tells us in this passage to armor up and prepare for battle. Take the offensive position instead of being neutral or in the defensive position. To take the offensive, and to be victorious over these thoughts, we fight Satan's lies with God's promises. Each component of the armor is a set of lessons to know and commit to memory. Let's source out all of God's promises in His Word and meditate on them so that the truth of His Word will be stamped into our minds each day, instead of Satan's lies. Let's have thoughts of overcoming and thoughts of victory, instead of thoughts of defeat. We won't be able to do this if we don't know God's promises in His Word. Once we know His promises, we command them into our lives through faith. When we work in the order of Christ in terms of managing our thoughts, we start seeing the kingdom life come alive in our day to day. We need to meditate on the good promises of God each day instead of marinating in Satan's lies.

This book of the law shall not depart from your mouth, but you shall meditate on it day and night, so that you may be careful to do according to all that is written in it; for then you will make your way prosperous, and then you will have success. (Joshua 1:8)

God speaks about meditating on Him and His promises in that verse, and He also mentions having those promises coming out of our mouths. That's precisely why I take time each morning, and all through the day, to declare His Words like I mentioned in the previous chapter. Those declarations are all of His promises found in specific scriptures that I meditate on day and night.

If we have defeat leaving our lips, because of what is in our minds, then defeat will inevitably come. If we are speaking strong words of victory from God's Word, then victory will come. That's God's promise. Let's take the time to really develop the ability to manage our thoughts and the words that leave our mouths. What kingdom will you let into your mind? Let's make a decision not to listen to the lies of the enemy from this day forward. Let's let the power of God's kingdom into our minds.

Although there are many more forms of worship in Christ's order that bring the victorious kingdom life, I believe the ones we have discussed are foundational to any believer's journey. These experiences in Christ's order will keep us on the right path, to live out victorious kingdom-life moments. We will inevitably discover and enjoy further experiences in Christ's order, releasing more and more moments of victory into our lives as we press in with intention. Let's be determined believers in our walks.

How beautiful on the mountains are the
feet of those <u>who bring the good news,</u>
who proclaim peace, who bring good
tidings, who proclaim salvation, who say
to Zion, "Your God reigns!"

—*Isaiah 52:7*

52/7 **final remarks**

**"PRIORITY"
IN PURPOSE**

I SAVED THE BEST for last, as far as I'm concerned. The first thing I love the most about that verse is the placing of it in Isaiah: "52/7" Perhaps this tells us that the golden nugget in our overall purpose is to be ready at all times to be "deployed." Prepared and ready to go to work fifty-two weeks a year and seven days a week in mission, thus fulfilling purpose. There will be *nothing* more effective to draw the power of God into our lives, in the most extreme way, than acknowledging the goodness of Jesus Christ to others—through discipleship with praise on our lips.

The Bible says,

> But in your hearts revere Christ as Lord. _Always be prepared to give an answer_ to everyone who asks you to give the reason for the hope that you have. But do this with gentleness and respect, keeping a clear conscience, so that those who speak maliciously against your good behavior in Christ may be ashamed of their slander. (1 Peter 3:15–16)

Not too long ago, I ran into an Arab man at the mall that was selling phone cases at a Kiosk. We were having a really nice time together, sharing a lot of smiles and jokes. He gave me an extraordinary deal on a three-pack of clear plastic covers that I needed for my new phone. Without even thinking about it, I said, "Well, praise the Lord," under my breath, as he gave me this nice deal.

He looked up at me and said, "Praise God." I suppose his words surprised me, as much as mine did to him. He asked me what I believed in. I knew what was about to come. A discussion about gods. He told me he was a Muslim, and I told him I was a Christian. This type of situation used to be tricky for me with Muslim believers. It isn't anymore. I _never_ debate God. This never works. I don't tell them about Jesus Christ only and then hope that they see something different than what they already see. I back it up.

He asked me why I believe in Jesus. I knew the door had been opened by the Holy Spirit. Muslims very rarely ask me a question that specific. I said,

> Two years ago, I stood on a chair with a rope around my neck. I wanted to die. In that moment, I had a power surge go through my mind and my body. I went to bed, and I was never the same. Weeks later, I confirmed that this was the power of Jesus Christ in my life. Ever since that night, I've seen proof of God's promises happen in my life as written in the Holy Bible. I have never been the same.

I told this man about the freedom from addiction, the restoration of relationships in my life, financial breakthroughs that God has done in my life. He could see the joy and the peace in my eyes. He could see victory. I showed him a few little scriptures that said this would happen in my life if I followed Jesus. I showed him the "power play" in my life since my "last night." I was going back and making reports about God's power, so to speak. He was moved by these stories. I could see that his eyes had become glazed over with some tears. The Holy Spirit moved right in. I could feel the power and anointing in me physically, right there in that moment. I said, "Have you ever had anything like this happen to you?"

He said, "No, not really."

I said, "Brother, Jesus was not just a prophet. He is the Son of Man. The King of kings. Our Lord and Savior."

I said, "Take a deeper look into Jesus, as written in the Holy Bible. It will blow your mind." He said he would.

I gave him a side-five, a man hug, chest bump—dropped down some cash with a tip, and walked away.

> *They triumphed over him by the blood of the Lamb*
> *and by the word of their testimony. (Revelations 12:11)*

The blood of the Lamb is Jesus Christ as our Lord and Savior. The word of our testimony is what will unleash the power from the blood of the Lamb. If we never see power, we will never have any testimony. If we don't have testimonies, we will have nothing to talk about. This is why Jesus said, "Seek first the kingdom." This is so we would have His power as the evidence to back up our words.

> *Because our Gospel came to you not simply with*
> *words but also with power, with the Holy Spirit and*
> *deep conviction. (1 Thessalonians 1:5)*

We won't be very effective disciples until we start having something to talk about to the lost. We can't be living the same lives as the lost and expect to move people's hearts without proof of His glory in our lives through His power. How will any of us trust God's Word if we don't actually see the evidence of it happening! The Holy Spirit was sent to us so that we could see the evidence, and then give evidence, of His existence through His power! Why should we be believers? Because it sounds good? Because we were born with Christian parents? Because we have heard about it? Even God knew the last three cases weren't the answer.

God will show us the proof of why we believe through the *power* of the Holy Spirit. The Bible says,

> *I raised you up for this very purpose, that I might display My power in you and that My name might be proclaimed in all the earth. (Romans 9:17)*

Power through love. Love is action, not just words. Our words need to be backed up with action, love, power, and glory. Many believers won't take action, because they haven't experienced God's power. I'm not on fire for the Lord, because of my personality. Before my "last night," I was completely opposite in personality, actually. I'm on fire because I see God's power show up and show out in my life almost every other day, one way or another. If we don't see God's power show up and show out, there likely won't be much to be fired up about. At that point, telling others about Jesus will have no power behind it. The words will be pretty empty, without action, power and a fire behind them. That is, testimony of God's love and power from real-life experiences. I could tell you that I love you all day long, but unless those words are backed up with some sort of action, the words will mean nothing. Well, it's the same with Jesus.

THE HARVEST SCALE (90 PERCENT)

As we see, we need to be ready. Earlier in this book, I mentioned that we could be obedient from the surrender section, all the way down to the managing our thought-lives section, in the form of worship. Then we discussed how we could forfeit the release of the smaller harvest moments if we had grumbling or complaining thoughts, words, and attitudes. God will not bless negative, complaining, and unfaithful postures. Even if we are doing some of the work. This becomes religious works. We know that God doesn't bless religious works. That's why many believers don't see breakthroughs and the victorious life playing out. God blesses the praises of His Saints that stand on His promises in faith, working in His order. It would be disheartening to put in all of the work and miss the target or a harvest. This is the harvest scale. The blessings in the harvest scale is the 90 percent that will power us up to do the last 10 percent effectively. This equals 100 percent.

THE KINGDOM SCALE (10 PERCENT)

I want to use the same comparison on a bigger scale now: The Kingdom Scale. What if we successfully operated and succeeded in all of the template experiences of God's order right from "surrender" to "managing our thought lives" in this book? We would be "built up," sure, but then what? What if we found some "levels" of victory and then didn't take selfless postures to multiply and to share the good news? What would be the point? And what may we forfeit?

The point, one of the answers is that we would miss the point of our purposes entirely. This is because it would become "all about me" if we didn't multiply. We need to get out of these mind-sets to be effective disciples for the Lord. If it is all about "me," we will be selfish people taking selfish postures. That's not what we are called to do. Our salvation isn't supposed to be a private matter, regardless of what we have convinced ourselves to believe. God's Word doesn't tell us to mind our own business so that we don't "offend" anyone if they have no belief or different beliefs. Have we convinced ourselves that we have a universal "love" toward humanity by keeping our hope private? Have we convinced ourselves that we are living in love if we are "respecting" others' beliefs, by keeping our hope to ourselves? Although this may be a good personal opinion, it's not Biblical, and it's not what we are called to do. We are called to share the goodness of God in our lives to others.

Pray also for me, that whenever I speak, words may be given me so that I will fearlessly make known the mystery of the Gospel, for which I am an ambassador in chains. Pray that I may declare it fearlessly, as I should. (Ephesians 6:19–20)

I don't think there is anything that we can do that will bring more power into our lives—nothing more than this. And just so we are clear, we are not called to be obnoxious about it, and we aren't called to force people to think the same way or treat them less or differently if they don't believe what we do. We are asked to "share the good news of salvation" and multiply the message so that it may save lives. This will make disciples. It says this right in His Word.

Forfeit. In the "harvest" scale mentioned earlier, what a waste it would be to do all the work along the way and then grumble and complain at the end with negative attitudes. There won't be much of a harvest until we sort that out. Let's talk about the kingdom scale now. How much more of a waste would it be if we did all the work along the way and <u>didn't grumble</u>, and we did receive the harvest moments *but* didn't multiply after all of this? You see, there will be evidence of God's power at different levels when we start getting busy in His order. That's a fact. I know this because I have watched many, including myself, in this journey experience different levels of His glory. That being said, the <u>real concentration</u> of His power comes available to us when we take it public.

"Harvest" is one thing. Life-altering moments in the "kingdom of God" is an entirely different experience. The turbo-boosted moments are kingdom life. They are mind-blowing breakthrough and kingdom moments of extreme victory. This is the bigger scale I was just speaking about. One scale, if executed, brings smaller harvests. The other scale, if executed, <u>brings the supercharged life-altering kingdom moments</u>. If we don't go public with the harvest experiences and witness them to the world, we are missing the entire point. We will also miss out on something else. We will miss out on the supercharged kingdom-powered lives. They won't happen to the *fullest* if we are not going public.

The Bible says,

> "Because he loves Me," says the Lord, "I will res-
> cue him; I will protect him, for he acknowledges My
> name. He will call on Me, and I will answer him; I will
> be with him in trouble, I will deliver him and honor
> him." (Psalm 91:14–15)

The secret in this verse is the acknowledgment. This is a two-part process. First, we acknowledge God personally in our lives as a part of our daily relationship. Let's not miss the hidden gem in the second part! Let's also acknowledge His goodness in our lives to others. This is where stuff really starts to happen. When we acknowledge the goodness of God in our lives to others and we have the courage to share the good news, there will be preferential treatment in our lives from the Lord. This is new-level kingdom power, and this is an absolute fact. Most believers don't recognize the power that is birthed when we proclaim the name of Jesus in our lives, in public, in a loving and proper way. And like everything else, the more we do it, the more we will see His glory in our lives.

For the believer, the signs of God's glory are meant to bring the "believing" community into a posture of merging the power together with the belief. As we talked about many times, a large portion of the believing community is unaware or not working in kingdom power. Evidence of this power edifies the believing community that may not be experiencing the victorious kingdom life. Obviously, and equally important, it's to lay seed for the unbelieving community as well, to attract them to the goodness of God.

Do we think Jesus performed all of those miracles to show off or to put on self-righteous healing clinics? Of course not! Jesus displayed His power and glory as evidence to lay the foundation of the Gospel! He knew that words would be dead without power or action behind them! Just the same, we are to show the same evidence of His power to the rest of the world! In turn, this would keep the cycle going which will include a kingdom type of life available to whoever would believe in Him and then walk in His order—truly walk in His order, that is. If we take this power public, we will see more power and more favor in our lives to take His glory public again. It's a cycle that's gets stronger and stronger as we pursue Him. There have been too many years with dead religious words being thrown out there, with no evident signs of His power and Glory. We need to tap into His power. This will change lives in a radical way for His glory.

I know this is a "petty" scale or illustration. It's for the sake of simplicity so we can easily understand. Let's picture everything in this book up to the *last* chapter as being 90 percent of the journey—*if* we did it. These are pretty good lives for those who are active in them. But how do we *really* tap into the kingdom of God in the fullest measure? Take the harvest scale public.

> I tell you, whoever publicly acknowledges Me before others, the Son of Man will also acknowledge before the angels of God. But whoever disowns Me before others will be disowned before the angels of God. (Luke 12:8–9)

Taking this life public is the 10 percent that many of us miss or do very little of. And to be honest, we forfeit the entire purpose in our journey by not taking it public. We also forfeit kingdom power as well. The last 10 percent is mind-blowing stuff. It is where the extremely set-apart moments of power, favor, and victory are birthed. Why is this? This is because taking it public is the single-most powerful thing we will ever do, mixed in with all the other forms of worship. It's love. It's the whole objective and our entire purpose. When we are doing what the Lord tells us to do, He will reward us. How do we know this for sure?

The Bible says,

> We are witnesses of these things, and so is the Holy Spirit, who God has given to those who <u>obey Him</u>. (Acts 5:32)

Having the Holy Spirit with us comes through obedience. Obedience is faith at work in our deeds. With the Holy Spirit, we have power. Without His power, we struggle to do any of this. So we see our deeds in obedience do matter. When we make the decisions to be obedient and put ourselves aside in selflessness, that's when we really see the entire picture come together. Putting ourselves aside will allow us to share the good news. When we share the good news, we are now making disciples. When we make disciples, we are multiplying the kingdom. When we multiply the kingdom in the *full* order of Christ, well . . . that's when we start to have these "blow our hair straight back" kingdom experiences. But not until then. Salvation is free, and the power is not.

The Bible says,

> He said to them, "Go into all the world and preach to Gospel to all creation. Whoever believes and is baptized will be saved, but whoever does not believe will be condemned. And these signs will accompany those who believe: In My name they will drive out demons; they will speak in new tongues; they will pick up snakes with their hands; and when they drink deadly poison, it will not hurt them at all; they will place their hands on sick people, and they will get well." After the Lord Jesus had spoken to them, He was taken up into heaven and He sat at the right hand of God.
>
> Then the disciples went out and preached everywhere, and the Lord worked with them and confirmed His word by the signs that accompanied it. (Mark 16:15–20)

All the evidence is in that one scripture alone. The 90 percent is operating in His order, in faith and obedience, talked about all through our book. The 90 percent will give us various "harvests." The 10 percent is to "take this story public." Go spread this news, and celebrate these harvests with others. That's a total of 100 percent. This is the kingdom of God summed up in one scripture. This is where real purpose and real power start taking root in our lives.

Seek first the kingdom. If we don't experience victory, His power, and His glory, we will have nothing to take public. "Hey, have your heard about my God? He sure loves us." I'm sorry, that's just not going to be a complete way to witness to unbelievers most of the time. We need to take the love (blood of the lamb) and back it up with the power (the word of our testimony). Without the words of our testimony, it won't be a very effective ministry. Also, Jesus didn't do it that way either. He always backed up His words with power. He showed His power as the proof of His awesome goodness! That's why God told His believers to seek first the kingdom of God! Seek first My power, after you believe, so you have something to actually talk about! Words are dead without action behind them. This is a simple reality in everyday life. Words without action won't mean a dang thing. Action or love won't come without His power! The 90 percent will no doubt bring results, but when we *really* dial into purpose and start preaching the good news and we take this news public, we start experiencing turbocharged kingdom-life experiences, because God said He would be with us in the last line of that verse.

> *And the Lord worked with them and confirmed His Word by signs that accompanied it.*

The fulfillment of our true "purpose" in life becomes complete, and we end up firing on all cylinders as we merge the entire purpose together.

That is "belief + power" + "going public" = Kingdom life.

Of course, results will be accordingly to the level of our efforts in obedience.

GO MAKE DISCIPLES

WHAT IS A DISCIPLE?

Making disciples is the nucleus of God's redemption plan. A disciple is someone who believes in Jesus Christ and the works of the Cross. A disciple is someone who believes the Word of God to be true. A disciple is someone who takes that belief and then goes out and does what God tells us to do. A disciple would need God's kingdom power to multiply and make other disciples. Being a disciple is a lifelong journey. Being a disciple is not easy. A disciple would be set apart. A disciple would be "in" the world, but they certainly won't be "of" this world. A disciple won't blend in with the world. A disciple will get rejected in this world, in some cases, for their message of hope. Disciples wouldn't waste an opportunity to share the "good news." A disciple heads out to tell people about the good news so they, too, will believe and be born again. A disciple will start their new life in the sanctification process, aligned with Gospel principles and teachings. A disciple's life would resemble the evidence of their belief. A true disciple will live with God's power. That new disciple would start the whole process all over again. *Multiply.* 52/7

Let's end with *Love.*

The Bible says,

> Love is patient, love is kind. It does not envy, it does not boast, it is not proud. It does not dishonor others, it is not self-seeking, it is not easily angered, it keeps no records of wrongs. Love does not delight in evil but rejoices with the truth. It always protects, always trusts, always hopes, always perseveres. Love never fails. (1 Corinthians 13:4)

Love is an action, not an emotion. Joy or happiness is an emotion. How do we actually spell the word love? T-I-M-E. Love will always take some of our time to execute. We need to pray for love to be in us so that it can flow through us. When we head out, we must go in love. Without love, none of this is possible, and it's all for nothing. Love is a process. Love will be learned. Love is hard work.

Love hurts. Love will cost. We will need love to access His power. The salvation, however? Salvation is free to us. It wasn't free for God and His Son. God loved us when we didn't love Him back. Love was the work on the Cross. Love sums up the entire message in God's book and brings the Gospel message to completion. Love puts a bow tie around the entire gift of salvation, kingdom power, and discipleship. The best disciples would use the fewest words. Silent sermons are the most powerful sermons. Let's preach more with our lives in His power and less with our words without it.

Let's multiply the message of Good News in Love.

> Lord, I have heard of Your fame; I stand in awe of Your deeds, Lord. Repeat them in our day, in our time make them known. (Habakkuk 3:2)

God bless.
The end

? the forgotten gift

A GIFT INSTEAD OF THE GRIND

A SABBATH, OR *THE* Sabbath? The Lord said, "Remember <u>the</u> Sabbath day." He didn't say, "Remember <u>a</u> Sabbath day" in Exodus 20:8. I wonder why God said, "Remember," instead of, "Thou shalt not," in only one of the Ten Commandments? This is because God knew that we would forget. God knew that mankind would be so consumed with the craziness of life that we would forget about the day He set aside for us as a *gift*.

What if Sabbath is "<u>*the*</u>" day, instead of "<u>*a*</u>" day?

What if God has a "set-apart" privilege, power, and favor for us by resting on "_the_" day, instead of "_a_" day? It's something to ponder, isn't it? As believers, shouldn't we be excited instead of critical about opportunity with the Lord? We can get blessed on any day of the week that we worship the Lord—that is a fact. But what if the "Sabbath" blessing was a different blessing?

Perhaps an opportunity for "different" power, favor, blessing, and peace for the rest of the week, that is. That's all I want us to ponder here, and that's why I will be brief on this topic. This topic could be a whole book alone.

God mentions the blessing on this day, even _before_ one Jew would ever walk this earth.

The Bible says,

> Thus the heavens and the Earth were completed in all their vast array. By the seventh day, God had finished the work He had been doing; so on the seventh day He rested from all of His work. Then <u>God blessed the seventh day</u> and made it holy, because on it He rested from all the work of creating that He had done.
> (Genesis 2:1–3)

God gave this day as a blessing at creation, to Adam and Eve, long before there were any Jews or Egyptians or Chinese or any other race. The Jewish race didn't exist until 2,300 years after creation—until Abraham, the first Jew. So I suppose, this day wasn't created for the "Jewish" community only. God had 2,300 years of prepared Sabbath blessing before a Jew would ever come to be. We also see the Sabbath day was a very specific day to the Jews and the Gentiles well after Christ died. In fact, Acts 13:14 shows us that the apostle Paul was teaching to the Jews and the Gentiles in the Synagogue on the Sabbath many years after Christ ascended to go be with the Father.

The Bible says,

> From Perga they went on to Pisidian Antioch. On the Sabbath they entered the synagogue and sat down.
> (Acts 13:14)

Then in verse 16 it says,

> *Standing up, Paul motioned with his hand and said:*
> *"Fellow Israelites and you gentiles who worship god,*
> *listen to me!" (Acts 13:16)*

Then in verse 42 it says,

> *As Paul and Barnabas were leaving the synagogue,*
> *the people invited them to speak further about these*
> *things on the next Sabbath. (Acts 13:42)*

And

> *On the next Sabbath almost the whole city gathered*
> *to hear the word of the Lord. When the Jews saw the*
> *crowds, they were filled with jealousy. They began to*
> *contradict what Paul was saying and heaped abuse on*
> *Him. Then Paul and Barnabas answered them boldly:*
> *"We had to speak the word of God to you first. Since*
> *you reject it and do not consider yourselves worthy of*
> *eternal life, we not <u>turn to the gentiles</u>." (Acts 13:44–46)*

What if we look at the Sabbath day as a gift instead of a religious topic? What if we didn't portray the Sabbath as being a random day or a random time—but an actual set-apart time and specific day that God has given to us as a *gift*. As mentioned before, there will be no power in religion or critical thinking or argument. I'm not suggesting for anyone to do this or for anyone to do that or change this or change that—as much as just opening our hearts about the Sabbath day, and letting the Holy Spirit talk to us. Perhaps there is a hidden gem here. We don't forfeit salvation or become "less than" if we are on one side or the other when it comes to the Sabbath day posture. That's not what this is about. This is exploration.

Exploration should be an exciting topic for a believer. Maybe it's not that exciting if we are covered over by a religious spirit. A fog, so to speak. The Sabbath day in the Bible is "symbolism" of a very specific day in our week, from Friday at sunset until Saturday at sunset. It doesn't matter what time zone we are in or how many leap years there have been or how many other reasons we want to use to say that Saturday isn't the day to use as the "symbolism" for the Sabbath day as mentioned all through the Bible. Time zones on earth have existed since night and day were created back in the first chapter of our Bibles. There will be a thousand reasons many scholars will try and reason around "the" day instead of "a" day. I just look to the Bible as I keep my heart open about the Sabbath day:

> *After the Sabbath, at dawn on the first day of the week, Mary Magdalene and the other Mary went to look at the tomb. (Matthew 28:1) (We call this Easter.)*

> *It was Preparation Day (that is, the day before the Sabbath). (Mark 15:42) (We call this Good Friday.)*

> *It was Preparation Day, and the Sabbath was about to begin. (Luke 23:54) (We call this good Friday)*

> *On the first day of the week, very early in the morning, the women took the spices they had prepared and went to the tomb. (Luke 24:1) (We call the first day of the week Sunday.)*

> *Now it was the day of Preparation, and the next day was to be a special Sabbath. (John 19:31) (We call this Good Friday.)*

> *Early on the first day of the week, while it was still dark, Mary Magdalene went to the tomb and saw that the stone had been removed from the entrance. (John 20:1) (We call the first day of the week Sunday.)*

We see that "Good Friday," as we recognize it today, would be the day that Jesus was crucified, as seen in the Word above. That's a Friday, and we all recognize it. Why do we recognize Good "Friday" as a very *specific* day every single year? Then we see that the Mary's would go to the tomb on the first day of the week *after* the Sabbath day, as mentioned in Matthew 28. Sunday is the first day of the week if Jesus was crucified on Friday and rested in His tomb on Saturday, or the Sabbath day.

Most of society recognizes Monday as the start of our weeks instead of Sunday, as mentioned in the scriptures, as the first day of the week. Even our own calendars tell us that Sunday is the first day of the week—yet it's the last day of the week in our spiritual walks, to most. Just saying. The real question? Why do we recognize any particular day in our lives with more "significance" than any other days and yet claim that there is no "significance" in "the" Sabbath day, as mentioned all through the scriptures? Good Friday, Jesus was crucified. He <u>rested</u> in His tomb on the Sabbath day. Then He rose on the first day of the week, which is Sunday. One day after the Sabbath. Most believers see the end of the week, or their day of worship, on what is in fact the first day of the week—Sunday.

Most will discredit the significance of a specific day, and yet we set special days to celebrate and show more honor at times of Advent, and at Christmas, Easter, and Good Friday and such. Ever notice how most believers will only wear suits or their nicest clothes to church on the Christmas Eve service? Why is this? Why do we hold these "days" in any higher form of honor than any other days of the year if "days" don't matter all that much in our walks with Christ? In other words, most believers claim that specific days don't mean a thing in terms of the "Sabbath" day, in our walks with Jesus, because we can celebrate Jesus on any day of the week.

Yet we set special celebrations for other days of the year. Kind of hypocritical in a sense, isn't it? To honor other days of the year and give no significance to the Sabbath day as mentioned about sixty times in the New Testament? Again, this is just to get our hearts marinating on the idea that there may be a treasure hidden in the Sabbath day blessing. Yes, we can, and we should be celebrating Jesus on every day of the week—no doubt. Not just one day. That's not what we are exploring here. What if the Sabbath blessing was so much different than a normal blessing? That's all this is about.

"A different blessing."

The Bible says,

*Six days do your work, but on the seventh day do
not work, so that your ox and your donkey may rest,
and so that the slave born in your household and
the foreigner living among you may be refreshed.
(Exodus 23:12)*

Refreshed, not Religion. Refreshed, not Rules. Why would God talk about one specific day all throughout the Bible? Ever notice how the majority of Western culture believers look so worn out, beat up, and stressed out from week to week? Maybe a part of the reason is that we give no regard to the Sabbath Day blessing that could result in a set-apart blessing and refreshing. Even in the New Testament, we see Jesus preaching and teaching on the Sabbath day in the Synagogues.

*He went to Nazareth, where He had been brought up,
and on the Sabbath day He went into the synagogue,
as was His custom. He stood up to read, and the scroll
of the prophet Isaiah was handed to Him. Unrolling it,
He found the place where it is written. (Luke 4:16–17)*

We also see that Jesus was telling us that the Sabbath was a gift for mankind. It wasn't for Himself; it was for us!

*Then He said to them, "The Sabbath was made for
man, not man for the Sabbath. So the Son of Man is
Lord even of the Sabbath." (Mark 2:27)*

This verse means that the Sabbath is a blessing for us (for man). Jesus doesn't need the Sabbath; we do. We need to see that *order* is opportunity, and God's ways don't prohibit us. They protect us from ourselves so that we can be a blessed and prosperous people. We can get all religious and offended with the topic of the Sabbath, or we can get our hearts wide open to see if there is a special gift of peace, power, and provision on the day that the Lord has set aside for us. Let's read the Ten Commandments in Exodus 20 again.

Why is it that we will attempt to honor and see true significance in every one of the commandments, except the Fourth Commandment? Remember the Sabbath day. It just doesn't make *any* sense why we want to reason our way out of the Fourth Commandment so bad when we agree with the other nine. How can we possibly say that one of these commandments doesn't mean anything today? We certainly have no problems defending the other nine commandments when it comes to obedience or opportunity or looking at the teachings of Jesus Himself, all through the Word. "Thou shalt not kill" is the sixth commandment. Yup, okay. "Though shalt not steal" is the eighth commandment. Yup, okay. "Thou shalt not commit adultery" is the seventh commandment. Yup, okay. Jesus taught us to obey every one of the Ten Commandments all through the Gospels in His very own teachings. He didn't miss one. Why would He *leave one out?*

Jesus was not incomplete in *anything*. He said all the commandments were made complete through love. Love completes order; it doesn't erase the order. This means we would follow Jesus and His ways in a heart posture of relationship now, *not religion.* That's what this means. The law turns into love. Order is love. We do them, because we love Him. We don't do it for "religious" reasons anymore after the cross. *No deed on earth will be worth anything if we don't do it, because we love and honor Jesus!*

All the commandments were summed up by love. This doesn't mean we lose the principles and teachings and fall into a "universalism" love, with some sort of mysterious "grace" that has no order attached to the promises. It means we obey and worship unto the Lord because we love Him! Love dissolves religion and rules and releases the reward. There will be no power in religion. Love for our Christ will make order whole. How the heck did we ever turn the gift of the Sabbath blessing into a religious topic, a lost blessing, or a denomination that creates division? Jesus brings the commandments to completion. He doesn't abolish them. Jesus is Lord of the Sabbath because everything is made complete through Him and through the love of Jesus through the Cross! We must realize that the Cross completes everything; it doesn't erase everything. We need to understand the difference. Jesus said that Himself.

The Bible says,

> Everyone who believes that Jesus is the Christ is born of God, and everyone who loves the Father loves His child as well. This is how we know that we love the children of God: By loving God and carrying out His commands. In fact, this love for God: To keep His commands. (1 John 5:1–3)

> Do not think that I have come to abolish the Law or the Prophets; I have not come to abolish them but to fulfill them. For truly I tell you, until heaven and Earth disappear, not the smallest letter, not the least stroke of a pen, will by any means disappear from the Law until everything is accomplished. (Matthew 5:17–18)

Jesus lived by example. The apostles followed Jesus's example after He left to go be with the Father. If Christ had changed the Sabbath day to Sunday or said the *day doesn't* matter, He would have made it clear—plain and simple. Surely, He or the apostles who followed in His footsteps would have given a very specific account of this change somewhere in the New Testament. Notice further on in the book of Acts.

The Bible says,

> As was his custom, Paul went into the synagogue, and on three Sabbath days he reasoned with them from the Scriptures, explaining and proving that the Messiah had to suffer and rise from the dead. (Acts 17:2)

We sure speak a lot about Jesus and His ways, and Paul and his ways. Perhaps no other apostle gets talked about more than the apostle Paul. And yet we see that Paul saw serious significance with the Sabbath Day. Not a random "Sabbath" day.

If we don't go after deeds and obedience in love and worship, it will be done in religion, which is bogus. It will be done with no significance in the actual purpose they were designed for by God. The purpose is to protect us and to prosper us. Not to prohibit us. We will not see this until we get free of the religious spirit. Our goal is to be living righteously that comes through the power of His grace—not living to look righteous. God's order is supposed to change us. It is supposed to bless us so that we can be a blessing to others.

The only time we see Jesus getting cranky about the Sabbath day truth is when the Pharisees were treating the Sabbath day religiously, instead of relationally. Maybe that's why we get cranky about the Sabbath day topic. They were getting all high and mighty about themselves and the Sabbath day with a religious attitude. This type of blowback will come back on us every time we try and act all high and mighty in any area of worship. Just because we see blowback about the Sabbath in the scriptures doesn't mean this day has been abolished.

The only time we see a negative spin about the Sabbath was when the Pharisees were involved. Critical religion again. They were trying to twist up Jesus with the very gift and provision that God created for His people! This was obedience turned *religious* again! Jesus said, "I desire mercy, not sacrifice," when He was talking to those guys about the Sabbath—when He healed a man's hand and was picking grain. In other words, *the Sabbath Day* is a gift for my people, so quit trying to put a religious twist on it!

The Sabbath day isn't a religion as some people have made it out to be. Again, this is where denominational beliefs come in. We start building religion around a blessing. What a waste! The Sabbath isn't for a religion; it is for a reward! It's a gift from God. The minute we try and push the day or make a religion out of it, we suck the power right out of the purpose, as far as I'm concerned. Jesus didn't create Seventh Day Adventists, or Lutherans, or Baptists, or Jehovah's Witnesses, or whatever domination we think is "better." Denomination is division, and that was made by man, not God. There is no kingdom power in man-made things.

As believers, I think we should take some time to pray about the Sabbath Day and see what the Holy Spirit tells each and every one of us about it. For me, if I'm not one hundred-percent complete in a teaching or a principle, I will err to the side of order every time, to the best of my ability. Not for religion but because it's a safe place with God. He looks at the heart. If I err to the side of order, with a heart in a position to please Him, *I am absolutely* convinced that my Father will reward me every single time, even if the principle is out a bit. Why? Like I mentioned earlier, the evidence is all throughout His Word. The only thing the Lord will be looking at when we are worshipping Him is where our hearts are positioned. Is it to please Him or please ourselves and others around us? To live in righteous order or living to look righteous?

> *I, the Lord, search the heart, I test the mind, even to give to each man according to his ways, according to the results of his deeds. (Jeremiah 17:10)*

What if our kids decided to go ahead and do the dishes without even being asked one day? On their own time, even though it wasn't actually one of the chores on their lists? For absolutely no other reason but to try and please us? Then if they missed a dish or two by accident or put the wrong cycle on in the dishwasher, with their hearts in a position to make us proud of them, would we be upset with them? Or would we reward them? I would give them a reward. I think that's how our Father treats His children as well. It's not about perfecting His order; it's about having our hearts in a posture of "all-in" for Him.

A promise *always* has a principle attached. We must have our hearts in a position of reverence, not religion, when it comes to carrying out these principles to see the promises come to pass. Every single time I hear a "religious" believer trying to discredit the Sabbath day significance, it's coming out of a defeated believer's mouth. Their lives show *no significant signs* of the Lord's mighty love, power and favor. They live natural lives, just the same as the rest of the world, in their believing postures. They seem to live with little joy as well. This is not evidence of the Holy Spirit's fruit. These are the same people who have no words coming out of their mouths during the praise and worship parts of our services as they come in late, and they stare around the room to watch what everyone else is doing.

Why would we argue about principles in God's Word that are designed to bless us? Why would we teach against God's commands? That's a pretty unstable posture, as far as I'm concerned. At minimum, if we aren't *sure*, let's err to the side of order or keep our mouths shut when arguing against God's commands, as a starting point. I'm sure that I am not complete in many principles in God's Word. That being said, if there is a promise associated with that principle or a removal of a promise in that principle, I will err to the side of putting my heart in a position to go after the obedience every single time to the best of my ability. Or at least keep my heart open in prayer about it. I don't dare criticize it. Perhaps that might be the most significant principle one could ever live within God's principles. Err to the side of *order* with our hearts in the right position, even if we aren't certain? I think God will give us the benefit every time if our hearts are in the position of relation, and not religion. There is power and provision in the promises, if we pursue the principles.

The power and favor would come for those dedicated enough to seek them out and then actually execute in them after the discovery. "Few would enter." Those who will be set apart and go against the grain for the sake of truth will be few in the body of Christ. In turn, they will see set-apart power, favor, and blessing if it's done with a heart in a posture to please our Lord. God isn't searching for people who will "follow the crowd," as the saying goes. He is looking for those who will lead the crowd in truth. Even if it is not comfortable or popular. Truth will always be rejected when it's designed to transform us out of the "status quo" of our popular or comfortable lives. Few will enter the special place of power, protection, privilege, and provision because we just wouldn't follow the principles. The promises are not automatic. Salvation is free; the power is not.

God bless you even more!

> There remains, then, a Sabbath-rest for the people of
> God; for anyone who enters God's rest also rests from
> their works, just as God did from His. Let us, there-
> fore, make every effort to enter that rest, so that no
> one will perish by following their example of disobedi-
> ence. (Hebrews 4:9–11)

Sidenote: Another common belief is that Pentecost was the "birth" of the church. I believe that the church was conceived at Pentecost and is still in conception. This based on some specific scriptures. This is a sidenote, so I will be brief. I didn't want to say "conception" in chapter 5 and then not explain why. Also, this won't be an important point to focus on for the purposes of our study.

I believe that the church was "conceived" at Pentecost, and that it is still in conception until the final return of Christ. I believe the church is "birthed" when the bride is brought together with the groom at His Second Coming. The reason I feel this way is based on Jacob's week of labor or what most believers call the seven-year tribulation period. Irrespective to all of the different debates about the tribulation period, most every believer will agree that there will be a seven-year tribulation period to come on earth, so say the scriptures. As we read Isaiah 66, we see a very significant point when it talks about this time period.

> Hear the uproar from the city; hear that noise from the temple! It is the sound of the Lord _repaying His enemies all they deserve._ _"Before she goes into labor, she gives birth; before the pains come upon her,_ she delivers a son. Who has ever heard of such things (giving birth before the labor)? Who has ever seen things like this? Can a country be born in a day or a nation be brought forth in a moment? Yet no sooner is Zion in labor than _she gives birth to her children._ (Isaiah 66:5-8)

I'll make this short and sweet:

Repaying His enemies all they deserve in Zion: His return to Israel and the last battle.

Before she goes into labor: she is Israel. Labor is the tribulation period.

She gives birth to her children: believers. The church is birthed when He comes for us.

Can a country be born in a day: Yes, 1948, after more than 1,900 years of being in exile, Israel miraculously and quickly established their nation again, fulfilling the scriptures.

Notice that she <u>births before</u> she labors. The church is birthed just before the labor starts. That is why Isaiah said, "Who has heard or seen such a thing?" So I believe we reunite with Jesus at His return. Then the labor starts. The birth at that point is why I belief the church goes from a conception at Pentecost to be birthed when Jesus returns. This topic could go a lot deeper, but that's what I see in the scriptures, contrary to popular belief. I believe that we are still in conception until the return of Christ.

ABOUT THE AUTHOR

AT AGE THIRTY-FOUR, RYAN Davis Shaw's life came to a terminal crossroads, which he calls his "last night." He was consumed by an unidentifiable desire to leave the misery called . . . life. Today, by God's grace, he lives a life completely free of depression, oppression, and addiction. Alongside this freedom, he has discovered power. He now enjoys living each and every day to the fullest.

Aside from staying busy with the daily requirements of running his business, Ryan loves to travel the world and experience all life has to offer. Ryan has a made-up mind to make it a priority of sharing his story of pain to freedom and power, even as he fishes the deepest oceans of the Caribbean or jumps off the tallest bungee platforms in South Africa. Ryan's passion to share God's glory takes precedence in every one of his day-to-day activities.

Ryan's career has included working as a millwright mechanic, a field and gas plant operator, and currently as an award-winning new home construction owner. Ryan is newly married to his beautiful wife Caitlin. Together, they reside in Alberta, Canada. They enjoy spending various parts of the year together in the Bahamas, doing ministry.

Made in the USA
Middletown, DE
09 October 2021